The
Dramatic
Writer's
Companion

T0288035

Books by Will Dunne

*The Dramatic Writer's Companion: Tools to Develop Characters,
Cause Scenes, and Build Stories*

*Character, Scene, and Story: New Tools from the Dramatic Writer's
Companion*

The Architecture of Story: A Technical Guide for the Dramatic Writer

The Dramatic Writer's Companion

TOOLS TO DEVELOP CHARACTERS, CAUSE SCENES, AND BUILD STORIES

2nd Edition

WILL DUNNE

THE UNIVERSITY OF CHICAGO PRESS

CHICAGO AND LONDON

The University of Chicago Press, Chicago 60637
The University of Chicago Press, Ltd., London
Published 2017
Printed in the United States of America

26 25 24 23 22 21 20   2 3 4 5

ISBN-13: 978-0-226-49408-1 (paper)
ISBN-13: 978-0-226-49411-1 (e-book)
DOI: 10.7208/chicago/9780226494111.001.00001

Library of Congress Cataloging-in-Publication Data

Names: Dunne, Will, author. | Supplement (work): Dunne, Will. Character, scene, story.
Title: The dramatic writer's companion : tools to develop characters, cause scenes, and build stories / Will Dunne.
Description: 2nd edition. | Chicago ; London : The University of Chicago Press, 2017.
Identifiers: LCCN 2017020150 | ISBN 9780226494081 (pbk. : alk. paper) | ISBN 9780226494111 (e-book)
Subjects: LCSH: Drama—Technique—Handbooks, manuals, etc. | Authorship—Handbooks, manuals, etc. | Playwriting—Handbooks, manuals, etc. | Motion picture authorship—Handbooks, manuals, etc.
Classification: LCC PN1661 .D86 2017 | DDC 808.2—dc23 LC record available at https://lccn.loc.gov/2017020150

♾ This paper meets the requirements of ANSI/NISO Z39.48-1992 (Permanence of Paper).

In honor of LLOYD RICHARDS

and with gratitude to MARY F. McCABE

CONTENTS

Basic Character Builder 3

Begin to create a new character by fleshing out key physical, psychological, and social traits and by identifying some of the important experiences that have shaped the character by the time the story begins.

What the Character Believes 8

The character's personal beliefs have a huge impact on how he or she sees the world, makes decisions, and behaves. Twenty topics lead you through an exploration of this credo and—like the next two parallel exercises—ask you to respond through your character's unique perceptions and voice.

Where the Character Lives 10

Whether or not story action actually takes place in the character's home, it is a personal domain that can reveal much about who your character is and isn't. Twenty questions lead you through this exploration.

Where the Character Works 13

The activities, culture, and experience of work provide another key source of character information—even if this work doesn't figure prominently in the story action. Twenty questions lead you through this exploration.

Getting Emotional 16

Dramatic characters tend to be driven by strong feelings. Learn more about your character by exploring his or her primal emotions—anger, fear, and love—and the stimuli that trigger them.

Into the Past 20

One key to a great story is a great backstory. What has your character experienced in the past that will shed new light on his or her behavior now? Starting at the precise moment the story begins, this exercise leads you backward through time, step by step, to discover important truths.

ABOUT THIS GUIDE

The Dramatic Writer's Companion is a creative and analytical reference tool that has helped thousands of writers develop new plays, screenplays, and other types of stories. It is composed not as a linear sequence of chapters but as a collection of self-contained writing exercises to help you explore and refine your own unique material. These tools can be used at any time in any order and can be repeated as often as you like to make new discoveries.

This second edition of the guide has been updated to include chapter-by-chapter references to related writing exercises in the complementary guide *Character, Scene, and Story: New Tools from the Dramatic Writer's Companion*, which uses a similar structure and approach to help you develop scripts. It is not necessary to have that guide in order to use this one, but having both expands the collection of writing tools at your disposal as you flesh out characters, scenes, and stories. Together, the two guides offer you more than one hundred script development tools.

For best results, please take the time to read this introduction, which explains more about this guide and how to use it.

■ TO THE DRAMATIC WRITER

As a dramatic writer working on a play or screenplay, you are engaged in the process of telling a story. It is a process both old and new—old because its roots stretch back through centuries and offer time-tested principles to guide you, and new because it must be adapted to an utterly unique set of dynamics: you and the story you want to tell.

This guide is designed to help you manage both the old and the new of the storytelling process. Written from a playwright's perspective and making room in its embrace for both playwrights and screenwriters, the guide offers sixty-two in-depth character, scene, and story development exercises. The purpose of these tools is to spark creativity and steer analysis as you develop your script.

TOOLS FOR LEAPING INTO BLANK PAGES

The exercises in this guide build on certain basic assumptions. First, though stage and film are each a distinct medium, the writers of plays and screenplays are more alike than different. Both must create the blueprint for an emotional experience that is meant to be seen and heard. Both must tackle the idea that "less is more" and convey a lot—often a character's entire lifetime—in one audience sitting. Both must use the present to imply the past. Both must figure out how to "show, not tell," the story so that the audience's knowledge of it comes not from hearing explanations but from observing and interpreting character behavior. Like storytellers of any kind, dramatic writers also must try to grab the audience from the start, keep them interested to the end, and communicate something meaningful along the way. It is common challenges like these that the exercises in this guide are designed to address.

Second, though there may be no rules for creating art, dramatic stories tend to reflect certain basic storytelling principles. For example, most plays and screenplays focus on the dramatic journey of one main character. This journey usually consists of a series of events that change the world of the story for better or worse. Most of these events are caused by the character's need to accomplish something important and are shaped by the conflicts and risks that stand in the way.

Some dramatic writers adhere faithfully to classic principles like these and produce great works like A *Streetcar Named Desire* and *Long Day's Journey into Night*. Other writers cherry-pick such principles—using some and ignoring others—to produce great plays like *Waiting for Godot*, where nothing really happens, and great films like *Crash*, which has no main character or central throughline. Whether you wish to use traditional techniques or ignore them, you can benefit from an understanding of storytelling principles that have proven to work. The exercises in this guide are designed to remind you of such principles and give you leeway to adapt them in whatever way best fits your specific needs and story.

American playwright and director Moss Hart once said that you never really learn how to write a play, you learn only how to write this *play.*

CHARACTER: THE HEART AND SOUL OF STORY

While emphasizing different aspects of the dramatic writing process, this guide draws from the theory that character is the root of scene and story. The more you know your characters and the world they inhabit, the better equipped you will be to discover and develop all of the other dramatic elements for your script.

Every exercise in this guide is, to some degree, a character exploration. Even when you are working through the details of a scene or building a story, you are making decisions about your characters: how each is unique and how each is universal. The success of your work will depend on how broadly and deeply you mine the truths of each character and use them to structure the dramatic journey. Such truths are most useful when you understand them emotionally as well as intellectually, especially when you are in the moment of a scene and need to know what each character will say and do next.

Plot is a critical element of any play or screenplay, but a script dictated by plot points may end up sacrificing truth for spectacle and result not in drama but in melodrama. By letting the plot evolve from the characters instead of forcing the characters into a prefabricated plot, you can keep the focus on truths that enlighten the human condition rather than exaggerated conflicts and emotions that exist only for dramatic effect.

Herein lies the simplest yet most powerful idea underlying this collection of dramatic writing exercises: The character is not something added to the scene or to the story. Rather, the character is the scene. The character is the story.

REAL STORY SOLUTIONS

Each exercise in this guide grew out of real issues that playwrights and screenwriters faced while working on scripts, side by side, in more than fifteen hundred dramatic writing workshops that I conducted over twenty years. Each exercise was then tested with different writer groups and refined as needed. The result is a collection of tools that translate dramatic theory into action steps and cover a range of topics from a variety of angles.

Some exercises focus on development details, such as defining a character's credo or figuring out her scenic objective. Others address the big picture of the story by helping you explore subject, theme, and throughline. Sometimes the approach is instinctual—you work "from the heart" to find new insights—and sometimes intellectual: you work "from the head" to evaluate material, fix problems, and reach writing goals.

Each exercise tackles its topic in depth and provides step-by-step guidance rather than general directives. Though the guide is meant to have both educational and motivational value, no exercise is solely a lesson or creative diversion for its own sake. Rather, each targets information that you can import to your story so that you are always exploring your own material—not someone else's. In effect, the exercises become part of your writing process rather than something you do in addition to it.

OTHER RELATED RESOURCES TO ENRICH YOUR WRITING PROCESS

This guide is complemented by two other guides that use a similar structure and approach to help you develop dramatic scripts. Both let you adapt writing tools to your needs by choosing the topics you want to explore at any given time during the writing or revision process.

- *Character, Scene, and Story: New Tools from the Dramatic Writer's Companion* (Chicago: University of Chicago Press, 2017) expands the collection of script development tools in this guide by addressing new topics and by exploring many of the same topics in more depth or from new angles. To facilitate this process, each exercise in each guide includes references to related tools in the other guide. Many of the tools in *Character, Scene, and Story* are visceral techniques that call for intuitive responses. For example, they help you dig deeper into your script by fleshing out visual images, exploring characters from emotional perspectives, and tapping the power of color and sense memory to trigger story ideas. The new guide concludes with a special troubleshooting section to help you tackle problem scenes.

- *The Architecture of Story: A Technical Guide for the Dramatic Writer* (Chicago: University of Chicago Press, 2016) helps you develop your own dramatic scripts by exploring storytelling tools and techniques that other writers have used. Three successful contemporary American plays—*Doubt: A Parable* by John Patrick Shanley, *Topdog/ Underdog* by Suzan-Lori Parks, and *The Clean House* by Sarah Ruhl— are each dismantled from a technical perspective to illustrate dramatic writing principles that you can adapt in countless ways to the scripts you develop. In addition to detailed analysis of these plays, the guide includes hundreds of questions to help you evaluate your own work.

■ HOW TO USE THIS GUIDE

You are welcome to sit down and read this guide from cover to cover, but that is not the intended use. Like any reference tool, the guide invites you to review its contents, select the specific information you need now, and use it to produce results.

NONLINEAR DESIGN: YOU CHOOSE WHICH EXERCISE TO DO NEXT

The exercises in this guide are each self-contained, so you can try them in any order at any time and repeat them at different times with different results. This approach reflects the idea that there is no single way to develop story and lets you adapt the guide to your individual writing process and level of experience.

ORGANIZATION FOR EASE OF USE

To help you manage the guide, the exercises are divided into three areas of content: character, scene, and story. Though character is the foundation of scene and story, the breakdown allows a different focus for each section.

Exercises within each section have been further divided into stages 1, 2, and 3. The purpose of these numbers is not to indicate degree of difficulty but to suggest the general stage of script development in which an exercise might be most appropriate, with stage 1 best suited to early development and stage 3 to later development. Attention to these numbers is optional. They are provided mainly for writers who prefer a more structured approach to choosing exercises.

At the end of this guide you will find a troubleshooting section that high-lights twenty common script problems and suggests specific exercises to help you address them. For quick reference, you also will find a glossary of terms to facilitate nonlinear use of this guide and also to highlight the dramatic principles woven throughout the exercises. For example, the term *beat* appears in many of the exercises. While it may refer elsewhere to a pause in dialogue for dramatic effect, *beat* is used in this guide only to mean "the smallest unit of dramatic action." Just as a dramatic story is made up of scenes, a scene is made up of beats. Each beat centers on one thing, such as one topic, one behavior, or one emotion. Beats bring variety to the dramatic action of a scene and determine its structure and rhythm.

EXERCISE ELEMENTS TO TRIGGER DISCOVERY

As you work with the guide, you will find that each exercise offers certain features to support your character, scene, or story exploration, including a summary, suggestion for when to use the exercise, topic introduction, exercise introduction, detailed action steps, and recap of key messages.

Since the exercises are designed to be self-contained and useful in any order, certain principles and questions are repeated among them. As you develop your script, these recurring elements can often lead to new discoveries. Use any recurring theory you encounter as an opportunity to reevaluate your current writing process, and any recurring question as an opportunity to rethink your material and gain new insights about your characters and story. Some exercises tackle the same subject but with different levels of depth or from different angles. Most exercises can be completed in about thirty minutes.

EXAMPLES TO ILLUSTRATE KEY PRINCIPLES

The guide is sprinkled with hundreds of examples from dramatic works, many of which have been developed as both plays and films. Some examples are quick references. Others include more detailed script analysis. The dramatic works used most often or in most depth include *Angels in America, Part One: Millennium Approaches* by Tony Kushner, *Ballad of the Sad Café* adapted by Edward Albee from a book by Carson McCullers, *The Bear* by Anton Chekhov, *The Beard of Avon* by Amy Freed, *Betrayal* by Harold Pinter, *Blasted* by Sarah Kane, *Crimes of the Heart* by Beth Henley, *Doubt* by John Patrick Shanley, *Edmond* by David Mamet, *The Elephant Man* by Bernard Pomerance, *Frozen* by Bryony Lavery, *Glengarry Glen Ross* by David Mamet, *Hamlet* by William Shakespeare, *The History Boys* by Alan Bennett, *Hotel Desperado* by Will Dunne, *How I Became an Interesting Person* by Will Dunne, *In the Blood* by Suzan-Lori Parks, *Long Day's Journey into Night* by Eugene O'Neill, *Loot* by Joe Orton, *The Merchant of Venice* by William Shakespeare, *Of Mice and Men* by John Steinbeck, *The Pianist* by Wladyslaw Szpilman and Ronald Harwood, *The Piano Lesson* by August Wilson, *The Pillowman* by Martin McDonagh, *Proof* by David Auburn, *Psycho* by Robert Bloch and Joseph Stefano, *The Real Thing* by Tom Stoppard, *Search and Destroy* by Howard Korder, *Topdog/Underdog* by Suzan-Lori Parks, *A Streetcar Named Desire* by Tennessee Williams, *True West* by Sam Shepard, *Waiting for Godot* by Samuel Beckett, *Who's Afraid of Virginia Woolf?* by Edward Albee, and *Wit* by Margaret Edson.

GETTING STARTED

How should you begin to develop a dramatic script? Different writers address this question in different ways. In the end, their answers indicate not what is "correct" in the storytelling universe but rather what works best for them. Here are suggestions for getting started with this guide and doing whatever works best for you.

1. *Select a section.* Think about where you are now in the development of your script. Trust your instinct and pick one of three areas to tackle: character, scene, or story. Then go to the matching section in the table of contents.

- Use "Developing Your Character" to flesh out, explore, and understand the important characters in your story. Exercises range from a basic character builder to in-depth character analysis.
- Use "Causing a Scene" to plan, write, or revise any scene in your story. Exercises range from a basic scene starter to more advanced tools for refining dramatic action and dialogue.
- Use "Building Your Story" to spark global thinking and figure out how to compose and connect dramatic events so that they add up to one story. Exercises range from deciding whose story you're writing to analyzing and revising the dramatic journey that emerged.

If you don't know much about your story yet, or if you're not sure what to try next, go to "Developing Your Character." The more you know your characters, the more your story will write itself.

2. *(Optional) Select a level.* Choose the level of exercise that best matches your current knowledge of the story.

- *Stage 1* starter tools can help lay the groundwork for a new character, new scene, or new story: you may use them any time in any order during writing or revision but might find them most helpful during early script development, when you have the most to figure out.
- *Stage 2* exploratory tools can help you learn more about a character, scene, or story you've started. You may use them any time in any order but might find them most helpful during the middle to later stages of script development, when you want to get deeper into your material.

- *Stage* 3 focusing tools can help you simplify, prioritize, and clarify your thoughts about a character, scene, or whole story. You may use them any time in any order but might find them most helpful during the later stages of story development, when you are more familiar with your script and have the most details to track and manage.

Some writers will choose to do stage 1 exercises first, stage 2 next, and stage 3 last. Others will gain more from ignoring these numbers and intuitively creating their own system of use. For example, you may wish to try a stage 1 exercise during later script development. The leap back to basics can help shake up material that has grown stale. Or you may wish to try a stage 3 during early script development even though you may not yet be prepared to complete many of the steps. The leap forward can help you plan the story or formulate questions to guide the work ahead.

3. **Select an exercise.** Scan the exercise summaries in this category at this level, and pick the most appealing one. Don't worry about whether you are making the right choice, because while you are using this guide you cannot make a mistake. You can gain something useful from whichever exercise you choose to do—even if you simply select one at random.

4. *(Optional) Explore the topic further.* By reviewing the table of contents or the streamlined "Exercises at a Glance," you may find other tools in this guide related to the topic at hand. If you also have *Character, Scene, and Story: New Tools from the Dramatic Writer's Companion*, you can continue exploring the topic or a related one in that guide as well. To keep you aware of what the other guide offers, each chapter in this second edition concludes with suggestions of exercises to consider.

◼ ONGOING USE OF THE GUIDE

You can use this guide periodically or every time you sit down to work on your story. Integrate the exercises into your writing process to help you warm up, find and explore new ideas, and analyze and solve script problems. Remember that you can use the same exercise at different times to find new material for your story.

> *As you become familiar with the guide, you can shortcut exercise selection by using "Exercises at a Glance" on page xxiii.*

While you write and rewrite, you may wish to use the troubleshooting section at the end of the guide to tackle specific script problems. Remember that if the meaning of a term is unclear, you can always check the glossary for a working definition.

■ GROUND RULES

Before you start any exercise in this guide, be sure you are familiar with the following guidelines. They provide a foundation for each exercise and are designed to help you get the most out of this guide. For best results, revisit these suggestions now and then, and keep them in mind each time you do an exercise:

1. *Trust your authority.* A basic principle of these exercises is to proceed with confidence and turn off the censor inside you who says your work isn't good enough. While doing each exercise—at least for that thirty minutes or so—you are infallible and simply cannot make a mistake. Enjoy it while it lasts.

2. *Work fast.* Another basic principle is to open up and let ideas flow by working as quickly as possible. Try to avoid thinking too much or getting too complicated. If you get stuck on a question, jot down any answer—even a bad one—and go on from there. Off-the-cuff responses sometimes have surprising payoffs later.

3. *Look for what's new.* Some exercises may focus on material that overlaps with other material you've already discovered through another exercise or on your own. Keep taking creative leaps, and try to avoid repeating or rehashing what you already know. Use the exercises to make discoveries, not relive them.

4. *Go one step at a time.* The exercises tend to work best if you don't know where they are leading. Once you get past the introductory material and into the action steps of the exercise, don't look ahead. Focus on here and now.

5. *Honor exercise limits.* Most of the exercises are designed to be done in one sitting. Some have word limits and other restrictions. These limits are designed to boost your creativity, not stifle it.

6. *Stay flexible.* Some exercises ask you to explore several different possibilities to find one solution. For best results, complete the exercise even if you think you've already found a solution that works. It's only an exercise, and the exploration could lead to valuable material where you least expect it.

7. *Think big.* These exercises are designed ultimately to help you discover and understand what matters most about your story. If you find yourself at a crossroads, unsure of which way to turn, always make the most dramatic choice.

8. *Have fun.* While some writers suffer in garrets and slave over their stories, others enjoy their work. The value of your script will not be measured by how much anguish you experienced in producing it. Dramatic writing is serious stuff—and it will often be challenging—but you can have a good time in the process.

EXERCISES AT A GLANCE

Stage 3: Seeing the Big Picture

Developing Your Character

Character is the heart and soul of story. This section can help you flesh out your characters as you prepare to write, make ongoing discoveries about them as your story unfolds, and focus on what matters most. Use these exercises any time. You can always benefit from knowing more about your characters, especially if you begin to lose interest in them, get stuck in a scene, or feel unsure about the direction in which your story should proceed.

BASIC CHARACTER BUILDER

THE QUICK VERSION
Start to flesh out a character

BEST TIME FOR THIS
During early story development or any time you add a new character

**CHARACTER: A MIX OF PHYSICAL,
PSYCHOLOGICAL, AND SOCIAL TRAITS**
You won't understand what your story is about until you understand who your characters are. Dramatist Henrik Ibsen felt he could not begin writing a play until he knew the characters inside out—as if he had lived with them for a month. To know a character is to know the complex blend of physical, psychological, and social traits that make him or her unique. The most important of these traits will be revealed to us through the character's actions under the increasing pressure of story events.

Great stories create extreme circumstances where characters are tested—and usually changed—and where they may do things, for better or for worse, that they never thought possible. To write such stories, you need to know your characters well enough to understand where in life they have come from, how they usually behave day-to-day, in what unexpected ways they might act under stress, and in what ways they would never under any circumstances behave.

ABOUT THE EXERCISE
Try this first with your main character. You can repeat it later with other principal characters in less detail. Don't overdevelop minor characters. They may steal the show if, after they come and go, we are waiting for them to return.

You don't need to write volumes as you answer the exercise questions. It's more about making choices and knowing what they are. For best results:

Set up a personal palette. For each character you build, choose one or two people whom you can use—in combination with yourself—as a source of information. Pick people who trigger strong positive or negative feelings. Give the character a name that embodies your choices and has special meaning for you.

Look for what matters most. The importance of each question will depend on the unique character you are developing. Try to find character facts that may influence story events. Don't waste time on details that will have no impact.

Focus on when the story begins. The character will undergo changes as the dramatic journey unfolds. The exercise is designed to help you flesh out who the character is before those changes begin to occur.

When basing a character on someone from your life, you may find the best material by using his or her real name in the early private stages of writing. Once you establish the character—and before others see your script—switch to a fictitious name.

■ YOUR CHARACTER'S PHYSICAL LIFE

Remember that "now" and "today" refer to when the story begins.

1. When was the character born and what is the character's age now?
2. Think about his or her other vital stats, such as gender, ethnicity, height, and weight. Which of these, if any, might matter in the story?
3. How would most people describe the character's physical appearance?
4. Good or bad, what is the character's most striking physical feature?
5. How would you describe the character's strength, endurance, and coordination when it comes to physical activity and sports?
6. What is the character's favorite sport or physical activity?
7. How is the character's health now, and what has most contributed to this?
8. Is the character on any medication now? If so, what is it, why is the character taking it, and how does it affect his or her behavior?
9. What significant diseases, if any, has the character had in the past and what impact does this medical history have on the character now?
10. Has the character ever sustained a serious physical injury? If so, what happened and how has this affected the character?
11. Does the character have any permanent physical defects, such as nearsightedness, or temporary ones, such as a broken leg? If so, what are they?
12. Of the character's most defining traits, which ones run in the family?
13. Does the character use nicotine, alcohol, or recreational drugs? If so, what is used in what quantities and how important is this in the character's daily life?
14. What is the character's greatest physical asset?
15. What is the character's greatest physical weakness or liability?

■ YOUR CHARACTER'S INNER LIFE

1. What is the character's IQ and how has this affected the character?
2. How would you describe the character's imagination?
3. How does the character rate in terms of common sense and sound judgment?
4. How would you describe the character's outlook on life?
5. Does the character tend to be dominant or submissive with others, and why?
6. How does the character usually approach major problems?
7. What is the character's greatest talent?
8. What is the character's greatest lack of talent?
9. What is the character's biggest success in life so far?
10. What is the character's biggest failure in life so far?
11. Up to now, what has been the character's main ambition?
12. What is the character's biggest delusion?
13. In order of importance, identify the character's three greatest fears.
14. In order of importance, name three things that make the character really angry.
15. What would make the character feel embarrassed, ashamed, or guilty?
16. How would you describe the character's moral standards?
17. What are three things that your character most values?
18. What are three things that your character least values?
19. What is the character's greatest virtue?
20. What is the character's greatest vice?
21. What are the spiritual and religious beliefs of the character?
22. Identify something unusual that the character might do—but only if most people would not know about it.
23. Name three things the character would never, ever do.
24. What is the character's biggest secret and why has this stayed hidden?
25. What turns the character on sexually?
26. What is the character's greatest psychological strength?
27. What is the character's greatest psychological weakness?

■ YOUR CHARACTER'S LIFE WITH OTHERS

1. Where did the character grow up and in what kind of home?
2. What was the character's social class and how did this affect the character?
3. During the character's early years, who was in the family and how did the character fit in with them?
4. What did the character's parents do for a living and how much did they earn?
5. What was the greatest strength and weakness of the character's father?

6. What was the greatest strength and weakness of the character's mother?
7. In a nutshell, how would you describe the character's childhood?
8. Inside or outside the family, positive or negative, who had the greatest impact on the character as a child and how would you describe this influence?
9. What kind of schools did the character attend and how well did he or she do?
10. What were the character's best and worst subjects in school?
11. How popular was the character through childhood and teenage years?
12. How actively did the character participate in social organizations at school?
13. Inside or outside the family, positive or negative, who had the greatest impact on the character as a teenager and how would you describe this influence?
14. Who was the character's first love, how did this relationship get started, and—if the character is no longer in that relationship—what ended it?
15. What was the character's first real job, why did the character get hired, and—if the character is no longer at that job—what caused it to end?
16. What does the character do now for a living, how much does he or she earn, and how well suited is the character to this line of work?
17. What is the character's social class and marital status now?
18. Where does the character live now and with whom (if anyone)?
19. How would you describe the character's home life now?
20. How has the character's sex life been lately?
21. Publicly or secretly, whom does the character find most sexually attractive?
22. Who is the character's best friend today, and why?
23. Who is the character's worst enemy today, and why?
24. Does the character have any hobbies now and, if so, what?
25. Other than hobbies, what does the character usually do for fun?
26. What is the last book that the character read?
27. What is the last film, if any, that the character saw?
28. When is the last time the character went to a party, whose party was it, and what kind of time did the character have there?
29. Whether spouse, lover, best friend, coworker, family member, or mentor, who is the most significant other person in the character's life today, and why?
30. What is the happiest moment the character has shared with that person?
31. What is the unhappiest moment the character has shared with that person?
32. How would you describe the character's politics?

33. How would you describe the character's position or role in society today?
34. If the character could change one thing about the world, what would it be?
35. Positive or negative, what were three of the most significant turning points in the character's life and how has each affected the character whom we first meet?

WRAP-UP

You've begun to create a unique identity by making specific choices about the character's physical life, inner life, and life with others. As you develop your story, continue asking questions like these so that your character can keep growing. Look for answers that are relevant to the dramatic journey and can help you better understand how this character will feel and act as the journey unfolds.

Other exercises in this section can help you flesh out specific aspects of your character—such as belief system, home life, and work life—in more depth. In some cases, you may be asked similar questions about the same character and find yourself wanting to give different answers. Know that your character is dynamic and will continue to evolve in new and often unexpected ways as you write and rewrite your story.

To explore the character further, write a biography that focuses on the key turning points in his or her life. Look for examples that will influence story action and are not just interesting experiences in themselves. Another useful exercise is to track a day in the life of the character just before the story begins. You will learn a lot by discovering what he or she typically does from morning to night.

Related tools in *Character, Scene, and Story.* To continue fleshing out a character, try any exercise in the "Developing Your Character" section, from "Character Interview" to "What Is the Character Doing Now?"

WHAT THE CHARACTER BELIEVES

THE QUICK VERSION
Learn more about your character by fleshing out his or her personal credo

BEST TIME FOR THIS
Any time you need to know a character better

THE CHARACTER'S CREDO: A DEEP SOURCE OF ACTION
To figure out the events of your story, you need to understand your character's belief system. This includes how your character sees the world, what your character values and doesn't value, what pushes your character's buttons, and why your character is likely to behave a certain way under certain circumstances.

ABOUT THE EXERCISE
Choose a character whom you wish to explore in more depth and imagine him or her around the time the story begins. Then use free associations to answer the following exercise questions from this character's perspective and in this character's voice, as if you were writing dialogue. Tell the truth as best you can. "Truth" here is whatever you, the character, *believe* is true when the story begins.

■ YOUR CHARACTER'S BELIEF SYSTEM
When the story begins, how do you, the character, feel about the following twenty topics? For each one, try to say as much as you can in one minute of fast writing.

Money	Sin	Violence	Beauty
Children	Success	Marriage	Death
Church	Family	Drugs	Friendship
Technology	Politics	Justice	Failure
Freedom	Love	Sex	God

A DEEPER LOOK AT THREE KEY BELIEFS
To you, the character, when the story begins:

1. Review your quick responses to the twenty exercise topics. Choose any three topics to explore in more detail.

2. For each topic you chose, take five more minutes to continue where you left off and express your unique point of view. Remember that there is

no right or wrong way to do this. Just be specific and stay true to what you, the character, believe. Try to include specific examples from your life to support your beliefs.

WRAP-UP

Your character's belief system is a key component of who the character is and what makes the character tick. This system is based on what the character has experienced in life, what the character has been taught by others, and how the character feels and thinks as a result of all this.

Like people, no two characters have identical belief systems. Each therefore will act in a unique way, especially under stress when true values tend to show themselves—whether the character likes it or not.

It's easiest to understand values that you and the character share, but what about values you don't share? Take extra time to explore these key differences and what led the character to embrace them.

Related tools in Character, Scene, and Story. To explore a character's credo in more depth, go to the "Developing Your Character" section and try "Beyond Belief."

WHERE THE CHARACTER LIVES

THE QUICK VERSION
Find important clues to your character's identity by exploring his or her home

BEST TIME FOR THIS
Any time you need to know a character better

YOUR CHARACTER'S HOME:
A GOLD MINE OF PERSONAL INFORMATION
The more you know your characters, the more your story will write itself. This exercise helps you flesh out your principal characters by exploring their most personal domains: their homes. Whether or not these dwellings figure directly into the story action, they are telling places that can reveal a lot about who your characters really are.

ABOUT THE EXERCISE
Choose a character whom you wish to explore in more depth and imagine him or her around the time the story begins. Then answer the exercise questions from this character's perspective and in this character's voice, as if you were writing dialogue. Tell the truth as best you can. "Truth" here is whatever you, the character, *believe* is true when the story begins.

■ **YOUR CHARACTER'S HOME LIFE**
To you, the character: when the story begins:
1. Where is your home located? If you were to get mail there, what information would be on it: your name and full mailing address.
2. What type of place is it—for example, house, apartment, trailer, hotel room, palace, cave, tent, forest, or space station—and how long have you lived there?
3. Identify the different rooms or distinct areas of your home—for example, living room, kitchenette, bathroom, patio.
4. How would you describe your neighborhood or immediate surroundings?
5. What is your financial relationship to your home—for example, do you own, rent, or stay there for free?
   • If you pay, what's the monthly cost and how easily do you manage this?
   • If it's "free," what are you expected to provide instead of money?
6. Who else, if anyone, lives with you? Write each one's name and

relationship—for example, lover, husband, or cellmate. If you have pets, include them, too.

7. Briefly describe your home relationships:
   - If you live alone, how do you like being by yourself?
   - If you live with others, how well do you get along?
8. Briefly describe how your home usually looks—for example, neat or messy, immaculate or filthy, cluttered or sparse, fixed up or run down.
9. Which is your favorite room or area at home, and why?
10. What room or area of your home do you like least, and why?
11. Name three of your favorite possessions at home. Tell what each one is, where you keep it, and why you like it so much.
12. Name three of the possessions that you most want to get rid of someday. Tell what each one is, where you keep it, and why you dislike it.
13. What was the most memorable intimate encounter you've ever had in your home? Include when this happened and who was involved.
14. Aside from that, what's one of the happiest experiences you've ever had in your home? Include when this happened and who was involved.
15. What was the most memorable violent, criminal, or terrible act in your home? Include when this happened and who was involved.
16. Aside from that, what's one of the most frightening experiences you've ever had in your home? Include when this happened and who was involved.
17. What's one of the saddest experiences you've ever had in your home? Include when this happened and who was involved.
18. Name an object in your home—a physical item—that you keep secret from most people. Include where you have it now and why it's hidden.
19. Name something you do—or have done—in your home that most people don't know about. Tell who else, if anyone, was involved, and why it's a secret.
20. Summing it all up, how do you feel about your home?
    - If you're happy living there, what do you most enjoy about it?
    - If you're unhappy there, what's wrong and where would you rather live?

WRAP-UP

The character's home is an often overlooked source of important character information. By answering these questions—even the simplest ones about address, living unit, and rooms—you've had to make many specific and complex choices about your character's life. By responding as the character, you've also taken this research out of the realm of the academic and into the world of your story. This has given you a chance not only to search for leads to new story ideas, but also to develop more of your character's unique outlook, personality, and voice.

Related tools in *Character, Scene, and Story.* The character's home may include things that are important to the story. To study these items and other physical life in the character's world, go to the "Developing Your Character" section and try "Objects of Interest." To explore the character's early home life, try "Meet the Parents" in the same section.

WHERE THE CHARACTER WORKS

THE QUICK VERSION
Learn more about your character by exploring his or her work life

BEST TIME FOR THIS
Any time you need to know a character better

YOUR CHARACTER'S TRADE AND THE IMPACT IT'S MADE
Even if you never show us your character on the job, you can discover a lot of useful story information by exploring what the character does—or did—for a living. Whether it's frying fries at a fast-food stand or ruling a nation from a throne, work is a profound influence that affects and reflects the character's social class, lifestyle, economics, power base, and opportunities for growth. Work also determines how the character spends a significant amount of time and whom the character meets and doesn't meet on a regular basis. All of this can affect to some degree the character's view of society, value system, and perhaps even vocabulary and dress.

Ideally, your character is unique, and no generalization always applies, but different trades tend to suggest different traits among those who ply them. For example, a temp secretary earning minimum wage might see the world differently from a corporate executive raking in top dollar. An accountant might prize organization more than an artist, who might value breaking rules. A computer programmer might speak and dress differently from a church minister, lawyer, or horse jockey. Know your character's trade and the impact it's made. You'll have a better handle on your character during the story—even when work is the last thing on his or her mind.

ABOUT THE EXERCISE
Choose a character whom you wish to explore in more depth and imagine him or her around the time the story begins. Then answer the exercise questions from this character's perspective and in this character's voice, as if you were writing dialogue. Tell the truth as best you can. "Truth" here is whatever you, the character, *believe* is true when the story begins.

■ **YOUR CHARACTER'S WORK LIFE**
To you, the character: when the story begins:
 1. Think about general work categories. What is your profession? Or, if you are currently unemployed or retired, what type of work have you mostly done?

2. What type of establishment do you work in, what is it called, and where is it located in relationship to your home?
3. How do you get to work, and how long is the commute each way?
4. What are your usual working hours?
5. What is your specific job title and how long have you had this particular job?
6. Name two or three qualifications that you needed to get this job.
7. How much do you usually make each month, and how does this pay fit your current needs and lifestyle?
8. What is one of your greatest strengths on the job?
9. What is one your greatest weaknesses on the job?
10. Overall, how well suited are you for the type of work that you do?
11. Give a specific example of one of your greatest successes on the job.
12. Give a specific example of one of your greatest failures on the job.
13. Give a specific example of how you have fun either on the job or with your coworkers after hours.
14. Think about the people you interact with during work—for example, your boss, coworkers, customers, or suppliers. Whom do you like most, and why?
15. Think again about the people you interact with during work. Whom do you like least, and why?
16. What is one of the greatest secrets that you keep from your coworkers, and why do you keep this hidden?
17. What is one of your greatest fears or concerns related to your job?
18. Think about your answers to the questions so far. What do you like most about the type of work that you do?
19. Overall, what do like least about the type of work that you do?
20. If you could be doing any other type of work, what would it be, and why?

If your character has a job that you have never had, you may gain new story insights by taking the time to research that line of work. Talk to people who do it. What do they most like and dislike about the job? What's unique about it? How does it affect the rest of their lives?

WRAP-UP

If your character has a full-time job, it could account for a third of his or her waking life. You may now have a better knowledge of how that valuable time is spent, what it's like for your character, and what impact it has made. Remember that characters function with a logic and motivation that reflects a whole life—not just the one we see during story events.

By responding as the character, you've taken your research out of the realm of the academic and into the realm of the dramatic. So, while learning about his or her work life, you have also developed more of your character's outlook, personality, and unique voice.

Related tools in *Character, Scene, and Story*. To learn more about your character, try any exercise in the "Developing Your Character" section. For example, use "Character Interview" to flesh out the character emotionally. Or use "Character Fact Sheet" to develop a more objective portrait of him or her.

GETTING EMOTIONAL

THE QUICK VERSION
Explore causes and effects of a character's emotional life

BEST TIME FOR THIS
Any time you need to know a character better or find new story ideas

USING EMOTION TO WEAVE STORY
When we see a great play or film, we are not just told the story, we experience it. We live through the characters and share their feelings. In the end, we may say that we are "moved." This is a movement which is primarily emotional and which pulls us from a place of detachment to a place of involvement. We start out with no knowledge of the characters and end up not only knowing them well, but also caring about them.

Dramatic characters can stir our feelings because they are themselves emotional in nature. When they have strong needs and face increasing pressures, they tend to experience a gamut of feelings that reveal different dimensions of who they are and lead them to different paths of action.

When choosing subjects to write about, look for people, events, and issues that trigger strong feelings in you. These will most likely lead to your best writing, and your passion for the subject can help carry you through many of the challenges of developing story. Since you also need to bring analytical vision to your work, however, beware of personal subjects that still feel too close or emotionally overwhelming. These will be great to write about later when you have enough psychological distance to understand them more clearly.

Whether positive or negative, emotions signal that a limit has been reached or crossed. The character has been shaken out of complacency to feel sympathy or love, irritation or anger, anxiety or fear. The stimulus may have been internal—such as an idea or memory—or external—such as a physical event or social interaction. Either way, the emotion can produce physical and psychological responses that can, in turn, affect the character's behavior and speech. Emotion is thus both a cause and an effect of dramatic action, as well as an essential fabric of story.

You are about to explore causes and effects of a character's three defining emotions: anger, fear, and love. Use the same character for the whole exercise, and try it first with your main character. For best results, stay true to what you already know about the character, but remember to keep looking for new insights in each round.

■ **YOUR CHARACTER AND ANGER**

I am so angry because . . .

What makes your character really mad? Anger is a powerful emotion that can range from annoyance to rage, and what stirs it can reveal much about who your character is. Use these steps to find three examples of what causes—or could cause—extreme anger in your character:

1. **Actual story.** Fireworks erupt in the Alexander Payne film *Sideways* when Stephanie finds out that her devoted new boyfriend Jack is secretly engaged to someone else—and the wedding is this weekend. Imagine how different characters might explain their anger in a similar situation. One might say: "I am so angry because . . . he's a selfish heartless bastard who lied to me and used me." Another might say: "I am so angry because . . . now I'll never be able to trust anyone ever again." And yet another might say: "I am so angry because . . . we had tickets for Vegas this weekend and they're not refundable."

Find the time in your story when your character gets most angry. Identify the reason for this anger in a line that begins "I am so angry because . . ." and is completed in your character's unique voice. See if you can find an explanation that surprises you.

2. **Backstory.** Step into the past. Find an important time when the character got boiling mad. Try to see and feel what happened as if it were now. Then let the character explain it in a line that begins "I am so angry because . . ." Look for an explanation that ties somehow to the here and now of the story.

3. **Possible story.** Return to the present and, as an exercise, find something new that would make sense for your unique character: an example of anger that is not actually in the script now but could possibly be added. Identify the cause of this possible anger in a line that begins "I am so angry because . . ." and is completed in the unique voice of your character.

Because I am so angry . . .

Strong feelings can lead characters to do things—good or bad—that they might not otherwise have done: tell the truth, tell a lie, give up drugs, cheat on a test, rescue someone from a burning building, or rob a bank. Emotion can thus evolve from an effect of experience to a cause of it. Use these steps to explore possible effects of your character's anger:

1. *Key anger.* Look back at your three anger examples and choose one to explore further—no longer as a response but as a stimulus.

2. *Responses to anger.* Imagine your character feeling this anger and wanting to do something about it. Any number of responses is possible. Each would reflect a different side of the character. When betrayed by a lover, for example, one character might decide, "Because I am so angry . . . I'll never speak to him or even look at his face ever again." Another might say, "Because I am so angry . . . I'll go out and meet someone new." And yet another might say, "Because I am so angry . . . I'll find him wherever he is and beat him to a pulp."

Each of these emotional responses would trigger a different chain of events. In *Sideways*, Stephanie goes for the third possibility and ends up breaking Jack's nose—an injury he will have to explain to his fiancée as they prepare for the wedding.

Imagine three things your character might do as a result of the specific anger you are exploring. Think of them as separate possibilities rather than as a sequence of steps. Identify each in a line that begins "Because I am so angry . . ." and is completed in your character's unique voice. Even if you are working with the actual story example, take creative leaps and look for new discoveries about what your character might do.

■ YOUR CHARACTER AND FEAR
I am so afraid because . . .

What makes your character afraid? Fear is another powerful emotion, and may range from caution to terror. Use these steps to find three examples of what causes—or could cause—extreme fear in your character:

1. *Actual story.* Find a time in your story now when your character is afraid. Explain why in the character's voice: "I am so afraid because . . ."

2. *Backstory.* Find a time in the backstory when your character got scared. Explain why in the character's voice: "I am so afraid because . . ."

3. *Possible story.* Find an example of fear that is not actually in the story now but could possibly be added. Explain the cause of this possible fear in the character's voice: "I am so afraid because . . ."

Because I am so afraid . . .

How might fear affect your character's actions at a critical time? Use these steps to explore some specific possibilities:

1. *Key fear.* Look back at your three fear examples and choose one to explore further—no longer as a response but as a stimulus.

2. *Responses to fear.* Imagine your character doing something as a result of this fear. Find three separate alternatives that could make sense for your character and identify each in his or her voice: "Because I am so afraid . . ."

■ YOUR CHARACTER AND LOVE

I am so loving because . . .

What would lead your character to love? The subject of countless stories through centuries of storytelling, love is a powerful emotion that may range from simple caring to true romance to spiritual love. Use these steps to find three examples of what causes—or could cause—love in your character.

1. *Actual story.* Find a time in your story when your character feels love. Explain why in his or her voice: "I am so loving because . . ."

2. *Backstory.* Find a time in the backstory when your character felt love. Explain why in his or her voice: "I am so loving because . . ."

3. *Possible story.* Find a new example of love that could possibly be added to the story. Then explain the cause of this possible love in the character's voice: "I am so loving because . . ."

Because I am so loving . . .

Love can make one foolish or wise, honest or deceitful, generous or possessive. It can turn cowards into heroes, and beasts into beauties. Use these steps to explore specific ways that love might affect your character:

1. *Key love.* Look back at your three love examples and choose one to explore further—no longer as a response but as a stimulus.

2. *Responses to love.* Imagine your character wanting to do something as a result of this love. In your character's voice, identify three separate alternatives that would make sense for him or her: "Because I am so loving . . ."

WRAP-UP

As you work on your script, continue to look for new opportunities to use emotions like anger, fear, and love to shape and reflect the dramatic action. Remember that there is no generic cause for any one emotion and no generic effect. You will learn a lot about your characters from how they feel in a certain situation, why they feel that way, and what they do about it.

> **Related tools in *Character, Scene, and Story.***
> To explore a character's emotional life in more depth, go to the "Developing Your Character" section and try "The Emotional Character." Or go to the "Causing a Scene" section and try "The Emotional Onion."

INTO THE PAST

THE QUICK VERSION
Explore the backstory of an important character

BEST TIME FOR THIS
During early story development

PAST IS PRESENT
A key ingredient of a great story is a great backstory. You don't need to know every single thing that ever happened in the character's past, but if you are aware of the most significant relationships and events in this history, you will have a rich source of material to tap as you chart the character's dramatic journey in the present.

ABOUT THE EXERCISE
Try this with your main character or a principal character. As you step back through time, focus on what's relevant to your story. If your character is in mourning like Madame Popova, the melodramatic widow in Anton Chekhov's comedy *The Bear*, for example, you might find more story action by going back to the time of death and seeing what actually happened.

■ STEP 1: SET THE CLOCK . . .
. . . to the "point of attack" time for your story. This is simply when the story begins. At a certain moment, something happens—a nervous soldier on a moonlit night hears a noise and asks "Who's there?"—and a chain of dramatic events is set into motion.

Your main character may or may not be present to your audience at the point-of-attack time. In *Hamlet*, for example, the title character is elsewhere doing something as the soldiers gather in the moonlight to wait for a ghost. In *Who's Afraid of Virginia Woolf?* on the other hand, we meet the main characters right away as they trip home at 2:00 a.m. from a Saturday-night party.

Most stories communicate a general sense of the point-of-attack time, but not a precise one, because the details of this time often don't matter to the audience. However, this is an exercise where time is of the essence, so the first step is to decide exactly and precisely when your story begins. Think about that opening moment and define it in time by identifying the hour of the day, day of the week, month, date, and year—for example, 11:57 a.m., Friday, April 1, 1894.

Whether or not your character is present to the audience at this time, he or she is somewhere in the world of the story. Locate the character and answer the following seven questions. Then move to step 2.

AT THIS MOMENT IN TIME

1. **What is your character doing now?** Whether it's trivial or profound, positive or negative, your character is doing something. Even just the act of sitting usually involves more than that: perhaps the character is resting, waiting, thinking, daydreaming, praying, listening to something, or watching something. The activity may or may not involve others. Briefly describe what your character is doing—for example, Madame Popova is dabbing tears from her eyes with a handkerchief as she studies a large photograph of her deceased husband Nikolai Mikhailovich.

2. **Where is your character doing this?** This may be a setting where important story action occurs, or it may be some place in the offstage world of the character. Briefly describe the setting—for example, the drawing room of Madame Popova's house in the country. Though it's a lovely spring morning outside, the curtains are drawn. The room feels like a tomb, stale and musty.

3. **When is your character doing this?** You have been given a general time frame. Flesh it out by adding specific circumstances—for example, today is the seven-month anniversary of her husband's death.

4. **Who else, if anyone, is here and what are they doing?** If others are present, identify them in relation to your character and briefly describe what they are doing—for example, the only other person here now is Lookah, her elderly manservant. He is trying desperately to cheer her up.

5. **How does your character feel now?** This may or may not be a moment of high emotion. Either way, the character feels something. Describe it—for example, Madame Popova is in deep mourning, as if her husband had just died the night before.

6. **What is your character thinking about now?** Whether it's deep thought or an idle daydream, something is on the character's mind. Briefly describe it—for example, Madame Popova is thinking about Nikolai Mikhailovich, and how lonely and dead she feels without him.

7. **What is the next thing your character says?** Your character's next line may be self-directed or to someone else. It may be the launch of a new subject or a response to something just said. It may occur here and now, or later on. In any event, it's the next line out of your character's mouth. Identify whom is being addressed and write the line—for example, to Lookah, who has been admonishing her for never leaving the house, Madame Popova says, "And I will never go out. Why should I? My life is over. He lies in his grave. I have buried myself in these four walls. We are both dead."

■ STEP 2: MOVE THE CLOCK BACK . . .

. . . one day from the point-of-attack time, give or take a few hours. Go back and answer the same "At this moment in time" questions again. Look for what's important and what's new here and now.

■ STEP 3: MOVE THE CLOCK BACK . . .

. . . one week from the point-of-attack time, give or take a few hours or even a day. Answer the "At this moment in time" questions again.

■ STEP 4: MOVE THE CLOCK BACK . . .

. . . one month from the point-of-attack time, give or take a few days. Answer the "At this moment in time" questions again.

■ STEP 5: MOVE THE CLOCK BACK . . .

. . . one year from the point-of-attack time, give or take a few days or weeks. Answer the "At this moment in time" questions again.

■ STEP 6: MOVE THE CLOCK BACK . . .

. . . five years from the point-of-attack time, give or take a few weeks or months. Answer the "At this moment in time" questions again.

■ STEP 7: MOVE THE CLOCK BACK . . .

. . . ten years from the point-of-attack time, give or take a few weeks or months. Answer the "At this moment in time" questions again.

WRAP-UP

The backstory offers a wealth of ideas and insights for your story. However, when you spend time figuring out the backstory, you may find yourself wanting to write as much of it as possible into the story so nothing is wasted. This can lead to a lot of explanations and enlightened analyses from the characters, and can be the dramatic equivalent of meeting a windbag at a party who wants to tell you his life story.

To keep the dramatic journey moving forward, try not to explain the past so much as suggest it. Remember that we will be making inferences about your characters and their lives as we follow story events and read between the lines. We are more likely to be emotionally engaged when we are leaning forward, piecing clues together, and figuring out the characters rather than being told about them.

Related tools in *Character, Scene, and Story*. To learn more about a character's backstory, go to the "Developing Your Character" section and try "Meet the Parents." Or go to the "Causing a Scene" section and try "The Past Barges In."

DEFINING TRAIT

THE QUICK VERSION
Explore one of your character's dominant traits and its impact on the story

BEST TIME FOR THIS
Any time you need to know a character better

THE BOLD STROKES OF THE CHARACTER
A complex character has a wealth of physiological, psychological, and sociological traits that are revealed scene by scene through the character's actions. Among these traits, some are more important than others: they dominate the mix and often play a pivotal role in story events.

For example, certain physiological traits may come to mind first when you think of Helen Keller from *The Miracle Worker* or the title characters of *Hunchback of Notre Dame* or *Edward Scissorhands*. However, when you think of Ophelia from *Hamlet*, McMurphy from *One Flew Over the Cuckoo's Nest*, or Norma Desmond from *Sunset Boulevard*, your strongest associations might be psychological traits. And, when you think of Walter Lee Younger from *A Raisin in the Sun* or the title characters of *Norma Rae* or *Erin Brockovich*, your strongest associations might be sociological traits.

Whether inherited or acquired, positive or negative, what traits most loudly and clearly define your characters? How might these traits alter the course of the story?

ABOUT THE EXERCISE
This discovery exercise can help you find new story ideas by exploring a defining trait of an important character. You may wish to do the exercise more than once to explore other traits of the same character or other traits of other characters. For best results, think of "defining trait" as a dominant feature of character identity that has—or could have—a significant impact on the dramatic journey. Most of the exercise examples are from *Long Day's Journey into Night* by Eugene O'Neill.

■ A TRAIT THAT DEFINES YOUR CHARACTER
In O'Neill's play, a defining trait of the father, James Tyrone, is his attitude toward money: he is a cheapskate. Many people may be stingy, and this quality may not matter much except occasionally to irritate others. In O'Neill's play, however, James Tyrone's stinginess is paramount to the story.

It's what has led to the ruin of his family and will incite the here-and-now crisis that erupts around the failing health of his son Edmund.

Think about the physiological, psychological, and sociological dimensions of your character, both positive and negative, and select a defining trait to investigate. Then describe it in a word or phrase. If your character were Helen Keller, for example, you might write "deaf mute." If your character were Ophelia, you might write "mentally unbalanced." If your character were Walter Lee Younger, you might write "economically deprived."

THE ROOTS OF THE DEFINING TRAIT

1. *Primary Cause.* Why is James Tyrone so stingy? The reasons lie in a backstory which we can infer from story events. Perhaps he grew up in a poor family with barely enough to eat and much suffering from lack along the way. This childhood poverty could have made him fearful of ending up that way again and might be the main reason for his stinginess now.

Think about your character's defining trait and how it might have developed. Its causes may be rooted in heredity or environment or both, and may trace back to the recent or distant past. You can probably find a number of different reasons that this trait has become so prominent now in your character's identity, but what is the main reason? Take a creative leap, find an explanation that makes sense, and briefly describe the primary cause of your character's defining trait.

2. *Secondary Causes.* Other factors besides childhood poverty may have contributed to James Tyrone's penny pinching. Perhaps his rise to fame as a commercial actor gave him a taste of wealth that makes it even more unbearable to lose. The fact that his income was tied to an unstable career— the life of an actor on the road—also must have made his good fortune seem all the more impermanent and easy to lose.

The roots of your character's defining trait probably include a number of other contributing factors as well. Take another creative leap, look for explanations that make sense, and briefly describe at least two secondary causes of this trait.

THE EFFECTS OF THE DEFINING TRAIT

1. *Backstory.* James Tyrone's stinginess has led him to make a lot of bad decisions that have, in turn, led to major family crises in the past. For example, when his wife Mary took ill, he searched for the cheapest doctor he could find and ended up with a quack who overprescribed morphine. Mary became addicted, had to be institutionalized, and has been struggling with addiction, on and off, ever since. Her addiction is, in part, an effect of her husband's stinginess.

Think about your character's dominant trait and how it may have affected the world of your character before the story begins. If you haven't thought much about the backstory, this is a prime time to do so. Take a creative leap, look for specific examples from the past that make sense, and briefly describe one important positive or negative consequence of your character's dominant trait.

2. **Actual story.** After the curtain goes up on *Long Day's Journey into Night*, James Tyrone's stinginess has an immediate impact on much of what we see. Some of the effects are small. In the dark of night, for example, he has a fit if anyone lights more than one lamp in the house. Other effects of his stinginess are far more significant. When his youngest son Edmund is diagnosed with tuberculosis, James Tyrone wants to send him to the cheapest possible treatment center. In other words, he would rather risk his son's health than spend the money needed for proper medical care. This decision unleashes the family's demons. It sends the older son Jamie into a drunken stupor, pushes his wife Mary back into morphine addiction, and leaves Edmund feeling alone and helpless.

Think about the effects of your character's dominant trait during the here and now of the story. If you haven't worked out much of the actual story events yet, this is an opportunity to explore some possibilities. Take a creative leap, look for specific examples from the story that make sense, and briefly describe one important positive or negative consequence of your character's dominant trait.

3. **Potential story.** Think about your character's dominant trait and how it could affect your story in ways you have not yet considered. Let this final step of the exercise be your biggest creative leap yet. Look for at least one new positive or negative event that could possibly occur as a result of your character's dominant trait. Try to make a choice that surprises you but still makes sense in the unique world of your story. Briefly describe what might happen.

WRAP-UP

As you develop your story, the dominant traits of your characters can guide you through deeper more complex explorations of who the characters are, what they have experienced in the past, and how they might behave and influence events in the present. These bold strokes also give you a simple way to compare and contrast your characters so that you can see how they work together as a story population.

Related tools in *Character, Scene, and Story.* To explore a character's true nature, try any exercise in the "Developing Your Character" section, particularly "Beyond Belief," "Nothing but the Truth," and "What Is the Character Doing Now?"

ALLIES: THEN AND NOW

THE QUICK VERSION
Use ally relationships to explore a character and find new story ideas

BEST TIME FOR THIS
After you are well into the story

HUMAN RELATIONSHIPS: THE HEART OF DRAMA
Through drama, we see how certain individuals connect or fail to connect in times of stress. We also see what they gain or lose in the process. Consider the relationships that have shaped your character's identity by the time the story ends. Among them, you will find significant allies who tried to help the character and either succeeded or failed. These relationships can be a rich source of character and story development.

Some allies may be family members or friends. Others may be less personally involved in the character's life. Either way, their power depends on the resources they have to offer. Such resources may be tangible—such as money, tools, or information—or intangible—such as wisdom, love, or political influence—and their worth is measured by the unique world around them. In most stories, for example, a box of dirt would have little value. In *Dracula*, however, where the title character must sleep by day in a coffin filled with earth from his homeland, a box of dirt is key to survival and he who guards it is a critical ally.

ABOUT THE EXERCISE
Use this exercise to explore the past and present allies of your main character or a principle character. As you do this, remember that the distinction between "ally" and "adversary" is not always easy to draw. Human behavior may change from day to day, a friend may cause harm, a foe may do good, or an action that seemed wrong at first may turn out to be right over time. This exercise gives you definitions to simplify all this so that you can learn more about your character's allies and how they might influence the dramatic journey—even if they do so from the backstory. For best results:

Define "ally" as anyone who wants to help the character. For the purposes of this exercise, therefore, allies are defined *not* by the results of their actions but by their intentions: they mean well. Allies may be individuals, such as a classmate, sweetheart, or spouse, or groups with a common purpose, such as a baseball team, business corporation, or law enforcement agency. Over time, allies may evolve into adversaries, and vice versa.

Interpret freely. As you explore ally categories, translate terms such as "close," "distant," "powerful," and "weak" any way that feels appropriate. A powerful ally might be a world leader in one story and captain of the patrol boys in another. Over time, one character may fit more than one category.

Remember that this exercise is designed to spark creativity, not test organizational skills. If you're not sure who fits what category, just make a choice that feels right and move on. Keep your focus on information that could carry into the story and help you understand why or how things happen.

■ YOUR CHARACTER'S ALLIES — THEN

Who are the most influential allies from your character's past? Use the following categories to trigger ideas as you explore the backstory:

Basic types of allies

Allies may be powerful or weak, close or distant. These qualities may combine in different ways to create at least four basic types of allies.

1. *Close, powerful ally.* This is the greatest of friends: one who has not only a strong personal investment in your character, but also the means to provide the kind of help that makes a difference. Suppose that the character is Jake and that one of his greatest past allies was his Uncle Billy. When Jake's mother couldn't afford to send Jake to college, Uncle Billy provided the cash to send him to beauty school. The result: Jake found a purpose in life—to become a beautician.

Who in your character's past acted as a close powerful ally? Identify the name and relationship. Then give an example of what this ally did for your character and what important effect resulted from that action.

2. *Powerful but distant ally.* This ally has the means to provide help, but isn't invested enough in your character's personal life to be an automatic source of support. Assistance must somehow be earned. A powerful but distant ally in Jake's life was Mrs. Jordon, an upper-middle-class woman for whom his mother did weekly ironing. After much pleading, Mrs. Jordon agreed to hire Jake as her chauffeur for the summer. The result: he began to see how the other half lives and developed a strong thirst for the rich life.

Who in your character's past acted as a powerful but distant ally? Identify the name and relationship. Then give an example of what this ally did and what important effect resulted from that action.

3. *Close but weak ally.* This friend means well and has a strong personal investment in your character, but often lacks the resources necessary to solve problems effectively. A close but weak ally in Jake's past was his mother Linda Louise. When Jake got arrested for possession of marijuana, Linda Louise couldn't handle the stress and got dead drunk instead of raising bail money. The result: Jake spent not one but two nights in the county

jail, where he met a guy named Stomper who would later introduce him to a life of petty crime.

Who in your character's past acted as a close but weak ally? Identify the name and relationship. Then give an example of what this ally did and what important effect resulted from that action.

4. *Weak, distant ally.* Though on your character's side, this friend is minimally involved in your character's personal life and has limited resources available. A weak distant ally in Jake's life, for example, was his father Joe. When Jake was seven, after a strange Christmas dinner, Joe took out the garbage and never returned. The result: Jake grew up with longing for a father, anger toward the world, and a deep fear of abandonment.

Who in your character's past acted as a weak distant ally? Identify the name and relationship. Then give an example of what this ally did and what important effect resulted from that action.

More complex types of allies

Whether powerful or weak, close or distant, some allies may have other distinctive characteristics that set them apart from the others in their category. For example:

1. *Dangerous ally.* This friend wants to be on your character's side and is full of the best intentions, but tends to cause more harm than good. A dangerous ally whom Jake met in the past, for example, was Art, an ex-con running a small-time extortion ring. After Jake dropped out of beauty school, Art took him on as a protégé and, like a father, taught him everything he knew. The result: Jake became hopelessly entrenched in a life of petty crime.

Who in your character's past acted as a dangerous ally? Identify the name and relationship. Then give an example of what this ally did and what important effect resulted from that action.

2. *Adversarial ally.* An ally is, by the exercise definition, one who wants to help. Sometimes, however, it is not assistance but opposition that your character needs for his or her own good—such as when the character is acting in error or doing something potentially harmful.

If your character is trying to punish the wrong person for an injustice, for example, or use dangerous drugs, or commit a criminal act, one trying to stop this effort may be an adversarial ally who has the action of a foe, to thwart, but the intention of a friend, to help. This is one who believes "You'll thank me for this some day." In Jake's life, Ms. Chin, his math teacher, was an adversarial ally who wouldn't let Jake coast through her class as a D student. Ms. Chin pushed, punished, and harassed Jake ruthlessly through senior year. The result: Jake earned his only A in high school and acquired a love of numbers.

Who in your character's past acted as an adversarial ally? Identify the name and relationship. Then give an example of what this ally did and what important effect resulted from that action.

■ YOUR CHARACTER'S ALLIES — NOW

Continue to think about your character's key allies as you look ahead to the story. For quick reference to types of allies used in the exercise, see the table.

TYPE OF ALLY	DESCRIPTION
Close, powerful	Always wants to help and has great resources
Powerful but distant	Has great resources but isn't always available
Close but weak	Wants to help but is often ineffectual
Weak, distant	Tends to be both unreliable and ineffectual
Dangerous	Means well but causes more harm than good
Adversarial	Tries to help in the long run by thwarting now

1. *Start of story*. Think about the allies you have identified from the back-story and how your character might see these relationships as the story begins. When Jake's story begins, for example, he might see his three most important allies as (1) Mrs. Baker, his client and powerful but distant ally; (2) Art, his boss and dangerous ally; and, (3) Linda Louise, his mother and close but weak ally. From your character's point of view—right or wrong—as the story begins:

- Who are the character's three most significant allies now in order of importance? For each, identify the ally's name, relationship, and type.
- For each ally, write a "because" statement to explain why he or she seems important—for example, "Because Mrs. Baker has agreed to slip Jake extra cash if he secretly gives the incriminating videotapes to her."
- Briefly describe what these relationships suggest about your character's values, beliefs, and situation here and now—for example, "Jake values money above all else, naively believes he can outwit his boss, and is putting himself into greater jeopardy than he could ever imagine."

2. *Midpoint.* If story events matter, your character's life is affected as the dramatic journey unfolds. Some things change. Some don't. Take a leap forward and think about what's happening or could be happening halfway through the story. From your character's point of view—right or wrong—at this midpoint:

- Who are the character's three most significant allies now in order of importance? For each, write the ally's name, relationship, and type. These may be the same allies in the same order as before, the same allies in a new order, or a new set of allies. Or, one type of ally may have become another—for example, a powerful ally once close may now be distant.

- Write a "because" statement to tell why each ally seems important now.
- Briefly describe what these relationships suggest about your character's values, beliefs, and situation here and now.

3. *End of story.* Ideally, your character's life has been profoundly changed—or profoundly unchanged—by the time the dramatic journey ends. Take another leap forward. Think about what's happening or could be happening at the end of the story. Compare this with life at the start of the story. From your character's point of view—right or wrong—as the story nears an end:

- Who are the character's three most significant allies now in order of importance? For each, write the ally's name, relationship, and type.
- Write a "because" statement to tell why each ally seems important now.
- Briefly describe what these relationships suggest about your character's values, beliefs, and situation here and now. How has the character changed as a result of the dramatic journey?

WRAP-UP

This exercise builds on the saying: "Birds of a feather flock together." You can learn a lot about your character by looking carefully at his or her most important allies and how these alliances change—or don't change—over time. Out of these key relationships come much of your character's experience of the world and many of the forces that will govern what happens during the dramatic journey.

> **Related tools in *Character, Scene, and Story.*** To use an important character relationship to map out dramatic action, go to the "Causing a Scene" section and try "Relationship Storyboard."

ADVERSARIES: THEN AND NOW

THE QUICK VERSION
Use adversarial relationships to explore a character and develop story ideas

BEST TIME FOR THIS
After you are well into the story

THOSE WHO OPPOSE
Your character's dramatic journey is affected not only by allies who try to provide help, but also by adversaries who try to stop the character from achieving vital objectives. Some foes may be fierce: they have made an intense, uncompromising commitment to stop, defeat, or destroy your character—perhaps a rival in love, political enemy, or home invader. Other foes may be more restrained in their approach: they stand opposed to the character but limit their efforts to block the character's progress—perhaps an ex-spouse, business rival, or angry neighbor. Like allies, adversaries may be strong or weak in resources and may pop up anywhere—in the character's family, work life, social world, or community.

ABOUT THE EXERCISE
Who are your character's most significant adversaries? This exercise complements the previous one by helping you learn more about your character's past and present foes and how they might influence the dramatic journey—even if they do so from the backstory. For best results:

Define "adversary" as anyone who tries to defeat or destroy your character. For the purposes of this exercise, therefore, adversaries are defined *not* by the results of their actions but by their intentions: they aim to thwart. Adversaries may be individuals acting alone or united in groups. Over time, an adversary may become an ally, and vice versa.

Interpret freely. As you explore the categories suggested below, translate terms such as "fierce," "restrained," "powerful," and "weak" any way that feels appropriate. In one world, a powerful adversary might be a prosecutor with evidence to convict. In another, it might be an overbearing mother with a psychological hold on her lonely daughter. Over time, one character may fit more than one category.

Remember that this exercise is designed to spark creativity, not test organizational skills. If you're not sure who fits what category, just make a choice that feels right and move on. Keep your focus on information that could carry into the story and help you understand why or how things happen.

■ YOUR CHARACTER'S ADVERSARIES — THEN

Who are the most significant adversaries from your character's past? Use the following categories to trigger ideas as you explore the backstory.

Basic types of adversaries

Adversaries may be fierce or restrained, and either poor or rich in resources. These qualities may combine in different ways to create at least four basic types of adversaries:

1. *Fierce, powerful adversary.* This is the worse kind of enemy to have: one who is actively committed to your character's demise and has the ability to wreak this destruction. Suppose that the character is Jake and that one of his fierce, powerful allies was Guy Blanchard, a classmate at Byford High who also happened to be son of the principal. Guy hated Jake for reasons he never explained and managed to make everyone believe that Jake had stolen important records from the principal's office. The result: Jake got expelled from Byford and ended up in reform school.

Who in your character's past acted as a fierce, powerful adversary? Identify the name and relationship. Then give an example of what the foe did to your character and what important effect resulted from that action.

2. *Powerful but restrained adversary.* Though able to defeat or destroy your character totally, this foe may not care enough to do so or has another more pressing agenda. In either case, the adversary restrains from full attack. A powerful but restrained adversary in Jake's life, for example, was the Honorable Judge Anderson Black. The judge could have sent Jake to prison on fraud charges, but chose to award him parole in exchange for a Florida vacation secretly financed by Jake's boss Art. The result: Jake came to believe that society is corrupt from top to bottom and everyone in it has a price.

Who in your character's past acted as a powerful but restrained adversary? Identify the name and relationship. Then give an example of what the foe did and what important effect resulted from that action.

3. *Fierce adversary with weak resources.* This foe doesn't have the means to totally defeat or destroy your character, but won't stop trying and may score lucky hits. When Jake was still in beauty school, for example, an envious student named Bob became one of his worst rivals. During the school's annual hairstyling competition, Bob tried to eliminate Jake by putting a sleeping pill into his coffee. The result: Jake got extremely tired and, instead of winning the competition as everyone expected, placed second to Bob's third.

Who in your character's past acted as a fierce adversary with weak resources? Identify the name and relationship. Then give an example of what the foe did and what important effect resulted from that action.

4. *Restrained adversary with weak resources.* This is a back-burner foe who doesn't have the motivation or means to cause significant harm, but still manages to make life unpleasant for your character. Jake's sister Jill was such an adversary. She disapproved of his lifestyle and used his mother's birthday—the only time they still gathered each year—to expose Jake as a crook in front of the family. The result: Jake rarely goes home to Milwaukee.

Who in your character's past acted as a restrained adversary with weak resources? Identify the name and relationship. Then give an example of what the foe did and what important effect resulted from that action.

More complex types of adversaries

Whether fierce or restrained, rich or poor in resources, some foes may have certain characteristics that set them apart from the others in their category. For example:

1. *Beneficial adversary.* Though acting with malice and seeking to inflict harm, this foe takes actions that lead unexpectedly to benefits for your character. One of Jake's most helpful enemies was his older brother Johnny, who used to make him pay weekly protection money to avoid getting beaten up. The result: Jake joined the work force at an early age, starting as a paper boy, and developed a sense of self-reliance and pride of accomplishment unmatched in his family.

Who in your character's past acted as a beneficial adversary? Identify the name and relationship. Then give an example of what the foe did and what important effect resulted from that action.

2. *Friendly foe.* An adversary is, by the exercise definition, one who wants to defeat or destroy your character. Some adversaries may do this by posing as friends who help the character in the short term in order to defeat the character in the long term. These false friends often cloak lies and deceptions in wit, charm, and friendship to encourage self-destructive traits, such as jealousy; self-destructive behavior, such as binge eating or drinking; and misguided courses of action, such as plotting to rob a bank to get out of debt.

In any case, the friendly foe's real intention is malicious, like that of a wolf in sheep's clothing. In Jake's life, one friendly foe was Buck Burke, a high school associate with eyes for Jake's fiancée Susan Mae Bender. Buck led Jake to believe incorrectly that Susan Mae had been unfaithful to him. The result: Jake broke off the engagement and moved from Milwaukee to Chicago.

Who in your character's past acted as a friendly foe? Identify the name and relationship. Then give an example of what this foe did and what important effect resulted from that action.

■ YOUR CHARACTER'S ADVERSARIES — NOW

Continue to think about your character's key adversaries as you look ahead to the story. For quick reference to types of adversaries, see the table.

TYPE OF ADVERSARY	DESCRIPTION
Fierce, powerful	Always wants to defeat and has great resources
Powerful but restrained	Sometimes wants to defeat and has great resources
Fierce with weak resources	Always wants to defeat but is often ineffectual
Restrained with weak resources	Sometimes wants to defeat but is often ineffectual
Beneficial	Intends to defeat, but causes success
Friendly foe	Harms in the long term by being helpful now

1. *Start of story*. Think about the adversaries you identified from the backstory and how your character might see these relationships as the story begins. When Jake's story begins, for example, he might see his top foes as: (1) Stomper, his partner in crime and fierce, powerful adversary; (2) the Chicago Police Department, a frequent pursuer and powerful but restrained adversary; and, (3) Edie Shaw, a client and friendly foe. From your character's point of view—right or wrong—as the story begins:
   - Who are the character's three most significant adversaries now in order of importance? For each, identify the foe's name, relationship, and type.
   - For each adversary, write a "because" statement to explain why he or she seems important—for example, "Because Stomper is jealous of Jake's relationship with their boss Art and is out to get Jake."
   - Briefly describe what these relationships suggest about your character's values, beliefs, and situation here and now—for example, "Jake values his advantageous position in the business, believes that Stomper is not to be trusted, and is plotting to get Stomper before Stomper gets him."

2. *Midpoint*. As the dramatic journey unfolds, some things will change and some won't. Take a leap forward and think about what's happening or could be happening halfway through the story. From your character's point of view—right or wrong—at this midpoint:
   - Who are the character's three most significant adversaries now in order of importance? For each, write the foe's name, relationship, and type. These may be the same adversaries in the same order

as before, the same adversaries in a new order, or a new set of adversaries. Or, one type of adversary may have become another—for example, a powerful but restrained adversary may now be a fierce enemy.

- Write a "because" statement to tell why each foe seems important now.
- Briefly describe what these relationships suggest about your character's values, beliefs, and situation here and now.

3. *End of story.* Take another leap forward. Think about what's happening or could be happening at the end of the story and how this compares with what was happening when the story began. From your character's point of view—right or wrong—as the story ends:

- Who are the character's three most significant adversaries now in order of importance? For each, write the foe's name, relationship, and type.
- Write a "because" statement to tell why each foe seems important now.
- Briefly describe what these relationships suggest about your character's values, beliefs, and situation here and now. How has the character changed as a result of the dramatic journey?

WRAP-UP

As you develop your story, keep thinking about who stands in your character's way, what motivates such opposition, and how this resistance affects the character's dramatic journey in a positive or negative way. If a character starts to feel flat or passive, it may be a sign that you have not created adversaries who are fierce enough and powerful enough to force the character to a more intense and meaningful level of action.

Related tools in *Character, Scene, and Story.* To explore conflict at the scenic level, go to the "Causing a Scene" section and try "Mother Conflict." To use an important character relationship to map out dramatic action, try "Relationship Storyboard" in the same section.

CHARACTERS IN CONTRAST

THE QUICK VERSION
Learn more about two important characters by comparing them

BEST TIME FOR THIS
After you have a working sense of the main character

THE DRAMATIC VALUE OF SIMILARITY AND CONTRAST
Whether friends or foes, characters in a relationship tend to be in some ways alike and in some ways different. Their similarities help explain what draws them together and motivates them to interact. Their differences make them each distinct and offer sources of conflict for the story.

Think about the traits, qualities, and beliefs of your characters. How well have you balanced the similarities and differences among them? If two characters are allies, for example, we need to see enough overlap between them to believe their relationship. If the characters are too alike, however, they may seem only like slightly different versions of each other and their dramatic functions may feel redundant.

If two characters are adversaries, we need to see enough contrast between them to understand why they fail to fit together. If the characters are too different, however, we may have trouble believing that they could ever end up in the same story.

Contrast also helps define characters by showing what they are not. For example, plays like *Buried Child* and films like *Rocky Horror Picture Show* introduce us to unusual families. In each case, their oddity is measured by the contrast that results when ordinary people enter their worlds, such as the son's girlfriend in *Buried Child* or the stranded newlyweds in *Rocky Horror*. In the play *Lakeboat*, we meet a crew of men who have lost their dreams. We understand this loss by seeing it in contrast to the bright future awaiting the college student who has come aboard for a summer job.

ABOUT THE EXERCISE
Use this exercise to compare your main character to another principal character in your story. You may wish to repeat the exercise with the main character and other principals, one at a time, so you can better understand how the main character fits into—and is defined by—the population of the story. For best results:

Focus on both similarities and differences. You are about to compare two characters in twenty-one categories. In each, decide first whether the characters are more alike or different in this area. Then look for appropriate examples that help explain why the characters connect or don't connect during the story.

Focus on character traits, qualities, or beliefs that could possibly affect the story. Try to avoid choices that will have no influence on story events and are only for their own sake.

List your responses in columns. Create one list for each character so that you can easily see how they compare. You will be asked first to respond objectively as the writer and later subjectively as each character.

Exercise examples are from *Topdog/Underdog* by Suzan-Lori Parks. The characters in contrast are Lincoln and Booth.

■ HOW THE WORLD SEES YOUR CHARACTERS

For each character, respond objectively as the all-seeing, all-knowing writer:

1. *Inherited physical trait.* The physical traits of your characters can have a significant effect on how they behave in your story. Some of these traits— such as gender, age, race, ethnicity, body type, and identifying facial features—have been determined by birth. In *Topdog/Underdog*, Lincoln and Booth have inherited certain physical similarities: they are both African American males in their thirties and they are biologically brothers. Birth also has determined that Lincoln is the "older brother" to Booth. These ties are part of what keeps them together and pushes them apart as they vie to be "topdog" in each other's eyes. Think about how your characters compare and contrast physically. For each character, identify an important inherited physical trait that could affect story events.

2. *Acquired physical trait.* Some of the physical traits, qualities, states, or conditions of your characters have been not inherited, but acquired as a result of environment, lifestyle, and experience. Such traits may be as temporary as a sunburn or as permanent as a scar. Lincoln and Booth both exhibit a manner of dress that physically reflects their professions and approaches to life. Lincoln enters the play in whiteface and an Abraham Lincoln costume, an outfit that he wears at the arcade shooting booth where he works as a target for customers pretending to be assassins. Later, Booth arrives home in a big coat that conceals two new suits—he wears one inside the other—sleeves full of shoes and belts, pockets full of neckties and whiskey, and pants hiding folded shirts and a pornographic magazine—all goods from a day's shoplifting. Think again about how your characters compare and contrast physically. For each character, identify an acquired physical trait, quality, state, or condition that might matter in the story.

3. *Psychological trait.* Lincoln and Booth are psychologically opposites in many ways. The pessimist Lincoln sees himself as a victim of bad luck. He has lost his parents, his business partner, and his wife. He has no money and no home of his own. When the play begins, he sees little in his future,

except a hearse. The optimist Booth, on the other hand, has reached a point in life where he wants more than he has now. He is hungry for success and determined at all costs to achieve it. Are your two characters psychologically similar or different? For each character, identify an important psychological trait.

4. *Social trait.* Lincoln and Booth are alike in their inability to maintain meaningful relationships with women. Lincoln has lost his wife Cookie, and Booth has been unsuccessful in wooing his ex-girlfriend Grace. "She's in love with me again," he tells his brother, "but she don't know it yet." The loneliness of the brothers keeps them dependent on each other for daily companionship. Are your characters socially similar or different? For each character, identify a key social trait.

5. *Economics.* Lincoln and Booth are also alike in their lack of spending power. Lincoln cannot afford a place of his own and has to stay at his brother's, where he must sleep at night in a recliner. Booth has managed to establish a home. However, it's only a seedily furnished room with no running water, and he needs his brother's income to pay the weekly rent. Are your characters economically similar or different? Identify the economics of each character.

6. *Morality.* Lincoln and Booth have defined their personal morality to suit their needs. Lincoln used to be a con artist—a three-card monte dealer—who saw his partner get shot and killed in front of him. This experience scared Lincoln into giving up the cards and trying to make an "honest living." Booth, on the other hand, is a petty thief with no qualms about stealing what he wants or hustling others out of their cash. Are your characters morally similar or different? For each character, identify a key moral stance.

7. *Extra special talent.* This is something at which your characters excel that could possibly affect what happens in the story. Lincoln is the best three-card monte dealer around. He has a magical gift for "throwing the cards." Booth has a knack for shoplifting or, as he calls it, "boosting." He can steal anything that will fit into his deep pockets or under his coat. Think about the special gifts of your characters and how they compare. For each of your characters, identify an extra special talent.

8. *Extra special lack of talent.* This is something which your characters cannot do well at all that could possibly affect what happens in the story. Lincoln has a hard time holding on to what he has managed to acquire— whether it's the Chinese takeout "skrimps" he had intended to eat for dinner, his job at the shooting arcade, or his wife Cookie. Booth has a dream of being a three-card monte dealer, but no dealer skills to back it up. His attempts at the three-card monte routine are "studied and awkward." In effect, he is unable to realize his dreams on his own. For each of your characters, identify an extra special lack of talent.

> *What the character cannot do is sometimes more important—and more telling—than what the character can do.*

9. *A distinguishing personal asset.* This is a trait that you haven't already identified; it defines something important about your characters and gives them a clear advantage in certain situations. Lincoln's troubled past has left him with a wisdom that enables him at times to transcend the trials of his existence. Even when he is working as a target in a shooting booth, he can muster up a sense of peacefulness and meaningful contemplation. Meanwhile Booth has drive and purpose. When life defeats him, as it often does, he always manages to get back on his feet. He's the type who never gives up. For each of your characters, identify a distinguishing personal asset.

10. *A distinguishing personal liability.* This is a trait that you haven't already identified; it also defines something important about your characters and puts them at a clear disadvantage in certain situations. Though Lincoln has sworn off the cards, for example, he is still addicted to them. Their presence in the room is a constant source of temptation despite the danger they pose. Booth's liability is his explosive temper. His inability to keep it in check may explain many of his problems with women as well as his feuding with his brother. For each of your characters, identify a distinguishing personal liability.

11. *Greatest single virtue.* Lincoln and Booth are alike in their loyalty to each other. Despite their rivalry and bickering, each has come to the other's aid in times of trouble. What is the greatest virtue of each of your characters?

12. *Greatest single vice.* Lincoln and Booth are also alike in their jealousy of each other. Despite the brotherly tie, they both constantly try to best the other. What is the greatest vice of each of your characters?

13. *Greatest life ambition.* Before the play begins, Lincoln's greatest ambition is to earn an honest living that will bring him the simple pleasures of life, such as a bed of his own. Booth's ambitions are loftier. He wants "topdog" status in society so he can live high on the hog with his ex-girlfriend Grace at his side. Think about what your characters want most out of life as your story begins. For each of your characters, identify his or her greatest ambition so far.

14. *Greatest fear.* Lincoln fears the dangers of the hustling world so much that he has given up the thing he does best: throwing the cards. Booth fears being alone. He would rather retreat to fantasies inspired by pornography rather than face the fact that his ex-girlfriend no longer wants him. Think about how your characters compare and contrast. What is each one's greatest fear?

15. *Greatest anger.* Lincoln and Booth are alike in the ire they feel toward being betrayed by a loved one, especially each other. Their anger stems from being abandoned by their parents. What most angers each of your characters?

16. *Greatest secret.* Interesting characters tend to have interesting secrets—some of which are revealed during the story and some of which are not. What your character chooses to hide from everyone or from most people reveals much and can be a powerful source of story ideas. One of Lincoln's biggest secrets is that he has become sexually dysfunctional. One of Booth's biggest secrets is that he knows about Lincoln's problem because he, Booth, slept with Lincoln's wife. What is the greatest secret of each of your characters?

17. **Most unusual fact.** Among the unusual facts that make Lincoln and Booth unique are the names they have had to carry through life, with Lincoln named after president Abraham Lincoln and Booth named after the assassin John Wilkes Booth. What's particularly odd is that their father gave them these names as a joke. What is most unusual about each of your characters?

■ **HOW YOUR CHARACTERS SEE THEMSELVES**

Now switch to the subjective—and not necessarily accurate—viewpoint of each character in self-reflection, and answer in their unique voices, as if writing dialogue. In a few sentences for each character, sum up the following beliefs:

1. *Philosophy of love.* When the story begins, what important conclusions has each character drawn about love?

2. *Family philosophy.* What has each character come to believe about family based on his or her experiences before the story begins?

3. *Political philosophy.* How would each character sum up his or her political beliefs when the story begins?

4. *Spiritual philosophy.* What does each character have to say about God, religion, spirituality, or the meaning of life?

WRAP-UP

Think about how your two characters compare and contrast. How similar or different are they? Think also about how they fit or don't fit together in the story. When all is said and done, do you see them primarily as friends or foes? You can analyze your findings in many ways, as long as they make sense to you and serve the story. A few thoughts to keep in mind about your findings:

- **If your characters are mostly friends,** do they have enough similarities to form a believable union, and enough differences to make them each distinct? Even if opposites attract, there are usually some points of commonality that explain how two individuals fit together.

If your characters seem too different, you may need to get a better understanding of them and how they connect. If they seem too much alike, you may need to rethink some of their traits, qualities, and beliefs to make them each more unique and interesting.

- *If your characters are mostly foes,* do they have enough contrast to fuel the conflict between them, and enough similarity to explain why they have to deal with each other? If the characters are too similar, you may need to focus more on the differences that contribute to the problems between them. If the characters are too different, you may need to focus more on the commonality that has trapped them in this adversarial relationship.

Related tools in *Character, Scene, and Story.* To continue exploring characters in relation to one another, go to the "Developing Your Character" section and try "Side by Side" or "Two Views of One Character."

FINDING THE CHARACTER'S VOICE

THE QUICK VERSION
Hone and contrast the unique voices of two characters

BEST TIME FOR THIS
Any time you need to know a character better

SPEECH: A KEY TO CHARACTER IDENTITY
Imagine three characters talking in a room: Nora Helmer from *A Doll's House*, Blanche DuBois from *A Streetcar Named Desire*, and Hester La Negrita from *In the Blood*. Even if the room suddenly went dark, we would always know who was speaking, because each of these characters has such a distinct voice. "Voice" here refers not to vocal quality but rather the manner in which a character expresses personal thoughts and feelings.

Ideally, your characters do not all talk the way you do. Nor do they all talk like one another. Each has an individual voice—a unique way of saying things—that like a fingerprint identifies the character and sets him or her apart from everyone else in the story. This voice grows out of who the character is and finds its shape through the word choices, figures of speech, references, and other language strategies that the character uses consciously or subconsciously in speech.

> *How distinct are the voices of your characters? One measure is the ease with which you can take a set of lines from one character and give them to another character during editing. If dialogue can be easily reassigned, you have not yet found the voices of your characters.*

ABOUT THE EXERCISE
Though speech is its focus, this exercise is not about writing dialogue so much as getting to know your characters. Ideally, a unique and consistent voice will emerge from each of them as you develop your story. Several factors will shape this voice. Some are long-term factors that affect the character at the story level. Some are short-term factors that affect the character at the scenic level.

Use this exercise to explore such influences on any two of your characters. By focusing on two characters rather than just one, you may gain a better sense of the contrast—or lack of contrast—between them. The greater the contrast in character voice, the greater the differentiation in character identity. Begin by choosing two characters whose voices you wish to explore in more depth.

■ LONG-TERM FACTORS THAT CAN SHAPE A CHARACTER'S VOICE

Among factors that influence how characters talk, some are so deeply part of the character's identity that they usually don't change over the course of the story. First and foremost, the character's unique traits and basic values will color most of his or her dialogue, including how the character communicates with others, what subjects the character stresses or ignores, and how the character explains or describes things. Within each character's deep identity, any or all of the following long-term factors can influence how the character talks:

1. *Ethnicity.* Your character's racial and cultural background may affect the character's voice in many ways. For example, the character may speak in a certain dialect and use cultural idioms and references. Voice also may be affected by whether the character is speaking in his or her native language.

2. *Age*. Children tend to speak differently from adults. Elders tend to speak differently from teenagers. Does the character's age have any bearing on his or her art of expression?

3. *Geography.* Some terms and expressions, especially slang, are regional or local in nature. In the United States, for example, the vocabulary, style, and rhythms of a southerner might be different from those of a northerner.

4. *History.* The events that have happened or not happened during the character's life may also affect personal expression, particularly in the use of slang and local references. If your story takes place in a different time period, country, or planet, you need to consider how these elements may affect the character's voice.

5. *Attitude toward life*. Does your character tend to be an optimist or pessimist? This general attitude can affect what topics the character chooses and how positively or negatively the character describes them.

6. *Education.* A high-school dropout tends to speak differently from a PhD. Your character's word choices and syntax may reveal the character's educational background without your having to explain it.

7. *Occupation.* Your character's work life may include jargon and technical terms that affect the character's word choices and use of metaphors or similes to describe life outside of work. For example, a banker might speak differently from a rock musician, or undertaker, or prostitute, or computer technician.

8. *Lifestyle.* Language choices can be affected by how easy or how hard life has been, how hip or not hip the character may be, and other personal lifestyle factors. If the character belongs to any social subcultures, such as a drug subculture, racetrack subculture, or sexual subculture, he or she may use terms and metaphors common in these microworlds.

9. *Special interests.* Hobbies and other special interests can affect how your character sees others and communicates with them. For example, a sports enthusiast might tend to use sports terms and analogies to express ideas and feelings.

10. *Political beliefs.* Politics can also influence how characters express themselves, the reverence or irreverence with which they speak about institutions or society, and the terms they use. Is the character conservative or liberal? Politically correct or incorrect? Racist? Sexist? Ageist? Homophobic?

11. *Religious beliefs.* The character's spiritual beliefs or lack of them may matter as well. Does the character use religious references and analogies to express ideas and feelings? How otherworldly or worldly is the character's speech?

■ SHORT-TERM INFLUENCES ON A CHARACTER'S VOICE

Some of the factors that influence a character's voice are short-lived: they come and go with the dramatic moment, sometimes on a moment-by-moment basis, such as:

1. **Who the listener is.** Characters tend to speak in different ways to different people. How the character addresses the boss at work, for example, might be quite different from how the character addresses an intimate friend, an attractive stranger in a single's bar, or a door-to-door salesperson. The current relationship with the listener may also matter. Are they on good terms or bad terms?

2. *Current physical state.* The character's physical condition can affect word choices, expression, and sentence construction. Is the character healthy, or under the weather, or deathly ill? High or sober? Tired or alert?

3. *Current emotional state.* How your character feels may influence personal expression as well. For example, fear, anger, surprise, suspicion, joy, sorrow, and other emotions affect how efficiently or inefficiently, how verbose or terse, how friendly or cold your character will be.

4. *Current mental state.* Your character's intellectual abilities and psychological functions are dynamic and can become impaired under stress. This factor can affect how well or poorly your character communicates with others and how interested or uninterested the character may be in certain subjects.

5. *This particular setting.* The immediate environment may affect how characters express themselves to others, just as characters in a funeral parlor tend to speak differently from characters at a football game, or characters in the bedroom tend to speak differently from characters in church.

6. *This particular time.* The time of day, such as early morning or late at night, and other circumstances, such as just before a political revolution or just after one, all can affect word choices, sentence constructions, and use of metaphors and references to express ideas and feelings.

7. *This particular topic.* The subject at hand is often a key influence as well. The character may speak passionately about some subjects and dispassionately about others. Some topics may be easy to discuss and others, very difficult.

8. *Dramatic elements now at work.* The character's current objective, problem, motivation, and strategy also affect how things are said or not said, and can change from scene to scene or from moment to moment within a scene.

■ HOW YOUR CHARACTERS' VOICES COMPARE

Get ready to translate ten generic statements into the unique voices of your characters. Translate each statement twice: first into Character 1's voice and then into Character 2's voice. You can imagine the characters in the same situation or different situations speaking to the same listener or different listeners. The focus here is on how they each talk, not on how they share experiences. Look for as much contrast between their individual voices as possible, using these three steps for each generic statement:

1. Read the generic statement and think about what it expresses. Imagine this statement as subtext for a single line of dialogue or a monologue.

2. Imagine the character in an appropriate situation from your story or backstory and identify an appropriate listener. Think about what's going on in the situation you chose. Remember that the listener may be an onstage or offstage character, friend or foe, close relationship or stranger.

3. Think again about the long-term and short-term factors that can shape the character's voice. Then translate the generic statement into a speech that reflects the unique voice of each character. Depending on what's appropriate for this character in this situation with this listener, this speech may range from a word or two to an in-depth monologue.

TEN STATEMENTS FOR TRANSLATION

I've got good news.	I'm afraid.
I've got bad news.	I'm angry.
I love you.	I'm happy.
I hate you.	I'm sad.
I never expected this.	I don't trust you.

■ LISTENING AGAIN TO EACH CHARACTER'S VOICE

In the last section, you focused on two characters, how they express themselves and how their voices contrast. As a last step:

1. *Go back and read all ten speeches that you wrote for Character 1.* Listen for continuity in this single voice. Do all of these lines really sound as if they're coming from the same character? If any speech does not seem true to this character, why not? How might the speech be changed?

2. *Do the same quick analysis for Character 2.*

If you have already begun to use these same characters in your script, you can try this same type of analysis with a scene in which they appear. First read only Character 1's speeches, then only Character 2's. How strong are the two different voices that emerge?

WRAP-UP

Ideally, each character's voice is so distinct that it would not make sense coming out of anyone else's mouth. Finding this voice is an important and ongoing part of the character development process. As you write and edit your script, continue to listen to your characters and how they distinguish themselves from one another in their speech. If their voices at times seem to blur, you may need to rethink the long-term and short-term factors at work and make some of these factors matter more.

Related tools in *Character, Scene, and Story*. To learn more about what makes each character distinct, go to the "Developing Your Character" section and try "Side by Side." To continue exploring how your character might express ideas and feelings, go to the "Causing a Scene" section and try "Phrase Book."

THREE CHARACTERS IN ONE

THE QUICK VERSION
Analyze a character from three different points of view

BEST TIME FOR THIS
After you have a working sense of who the characters are

THE VALUE OF CHARACTER OPINIONS — RIGHT OR WRONG
When characters look at themselves, one another, or the world around them, they may or may not reach similar conclusions about what they see. Each has a certain opinion that reflects the character's unique identity, life experience, needs, problems, feelings, and present circumstances. Few characters are always right or always wrong. Most have some ability to be accurate or mistaken, to embrace the facts or flee from them, to uncover truths or foster delusions. Right or wrong, their perceptions say a lot about who they each are and how they fit together.

ABOUT THE EXERCISE
Get ready to look at one character from three different perspectives: that of the character, that of another character in the story, and that of a more objective observer from outside the story, such as yourself. Among these perspectives, each point of agreement or disagreement is an opportunity to learn more not only about the chosen characters but also about their relationship. Exercise examples are from A *Streetcar Named Desire* by Tennessee Williams. To begin:

Choose Character 1. This will be your focus for the entire exercise. Use a principal character, preferably your main character, and write down his or her name—for example, Blanche.

Choose Character 2. Find someone from the story who knows Character 1 well—or at least thinks so. This second character might be a friend who tends to see the good in Character 1, or a foe who tends to see the bad, or someone in between who is less biased. Identify Character 2's name and relationship—for example, Stanley, her brother-in-law.

Use yourself as the objective outside observer. Remember that you are the final word on what's true and not true in the world of your story.

■ THREE DIFFERENT VIEWS OF THE SAME CHARACTER

Answer each question three times: first as Character 1, then as Character 2, and then as an outside observer. Look for similarities and contrasts in these responses.

1. *One word.* If Blanche had to describe herself in one word, she might say "genteel." Her brother-in-law Stanley, on the other hand, might say "whore." An outside observer might say "needy." In one word—noun or adjective—how would your Character 1 be described from each of the three perspectives?

2. *Two words.* If a second word were added to the first for greater meaning, Blanche might describe herself as a "genteel aristocrat." Stanley might see her not just as a "whore" but as a "phony whore." An outside observer might see her not just as "needy" but as "desperately needy." From each of the three perspectives describing Character 1, add a second word that qualifies and adds significant meaning to the first word.

3. *Description.* If Blanche could be a little more verbose, she might describe herself as a genteel and misunderstood aristocrat unjustly abandoned in a cold, cruel world. Stanley might see her as a phony, lying, homewrecking whore who must be driven out. An outside observer might see her as a needy lost soul desperate for the love and kindness the world has denied her. From each of the three perspectives, write a brief description of Character 1 that includes the original two words—or versions of them—in any order.

4. *Metaphor.* A metaphor is a figure of speech in which a subject is described poetically by suggesting its resemblance to something else—for example, a person might be a sly fox, diamond in the rough, or ray of sunshine. The implied comparison tells us something important about the subject. Blanche might see herself as a lily waiting to bloom. Stanley might see her as a rat running around loose in his cupboard. An outside observer might see her as a streetcar named "Desire." From each of the three perspectives, find an apt metaphor to describe Character 1.

5. *Positive action.* From Blanche's perspective, one of her most positive actions in the story is to try to convince Stella to leave Stanley. Why might Blanche see that as good? Because he is a Neanderthal. From Stanley's point of view, one of Blanche's most positive actions is to allow herself to be institutionalized. Why might he see that as good? Because it finally gets her out of his hair. For an outside observer, one of Blanche's most positive actions might be to woo Mitch. Why? Because she is trying to pick up the pieces of her life and build a new future. From each of the three perspectives, identify a positive action of Character 1 and explain why it's a good thing.

6. *Negative action.* From Blanche's point of view, one of her most negative actions in the story is to come to Stella's home in the first place. Why might Blanche see this as bad? Because it's a one-room hovel with no room for her. Stanley might agree that her coming there was a bad thing. Why?

Because she is a threat to his marriage. An outside observer might say that one of Blanche's most negative actions is to insult Stanley. Why is this a bad thing? Because she creates an enemy whom she cannot conquer. From each of the three perspectives, identify a negative action of Character 1 and explain why it's a bad thing.

7. *Positive trait.* If Blanche had to name one of her greatest assets, she might say it's her cultural refinement. From Stanley's point of view, one of Blanche's assets might be a shapely figure. For an outside observer, one asset might be her ability to wield fragility like a powerful weapon. In your story, from each of the three perspectives, identify an important positive trait of Character 1.

8. *Negative trait.* If Blanche had to name one of her greatest liabilities, she might say that it's the tawdry past she must keep hidden. From Stanley's perspective, one of Blanche's negative traits is her high-and-mighty manner. For an outside observer, one weakness might be her inability to face the truth. In your story, from each of the three perspectives, identify an important negative trait of Character 1.

9. *Summary.* Think about your responses to the exercise questions. What have you learned about Character 1? What have you learned about Character 2? What have you learned about the relationship between them? Sum up your key discoveries.

WRAP-UP

Whether they are thinking about themselves, each other, or the world around them, your characters have different views of the dramatic events that are unfolding. Try to stay aware of these individual perceptions, how they compare and contrast, and how they might influence not only what's happening now in the story but also what might happen next.

Related tools in *Character, Scene, and Story.* For another look at how characters view each other, go to the "Developing Your Character" section and try "Two Views of One Character."

THE SECRET LIVES OF CHARACTERS

THE QUICK VERSION
Explore character secrets and their potential impact on your story

BEST TIME FOR THIS
Any time you need to know a character better

THE DRAMA OF SECRETS
Whether they are hiding something good or bad, secret keepers are engaged in dramatic action. They have an objective (to conceal), a problem (the risk of exposure), and a motivation (enough at stake to require privacy). Having secrets implies vulnerability (someone will be affected in an unwanted way if the secret is exposed), inner life (the keeping of a secret is often woven with strong emotion), and power (to keep a secret from others is to limit and control their knowledge in order to achieve a certain end). The dramatic nature of secrets may help explain why so many dramatic characters have them.

To know what characters are hiding is to know them in a more profound way, since their secrets often suggest a lot about what they value and what they fear. What are the secrets of your characters? How might these secrets affect character behavior and story events?

ABOUT THE EXERCISE
Use this exercise to explore the secrets of your characters and find new story ideas. For best results:

Develop two work lists. For A, list the names of your onstage characters. If you have a large cast, limit the list to the six most important characters. For B, list the names of at least three offstage characters from the past or present who may significantly influence the onstage story.

In each round, imagine a certain type of secret and use it to uncover an important truth that at least one of your characters is hiding at any time in your story or backstory. As you choose characters to explore, focus first on the A list and use the B list as a backup. Feel free to choose the same character any number of times. In the end, you may find that some of your characters have many secrets, and others have none.

Focus on each secret two ways. First express it in the character's voice. Then analyze it from an objective third-person point of view. Remember that, if a particular type of secret doesn't fit your story, it could still have an important function in the backstory.

■ **CHARACTER CONFIDENTIAL**

1. *I've got a secret about who I am.* For example, I am Joe in *Angels in America*. I'm married to Harper and most people think of me as straight, but I am secretly gay.

Which of your characters is concealing important information about his or her identity at any point in your story or backstory? What self-truth is being hidden? Remember to state the secret in your character's voice.

- *What values does this secret imply?* Secrets tend to suggest certain aspects of the secret keeper's value system. Joe's efforts to hide his sexual identity imply that he considers heterosexuality more desirable than homosexuality. This view reflects his Mormon upbringing and conservative Republican background. Joe's secrecy also implies that he values having a certain image at home, at work, and in public. Think about your character's secret. What values does it suggest?
- *What fears does this secret imply?* Secrets are often mixed with the worry that something important will be lost if the secret is not properly managed. Joe's secrecy suggests a fear of being rejected by his family, coworkers, and friends as well as a concern about damaging his political career. Justified or not, what fears are implied by your character's secrecy?
- *What actions might this secret trigger?* Secrets may lead characters to do things they might not otherwise do. Some of these actions can be telling indicators of the character's true nature. Joe's secret leads him to marry someone he doesn't love and to lead a double life of furtive sexual activity with other men. What might your character do as a result of his or her secret? Look for new story possibilities that make sense for your character.

2. *I've got a secret about how I am.* I am Blanche in *A Streetcar Named Desire*. When I first arrive in the French Quarter, no one else here knows that I'm penniless and homeless, that I lost my teaching job due to a sex scandal, and that I have been working as a prostitute.

Which of your characters is concealing important information about his or her current situation? State the secret in your character's voice.

Blanche's efforts to hide her dire circumstances suggest that she values her reputation, and fears the shame and isolation that could result from exposure. Her secret leads her to tell lies, drink in private, and use elaborate deceptions to manipulate others into helping her. What values and fears are implied by your character's secret? What might your character do as a result of this secret?

3. *I've got a secret about something I did in the past.* I am Claudius in *Hamlet*. I killed Hamlet's father, the king, so I could marry his wife and assume the throne of Denmark.

Which of your characters is covering up a significant deed—good or bad—from the recent or distant past? What did the character do? State the secret in your character's voice.

Claudius's secret suggests that he values power above all else and that he fears the disgrace and punishment that his crime, if discovered, could produce. His secret motivates him to exile the suspicious Hamlet and to plot his death. What values and fears are implied by your character's secret? What might your character do as a result of this secret?

4. *I've got a secret about something I am doing now.* I am Emma in *Betrayal* and I am having an affair with my husband's best friend Jerry.

Which of your characters is covering up a current activity? What is the character secretly doing?

Emma's secret suggests that she treasures the freedom to follow her heart's desire, but still values her marriage enough to hide uncomfortable truths that may damage it. Her secrecy also implies a fear of losing her husband's love and respect. The secret leads her down a trail of omissions and lies to a rented flat in another town which she and Jerry use for afternoon trysts. What values and fears are implied by your character's secret? What might your character do as a result of this secret?

5. *I've got a secret about something I plan to do in the future.* I am Boy Willie at the beginning of *The Piano Lesson* and I am planning to sell the family piano, even though I only own half of it and I know my sister will refuse to sell the other half. The money will go toward buying some land in Mississippi that my ancestors once worked as slaves.

Which of your characters has a secret plan in the works? What is the plan?

Boy Willie's plan implies that he values the future more than the past: he would sacrifice an important family heirloom and his relationship with his sister in order to gain the social status and income that a landowner can achieve. His plan also implies a fear of ending up on the "bottom of life" if he does nothing to advance himself. The secret has led him to return to his Pittsburgh home after three years with a truck and a friend to get the piano. What values and fears are implied by your character's secret? What might your character do as a result of this secret?

6. *I've got a secret about something I desire.* I am Sister Aloysius in *Doubt.* I can't say this openly because of the scandal it could cause, but I want to find out if the new priest Father Flynn is having an inappropriate relationship with one of the students in my school.

Which of your characters has a secret desire? What is it?

Aloysius's secret implies that she values her duties as a school principal and the image of the school and church in her community. Her secret also implies the fear of a child in danger. As a result of her secret, Aloysius puts her staff on high alert for any unusual activity in the school and focuses aggressively on a questionable report about Flynn. What values and fears are implied by your character's secret? What might your character do as a result of this secret?

7. *I've got a secret about you and me (something we share).* I am George in *Who's Afraid of Virginia Woolf?* and you are my wife Martha. We have been sharing a secret for years: we have an imaginary son. He is part of a game we love to play.

Which of your characters share a secret about themselves? What is it?

George and Martha's secret suggests that they value their relationship and the intimacy that a shared fantasy can nurture. Their secret also suggests fears of reality and separation. The secret leads them to play elaborate and competitive games to keep their fantasy world alive. What values and fears are implied by the secret your characters share? What might they do as a result of this secret?

8. *I've got a secret about you (something you don't know).* I am Cole in *The Sixth Sense* and I see dead people. You are my child psychologist Dr. Malcolm Crowe. You don't realize it, but you are a ghost unable to face the fact that you were murdered two years ago by a former patient.

Which of your characters know something about someone else that the other character does not realize? What is the secret?

Cole's secret suggests that he values his personal safety and that he fears what might happen if this unpredictable stranger were to find out the truth about himself. Cole's secret leads him to be cautious, withdrawn, and uncooperative in his meetings with Dr. Crowe. What values and fears are implied by your character's secret? What might your character do as a result of this secret?

9. *I've got a secret about my family.* I am Dodge in the backstory of *Buried Child.* Though my wife Hallie and I no longer sleep together, she is now pregnant. This news triggers the revelation that she has had an incestuous relationship with my son Tilden.

Which of your characters has a family secret? What is it?

The desire to hide the incest of his wife and son suggests that Dodge values family and fears the destruction of his home. The secret leads him to drown the unwanted child and bury it in the backyard. What values and fears are implied by your character's secret? What might your character do as a result of this secret?

10. *I've got a secret about something that happened in my community.* I am Vicarro in *27 Wagons Full of Cotton* (adapted later into the film *Baby Doll*). I will not report this to the authorities, but I know that my neighbor burned down my cotton gin in order to boost his own cotton business.

Which of your characters has a secret about one or more others in the community? What is the secret?

Vicarro's secrecy suggests that he values both revenge and vigilante justice. His secrecy also implies the fear that an enemy who has hurt him may not only go free, but also prosper. The secret leads Vicarro to exact his revenge by seducing his neighbor's wife. What values and fears are implied by your character's secret? What might your character do as a result of this secret?

WRAP-UP

One key to a fascinating character is a fascinating secret life that drives character behavior but is not revealed until it has raised important questions that we in the audience want answered. As you work on your script, continue to look for hidden truths that may help explain why your characters see the world a certain way, or have certain feelings, or do certain things. These truths can not only deepen your understanding of the characters, but also open the door to unexpected story ideas.

> **Related tools in _Character, Scene, and Story_.**
> To uncover more character secrets, go to the "Developing Your Character" section and try "Nothing but the Truth." Or go to the "Causing a Scene" section and try "Classified Information" or "Better Left Unsaid."

THE NOBLE CHARACTER

THE QUICK VERSION
Add dramatic impact to your story by raising the bar for your main character

BEST TIME FOR THIS
After you have a working sense of who the characters are

CHARACTERS OF GOLD AND SILVER
Great characters tend to be noble in nature. Even if they ultimately reach an unhappy end, such as Ophelia, or succumb to terrible deeds, such as Macbeth, they have a greatness of spirit that makes their flaws ever the more tragic or loathsome. From Didi and Gogo in *Waiting for Godot* to George and Martha *in Who's Afraid of Virginia Woolf?*, great characters are full of contradictions, with their noble qualities a sharp contrast to their weaknesses and crimes.

Among dictionary definitions of "noble," one that comes closest to describing great characters is "having eminence, high moral qualities, or ideals." Even if these high qualities and ideals are mixed with petty needs and base traits, their presence elevates the character and adds importance and dimension to the story.

Some great characters remain noble from beginning to end. Some lose their nobility as the dramatic journey unfolds. Some acquire it along the way. Regardless of their journeys, they reveal their nobility to us at some time. It may be expressed as an ongoing approach to life that we see throughout the story, or it may be fleeting, a nobility that rises up only in a single moment of critical importance.

Whether it is expressed in love, courage, compassion, or other qualities, the nobility of a character is almost always a form of generosity.

Even Shylock, often considered one of the greediest of villains, can be seen as a noble character when we first meet him in *The Merchant of Venice*. He is a man trying to defend his money and possessions in an environment where, because of his Jewish heritage, he cannot own land and is excluded from many professions. In his eagerness for acceptance, he is willing to lend money without interest to an abusive anti-Semite and, to create a "merry bond," asks for only a symbolic collateral—a pound of flesh—to protect the loan. His reliance on contracts reflects his respect for law and yearning for justice, and his unhappiness later over the loss of a turquoise ring shows a capacity to value sentiment over monetary value. However, Shylock's nobility is consumed by rage as he suffers insult, prejudice, the betrayal of a daughter, and other abuses from a powerful society that refuses to recognize his generosity or accept him as an equal member.

The nobility of characters is often tested—and measured—by the kinds of decisions they make. Sometimes it is the nature of the decision itself that reveals the truth. For example, Shylock's decision in the end to demand the pound of flesh for his unpaid debt puts the life of Antonio, the debtor, in jeopardy and shows us that Shylock's loss of nobility is complete.

Sometimes it is the size of the decision that tests the character. As a general rule, the greater the number of people affected by a decision, the greater the decision is. For example, an alcoholic must decide whether or not to stop drinking. This is important because her well-being is at risk. The importance escalates, however, if the alcoholic is pregnant—now the well-being of the fetus is also at risk—or if the alcoholic is a surgeon who must rely on clarity and precision to save lives. Why do so many stories focus on doctors, police, lawyers, politicians, kings, and queens? Because they make decisions that have consequences beyond themselves.

You don't need to write about a pregnant surgeon with a drinking problem to create these dynamics. Look for ways to structure your character relationships and story events so that your main character must make a decision with multiple and far-reaching effects. Even if it's only one or two others who will be affected, a decision with more than one consequence will up the stakes for your character and make us more likely to await its outcome.

Another dictionary definition for "noble" is "not corroding or deteriorating rapidly; precious; pure; said of metals, especially gold and silver." What is the gold or silver of your character? If your character's journey is upward, the presence of this trait may play a key role in the character's success. If your character's journey is downward, the loss or erosion of this trait may be what's responsible for the character's failure.

ABOUT THE EXERCISE

This exercise can help you explore the actual and potential nobility of a character. Try it first with your main character. For best results, build on what you know so far to find new possibilities for your story.

■ WHO YOUR CHARACTER IS NOW

1. *Noble trait.* Have you given your main character at least one noble trait? You may define "noble" any way you wish, as long as you personally see it as a lofty quality: a characteristic of greatness among the many qualities that make up who your character is. This noble trait may already

be present in your character when the story begins, or it may be acquired through the dramatic journey. It may be a trait which survives when tested or which collapses under stress. In a word or phrase, identify your character's most noble trait now—for example, wisdom. There is no wrong answer and "most noble" is relative to the character's world.

2. *Noble deed.* Have you given your character the opportunity to perform at least one noble deed during the story? The operative word here is "opportunity." Whether the character actually performs this noble deed or not, the opportunity to rise to greatness will not only make the story more interesting, but also expand the dimensions of your work and make the character's final success or failure all the more meaningful.

In a sentence or so, give a specific example of a noble deed that your character has the opportunity to perform at any time in the story. Try to tie this opportunity to the noble trait you just named. Remember that you're focusing here on opportunity and not necessarily actual action. Whether your character seizes the opportunity or not, it is a time when we see the character's most noble trait being tested. In *The Silence of the Lambs*, for example, one of Hannibal Lecter's most noble qualities is wisdom. This is tested when he has the opportunity to help FBI agent Clarice Starling figure out the identify of a serial killer at large.

■ WHO YOUR CHARACTER COULD BE

1. *Noble trait.* Think some more about your character. For the sake of exercise, be creative and imagine a totally new noble trait or quality for this character: something that you haven't considered yet but that could possibly be added to this unique character's nature—either coming into the story or acquired during the story. In a word or phrase, what new noble trait could you possibly give this character?

If you went with this choice, would it be a new trait that already exists when the story begins, or would it be acquired during the story as a result of what your character experiences?

2. *Noble deed.* Think about your story events and how they could unfold in a somewhat different way. In a sentence, give a specific example of a new noble deed that your character could have the opportunity to perform at any time during the story. Try to tie this opportunity to the new noble trait you just named. Again, focus on opportunity and not necessarily actual action. Whether your character would seize the opportunity or not, it would be a time when we could see the character's new noble trait being tested. Identify the potential example in one sentence: this is an opportunity that is not in your story now.

■ HOW YOUR CHARACTER COULD AFFECT OTHERS

1. *Critical decision.* Think about the important decisions your character makes during the story. Does the character ever have to make a decision

that immediately and critically affects at least one other character? In other words, is there an important decision with a significant ripple effect?

- *If you answered "yes" to the ripple effect:*
  - Identify who else is immediately and critically affected by your character's decision. For each person affected, write his or her name and relationship to the character.
  - Describe the decision and include specifically what alternatives your character must choose between.
- *If you answered "no" to the ripple effect:*
  - Imagine new possibilities. If the story were to unfold somewhat differently, who else could be critically affected by a decision of your character? For each person that could possibly be affected, write his or her name and relationship to the character.
  - Be creative and think about a possible new decision that your character would have to make: a decision that could have a significant ripple effect on the other character or characters you just named. Identify the options that your character could possibly face.

2. **More critical decision.** Think about the actual or possible decision you've just been exploring. Is there any way to make this decision bigger and more important by increasing or expanding its effects? For example, you could make the decision bigger and more important by having it affect a greater number of people, or by having it affect the same people but in a more critical way. As an exercise, how might you increase the size and scope of your character's decision?

WRAP-UP

This has been an exercise in growing your character: finding new ways to make him or her taller so that your work will be more likely to command our attention, stir up our deepest feelings, and mean something important to us during and after the story. Keep looking for opportunities to raise the bar for your character—even if he or she is a tragic figure who fails to meet the challenges of the journey.

> **Related tools in *Character, Scene, and Story*.** To learn more about a character's true nature, try any exercise in the "Developing Your Character" section, particularly "Character Interview," "Character Fact Sheet," or "Nothing but the Truth."

SEVEN DEADLY SINS

THE QUICK VERSION
Examine character strengths and weaknesses

BEST TIME FOR THIS
After you have a working sense of who your characters are

THE VIRTUES OF SIN
From Shannon in *Night of the Iguana*, to Reverend Parris in *The Crucible*, to the title character of *Elmer Gantry*, preachers in drama have warned us about the evils and dangers of sin. From a dramatic writer's perspective, however, the temptation to sin is an opportunity to test the strengths and weaknesses of characters and to reveal something important—positive or negative—about their true natures.

Even if your characters are not religious, you can use the concept of sin as a tool for character development. And, since you are a dramatic writer, you may find the best material by tackling the most dramatic of sins: the seven deadly ones. Through the ages, the traditional seven deadly sins— envy, gluttony, greed, lust, pride, sloth, and wrath—have provided fodder for countless dramatic stories, such as the classic drama *Faustus* by Christopher Marlowe and the modern comedy *Sin* by Wendy McLeod.

ABOUT THE EXERCISE
To begin, choose a character whom you have begun to develop and want to know in more depth. You may wish to explore more than one character at the same time so that you can compare weaknesses and strengths as you think about character sins.

"Sin" here is defined as "fault" or "wrong" in the broadest sense: any thought, word, or deed that could lead to a downfall of any kind—if not moral, then perhaps physical, economic, or social. Since the sins under scrutiny are "deadly," the focus will be on extreme faults and wrongs, and significant outcomes.

■ **THE TRADITIONAL SEVEN DEADLY SINS**
Think about your character in relationship to each of the seven deadly sins:
1. **Envy** is a feeling of discontent and ill will due to someone else's success or possessions. To envy is to have a resentful dislike of someone because he or she has something desirable. In *Amadeus* by Peter Shaffer, for

example, the composer Salieri orchestrates Mozart's fall from grace because of his envy of Mozart's talent.

2. *Gluttony* is the act or habit of eating or drinking way too much. In *The Merry Wives of Windsor* by William Shakespeare, gluttony is among the sins most noticeably embodied by the portly character of Falstaff.

3. *Greed* is an excessive desire for acquiring or having, or, put another way, the longing for more than one needs or deserves. In *Cat on a Hot Tin Roof* by Tennessee Williams, greed for Big Daddy's future estate is what pits family members against one another.

4. *Lust* is excessive sexual desire. To lust is to seek unrestrained pleasure—even at the cost of harm to oneself or others. In *A View from the Bridge* by Arthur Miller, a father risks the well-being of his whole family because of the lust that has tainted his affection for his daughter.

5. *Pride* can be a positive attribute, but it becomes negative when there's too much of it. The sin of pride is an excessive belief in one's own worth or merit: an exaggerated self-esteem, conceit, or vanity. In *King Lear*, by William Shakespeare, it may be pride that keeps the king from facing the error of his ways.

6. *Sloth* is extreme sluggishness. When one is slothful, one is disinclined to work or exert oneself. In Anton Chekhov's play, *The Cherry Orchard*, the aristocratic ennui of Mrs. Ranevsky and her family leads to the loss of their beloved estate.

7. *Wrath* is emotional agitation that is aroused by great displeasure and leads to loss of self-control. In *Electra* by Sophocles, a wrathful woman is consumed by obsessive dreams of retribution for her husband's death.

■ THE SINS OF YOUR CHARACTER

List the seven deadly sins. Then do a quick armchair analysis of your character by answering the following questions about his or her relationship to these sins:

1. *Most likely sins.* Think about your character's weaknesses. Of the seven deadly sins, which two would your unique character be most inclined to commit if circumstances led to temptation? As you select the two most likely sins, do not feel confined by actual scenarios from your story. Think about the whole life of the character. Remember that the past is a rich source of character information, and that the present and future are full of possibilities you haven't considered yet. Write a 1 beside your character's most likely sin, and 2 beside your character's second most likely sin.

2. *Least likely sins.* Now think about the same character's strengths. Of the seven deadly sins, which two would your character be least inclined to commit? As before, think about the character's whole life. Write a 7 beside your character's least likely sin and a 6 beside the second least likely sin.

3. *Middle sins.* Though you have written only four numbers, your choices

already reflect a wealth of information about your character. The most likely sins reveal defining character weaknesses. The least likely sins reveal defining character strengths. But what about the middle sins that didn't make it to either ranking? This gray zone may suggest an area that you need to explore further. Look again at these three middle sins. In what order might they be most likely to occur? Trust your first instinct and write a 3, 4, and 5 beside the three remaining sins on your list.

A DEEPER LOOK AT CHARACTER STRENGTHS AND WEAKNESSES

Use the following steps to find new story ideas. For best results, do the full set of steps at least three times. Focus first on a most likely sin (1 or 2), then on a middle sin (3, 4, or 5), and finally on a least likely sin (6 or 7). Each will tell you something different about your character. In each round, trust your first instinct and imagine your character at an important time in his or her life—past, present, or future—without feeling constrained by the dictates of your plot.

1. *Setting.* Think about your unique character and the particular sin you are exploring now. Locate a setting in which you could imagine the character being tempted to commit this sin. See if you can find a place that feels integral to this specific character and this specific temptation. Identify the setting and briefly describe it from your character's point of view.

2. *Circumstances.* Think about when the temptation might strike. Briefly identify the time of this temptation and the specific circumstances under which it might occur. The ingredients of this temptation are keys to your character's needs, values, and beliefs as well as his or her weaknesses.

3. *Other characters.* Who else, if anyone, is involved in this particular temptation or sin? Identify the name and relationship of any others who played an important role in this experience. Then describe the others from your character's point of view.

4. *Physical life.* Imagine that a certain physical object or element is pivotal to either the temptation or the sin. Identify this physical object or element, and briefly describe it from the character's point of view.

5. *Sense memory.* Imagine yourself as the character looking back at the temptation or the sin. Find one sense memory of this experience: something significant and specific that you can see, or hear, or smell, or taste, or feel. Identify it and describe it from your character's point of view.

6. *Action and motivation.* In this specific time and place, and under this particular set of circumstances, would your character succumb to the temptation of this sin or not? Imagine what might happen and sum it up in a few sentences from your character's point of view. Include why the character finally gave in to this temptation or finally resisted it.

7. *Consequences.* Long term or short term, what was the most important result of your character's action? Look for an outcome that might affect

how your story unfolds. Describe this outcome from your character's point of view. Include how your character feels now about what happened.

WRAP-UP

To know your characters is to know what they are most likely to do in life, what they might be willing to do under certain circumstances, and what they would never do.

In this exercise, you have been using a broad concept of "sin" to find out more about your character's inclinations and limits. Your ranking of the seven deadly sins offers a telling capsule portrait of what you now know.

> **Related tools in *Character, Scene, and Story.***
> To explore your character's flaws and vulnerabilities in more depth, go to the "Developing a Character" section and try "The Imperfect Character."

THE DRAMATIC TRIANGLE

THE QUICK VERSION
Flesh out a two-character relationship as a triangle that involves a third party

BEST TIME FOR THIS
After you are well into the story

THE GEOMETRY OF CHARACTER RELATIONSHIPS
When you put two characters into a story, you create a relationship that shows how they fit or don't fit together. Such relationships are often tested by the demands of the story and undergo changes that affect each character in a positive or negative way. If you were to look at the geometry of this relationship, you might see it as a line that connects two points. It might be a short line that holds the characters close, or a long line that keeps them apart and makes communication difficult.

If you were to broaden your view of the relationship and think about its most immediate influences, you might imagine any number of geometric shapes to describe its complexity. From a storytelling perspective, one of the most powerful ways to view a character relationship is not as a line connecting two points but as a triangle connecting three points. The metaphor suggests that, in a relationship between any two characters at any given time, there is often a third party affecting what happens between them: there is a dramatic triangle at work.

Almost every two-character relationship is a dramatic triangle that includes a third party. Sometimes this third party is physically present, as in Beth Henley's *Crimes of the Heart*, where the relationship between two sisters in a small Mississippi town is reconfigured by the return of a third sister who has been living in Los Angeles. In many cases, however, the third party to the relationship is not physically present. In Samuel Beckett's *Waiting for Godot*, for example, the title character never appears, yet influences almost everything that happens between the two men waiting for him. In Sam Shepard's *True West*, the feud between two brothers is greatly defined by their offstage father. In David Lindsay-Abaire's *Rabbit Hole*, the tentative relationship between two sisters is governed by a dead child who was son to one and nephew to the other.

Dramatic triangles are dynamic. The role of third party can be played by different characters from scene to scene, or even from moment to moment within a scene. As you develop your script, keep in mind that the relationship between any two characters may be bigger than the both of them. There is almost always someone else present—physically or psychologically. Your awareness of this presence can lead to many new character insights and story ideas.

ABOUT THE EXERCISE

You will need a two-character relationship to explore as a dramatic triangle. If it is an important relationship, it will probably change over the course of the story, so, for the sake of the exercise, you will also need to find a specific point in time to analyze these two characters in relationship to each other. For best results, find an important time between them—for example, in the backstory, or near the beginning or end of an act. Your analysis may later lead to a scene, but, for now, think of this as character exploration more than scene development.

Exercise examples are from Alan Bennett's *The History Boys*. Character 1 is Hector, a sixty-something maverick teacher of general studies at an all-boys English school. Character 2 is Posner, an eighteen-year-old boy who will soon be taking university admission exams. Their relationship: Posner is Hector's student and also one of the few students in the school that Hector does not find physically attractive. Their relationship will be examined at the end of act 1, when, alone in the classroom, they suddenly find themselves in an intense moment of connection which leaves Hector in flight, and Posner in confusion.

To begin, identify your Characters 1 and 2, the nature of their relationship, and the specific point in time when you will focus on it.

■ **CIRCUMSTANCES RELEVANT TO
THE CHARACTER RELATIONSHIP**

As *The History Boys* approaches the end of act 1, there have been a number of important developments in the individual lives of Hector and Posner—for example:

- Hector drives a motorcycle and likes to give rides to his favorite students after school. However, the headmaster recently received a report that Hector had been seen "fiddling" with a student on the back of his bike while they were stopped at a street light. The headmaster has since informed Hector that, to avoid scandal, he must submit his resignation at the end of the term. For Hector, who loves teaching more than anything else, this is akin to a death sentence.
- Posner has recently come to the conclusion that he is gay and has a crush on a fellow student named Dakir, who couldn't care less about him. Posner is now suffering the pangs of unrequited love.

Think about the character relationship you are exploring. What's been going on lately in the lives of the characters outside of this relationship? For each character, identify at least one important fact that could affect how he or she interacts with the other character.

■ HOW THE TWO CHARACTERS FIT TOGETHER NOW

You might describe your characters' relationship as personal or professional, positive or negative, deep or shallow. You may see it as a relationship with no future, or a long-term commitment with far-reaching effects. Regardless of how you define this connection, it is what either holds the characters together or pushes them apart, and it provides a context for what they do in the story. Use the following questions to flesh out your characters' relationship at this time in the story or backstory:

The relationship between Characters 1 and 2

1. While Hector often has strong personal feelings about his boys, he has never seen Posner as anything more than one of the crowd. Their relationship has been more academic than personal. Building on what you know about your Characters 1 and 2, how would you describe their relationship?

2. The last significant experience that Hector and Posner shared was a French lesson where Posner played the singing madam of a brothel—in French—while other boys played prostitutes and johns. For Hector, unusual lessons like this are routine, but for Posner, it was a moment in the sun that boosted his confidence and fueled his desire for more attention from his teachers. This desire has motivated Posner to memorize and recite an extra-long poem for Hector. Written by Thomas Hardy, the poem is called "Drummer Hodge" and it's one of Hector's favorites. What is the last significant experience that your two characters shared either onstage or off? What was one important outcome of this experience for either or both of them?

3. The importance of a relationship between any two characters at any given time is often not equal. One values the relationship more than the other. The relationship between Hector and Posner means much more to Posner, the student, than to Hector, the teacher. This fact will contribute to Posner's need to impress Hector by reciting the Hardy poem perfectly. Which of your two characters places the most importance on their relationship? How might this fact motivate his or her behavior in the story?

Character 1 in the relationship

1. Different relationships nurture different traits and qualities. One relationship can bring out a character's good side while another brings out the bad side. The teacher-student relationship fosters something noble in Hector: a true desire to instill in others the love of knowledge. Think about how your characters' relationship affects your Character 1 physically, psychologically, or socially. Identify one important trait or quality that this relationship fosters.

2. Hector likes Posner's singing voice and his ability in class to act out melodramatic scenes from famous movies. What does your Character 1 like most about your Character 2?

3. Hector doesn't dislike Posner, but tends to ignore him because of the boy's small stature and general lack of charisma. What does your Character 1 like least about your Character 2?

4. Hector feels disappointed when Posner is present. Hector would rather be alone with one of his pet students. How does your Character 1 feel about your Character 2 at the time you have chosen? Why does Character 1 feel this way?

5. Posner doesn't know that Hector is being forced to resign at the end of the term. Identify one important fact about your Character 1 that the other character does not know at this time. Look for a fact that could affect story action and see if you can discover something new.

Character 2 in the relationship

1. For Posner, the teacher-student relationship brings out his need to please and be liked. Think about how your characters' relationship affects your Character 2 physically, psychologically, or socially. Identify one important trait or quality that this relationship fosters.

2. Posner is emotionally stirred by Hector's love of knowledge for its own sake. What does your Character 2 like most about your Character 1?

3. Posner dislikes Hector's disregard of him. Posner is one of the few boys who never gets asked to ride on Hector's motorcycle after school. What does your Character 2 like least about your Character 1?

4. Though Posner is a bit of a traitor—he has begun to ally himself with one of Hector's faculty rivals—Posner is still in awe of Hector. The teacher is one of the most unusual and inspiring people that Posner has ever met. How does your Character 2 feel about your Character 1 at the time you have chosen? Why does Character 2 feel this way?

5. Hector doesn't know that Posner has a crush on his fellow student Dakir and is suffering the pangs of unrequited love. Identify one important fact about your Character 2 that Character 1 does not know at this time. Look for a fact that will affect story action and see if you can discover something new.

■ THE RELATIONSHIP AS A DRAMATIC TRIANGLE

As act 1 of *The History Boys* nears an end, the relationship between Hector and Posner is influenced by a third party, who, in this case, is not a real person but a fictional one: the subject of the Thomas Hardy poem that Posner recites and that Hector uses to teach a lesson. In effect, the third party in their dramatic triangle is Drummer Hodge, an unknown drummer boy who dies as a casualty of war and is buried without ceremony in a foreign land. Both Hector and Posner relate to this boy in a way that will deepen their relationship to each other—though only for a moment.

Think about your characters' relationship as a dramatic triangle. If your Character 1 is one point of the triangle, and Character 2 is a second point, who is the third point at the time you have chosen? Identify the third party who will influence your characters' relationship from onstage or off. As you do this, see if you can make any new discoveries about your characters and how they connect or don't connect. Who will influence them most now? Will this character's presence be physical or psychological?

■ EXPLORING THE DRAMATIC TRIANGLE

If you are focused on only two characters, you have created one relationship to help you make the story happen. By adding just one more character to the mix, even if only an offstage character, the number of relationships—and story opportunities—quadruples. In addition to the relationship between Characters 1 and 2, there now exists a relationship between Characters 1 and 3, 2 and 3, and the whole group of 1, 2, and 3. Here are some questions to help you flesh out the additional relationships that the dramatic triangle has created:

The relationship between Characters 1 and 3

1. Since Hector is a teacher and Drummer Hodge is a fictional character in a poem that will be taught, the relationship between them is academic. What is the nature of the relationship between your Characters 1 and 3? Objectively define it.

2. Hector sees the drummer boy as a symbol of the tragedy and waste of war, and as a metaphor for his own feelings now as he faces the loss of his job. Building on what you know about your characters, how would you subjectively describe the relationship between Characters 1 and 3?

3. When the subject of the poem "Drummer Hodge" comes up, Hector is enlivened. Hardy is one of his favorite writers. How does your Character 1 feel about your Character 3? Why does Character 1 feel this way?

4. The drummer boy will become a important tool for Hector to escape his problems and arouse Posner's thirst for knowledge. How will your Character 3 influence Character 1?

The relationship between Characters 2 and 3

1. The relationship between Posner and Drummer Hodge is academic. How would you objectively define the relationship between your Characters 2 and 3?

2. Posner sees the poem about the drummer boy as an opportunity to impress his teacher. Building on what you know about your Characters 2 and 3, how would you subjectively describe their relationship?

3. Posner feels sorry for the drummer boy and curious about his fate in the lonely foreign grave. How does your Character 2 feel about your Character 3? Why does Character 2 feel this way?

4. Posner will recite the poem perfectly and the drummer boy in it will move Posner emotionally: he will become more vulnerable to feelings of being separate and alone, and "not in the swim." How will your Character 3 influence your Character 2?

The group relationship between Characters 1, 2, and 3

1. Literally or figuratively, Hector, Posner, and Drummer Hodge are all casualties of war. Hector is embroiled in the school scandal that is threatening to end everything he loves. Posner is suffering from unrequited love. The drummer boy has been killed and buried without even a coffin in a foreign land. What is the strongest common denominator between your three characters?

2. One of the most positive aspects of the relationship between Hector, Posner, and Drummer Hodge is the emotional strength that comes from realizing that human misery is not new or uncommon: others through the ages have suffered similar problems. What is the most positive aspect of the relationship between your three characters?

3. One of the most negative aspects of the relationship between Hector, Posner, and Drummer Hodge is its painfully short life. Like a blinding flash, the warmth and comfort of this relationship will come and go. What is the most negative aspect of the relationship between your three characters?

4. In the dramatic triangle of Hector, Posner, and Drummer Hodge, the closest two characters are Hector and the drummer boy. Hector empathizes and identifies with the fictional boy more than he does with the real-life boy. Of your three characters at the time in the story that you have chosen, which two are the closest?

5. In the dramatic triangle of Hector, Posner, and Drummer Hodge, Hector has the most power. He is the teacher in charge of the classroom and has the most knowledge about the poem. In your dramatic triangle at this time in the story, which of your three characters has the most power?

6. Hector and Posner connect through their individual empathy with the lost drummer boy. This will move Hector to reach out literally to Posner for a type of connection that Posner is not ready to understand or accept. During this offer, the power will shift to Posner, for it will be the student—not the teacher—who decides whether a deeper relationship will develop. In your dramatic triangle, what is the biggest change that occurs—or could occur—between your characters at this time in the story? What does this change reveal about each of your characters?

WRAP-UP

Remember the power of three as you explore character relationships and how they are affected by other characters and story events. Keep in mind, too, that a third party who is not physically present in a dramatic triangle can sometimes be a more potent force than one who is.

Related tools in *Character, Scene, and Story.* To learn more about important characters who affect dramatic action from afar, go to the "Developing Your Character" section and try "The Invisible Character."

SPINAL TAP

THE QUICK VERSION
Use the root action or "spine" of a character to find new story material

BEST TIME FOR THIS
After you are well into the story

ROOT ACTION: THE SPINE OF THE CHARACTER
Dramatic characters tend to be active beings. They do things because they want things, and they cause stories to happen. From a technical point of view, their behavior has two functions: to show us who they really are—especially when they say one thing but do another—and to move the dramatic journey forward. In a great story, these functions have been so seamlessly combined that one rarely occurs without the other: character revelation and story movement go hand in hand.

Dramatic action may include physical tasks, such as rescuing a climber from a ledge of Mount Everest or chasing a smuggler through the streets of San Francisco. More often than not, however, it refers to interpersonal behavior in which one character is trying to affect another character in some important way. This action is dramatic if it is blocked by significant obstacles and driven by high stakes so that the characters must try various and increasingly risky strategies to get what they want.

Through the course of a story, a multidimensional character will act many different ways for many different reasons. Even if some of these actions seem contradictory—and they often do in a great character—they all flow from the same source: the root action or "spine" of the character.

If you look deep enough into the soul of any character, you can find one primal need that broadly defines who the character is and fundamentally drives what he or she does, though not always in obvious ways. By identifying this fountainhead of behavior, you can get a clearer big picture not only of your character, but also of the dramatic journey and what could happen in it.

ABOUT THE EXERCISE
To do this exercise, you need a working sense of your story and the character whom you will explore in more depth. You may wish to try this exercise with each of your principal characters, starting with your main character, and see how they compare and contrast. For best results, build on what you already know about each character.

1. *Identify important actions.* What are the doings of your character? In John Steinbeck's *Of Mice and Men*, the main character George does a number of things. Most involve his slow-witted partner Lennie. For example, George takes away the dead mouse Lennie wants to pet, inspires him with tales about the farm they hope to own one day, tries to teach him how to keep out of trouble at their new job, works to stop a fight between Lennie and the boss's son Curley, and, in the end, after Lennie has accidentally murdered Curley's wife, puts a pistol to the back of Lennie's head and kills him at a peaceful riverside before Curley can exact a vicious revenge.

Think about what your character does in your story and list as many specific actions as you can—up to about a dozen—in whatever order they come to you. Identify each action in a present-tense phrase that starts with a verb. Remember that the focus is not on what the character says or explains, but rather on what the character does. Look for what matters most.

2. *Prioritize actions*. Look at your list of character doings. Which ones speak loudest to you right now and seem most interesting? Pick five and number them in order of their importance from 1 to 5, with 1 meaning most important.

3. *Find a connection.* These five doings—especially the number 1 action—are key clues to your character's spine. When viewed together in order of importance, they begin to suggest a common denominator: a basic need of some kind that your character wants to satisfy. If two of the most important actions seem contrary or contradictory, one is pointing to that need while the other is masking it by pointing away. You need to figure out which of the two directions leads to the real need which is actually driving both behaviors.

In *Of Mice and Men*, George stokes up plans and dreams, gives advice, and solves problems—all for his partner Lennie, who has trouble taking care of himself. What connects these actions is a need to keep Lennie out of trouble so that they can earn enough money to defeat poverty and loneliness, and achieve their dream of owning a farm together. One of George's most important doings is the killing of Lennie at the end of the story—an action that seems contradictory to his earlier efforts to protect Lennie from harm. Yet the story has brought George to a crisis where the shooting is an act not of destruction but of protection. It's George's only way to save Lennie from an angry lynch mob.

Think about the five most important doings of your character and find one specific need that relates directly or indirectly to all of them.

4. *Extract one action*. You can boil the specific need down to a simple infinitive that describes one action. For example, the analysis of George's need—"to keep Lennie out of trouble so that they can earn enough money to defeat poverty and loneliness, and achieve their dream of owning a farm

together"—can be boiled down to the infinitive "to protect." This sums up what George is doing most of the time during the story. It also reflects his overall story objective. What infinitive best sums up what your character is doing most of the time during your story?

5. *Explore the action*. You may have discovered the spine of your character in the infinitive you just chose. Or, you may want to see if there is a more precise and descriptive way to express the root action. For example, suppose that the common denominator is "to protect." With the help of some imagination and a thesaurus, this action can be restated to highlight different ways to protect, from providing shade to providing safeguard to providing defense:

To shade	To curtain	To nestle	To secure
To shutter	To harbor	To father	To veil
To shroud	To nurture	To shield	To cloak
To arm	To screen	To defend	To ensconce
To shelter	To guard	To fence	To flank

Each of these is a more precise version of "to protect" and—literally and figuratively—may begin to suggest new traits, actions, and images for the character. George protects Lennie by teaching him how to act, rewarding good behavior, punishing bad behavior, and getting him to sleep at night by telling him the same bedtime story over and over. Though couched in the terms of migrant farmworkers, these are the kinds of things a parent typically does for a child. The way George protects, therefore, is "to father." His story decisions and actions all flow from this root action: he fathers Lennie, fathers their plans and dreams, and fathers solutions when their best laid plans go astray.

In the same story, Lennie spends a lot of time trying to touch things that look soft and pretty, such as mice, puppies, rabbits, and the shiny blonde hair of Curley's wife. The root action or spine of the character Lennie might be "to pet." It is the primal source of his decisions and actions in the story. Curley, on the other hand, is not only the boss's son but also an ex-boxer who likes to pick fights, especially with those like Lennie who are taller than him. The root action or spine of the character Curley might be "to poke."

What is the root action or spine of your character?

■ TAPPING THE SPINE OF YOUR CHARACTER

1. *Use the spine to find new traits*. Think more about the root action you just identified and the different traits that could literally and figuratively flow from it. If George's spine is "to father," for example, he might—like a loving parent—be a provider with beans for the hungry and dreams for the distressed. He might also have a tendency—like a frustrated parent—to be scolding and guilt producing when he feels disobeyed or let down. Try to find one positive and one negative new trait that could possibly flow from your character's root action or spine.

2. *Use the spine to find new actions.* Think about specific character actions that are not in your story now but might be added because they could flow literally or figuratively from this same spine. If George's root action is "to father," for example, he might do such things as stop Lennie from drinking bad river water, speak for Lennie when he is being questioned by Curley, and warn Lennie to avoid Curley's wife after she flirts with him. See what new possibilities you can discover by identifying three specific actions—positive or negative—that could possibly be added to your story later because they flow from the character spine.

3. *Use the spine to find a new image.* What new images of your character come to mind when you think about the root action within the specific world of your story? Many images in *Of Mice and Men* show us George as one who fathers. One of the most memorable is the early image of him flinging away the dead mouse that Lennie has reluctantly surrendered from his pocket. Find one interesting new image of your character that reveals the root action and could possibly be added to your story later. Describe the image in detail.

WRAP-UP

By identifying the root action of your most important characters, you have a simple way to understand who they each are and how they compare and contrast. You also have a new source of story ideas and a guide to steer your characters in the directions most appropriate for them.

Related tools in *Character, Scene, and Story.* To continue exploring character behavior, go to the "Developing Your Character" section and try "What Is the Character Doing Now?" To compare one character to another, try "Side by Side" in the same section.

CHARACTER AS PARADOX

THE QUICK VERSION
Use paradox to learn more about a character and find new story ideas

BEST TIME FOR THIS
After you have a working sense of who the characters are

WHEN SOMETHING IS WHAT IT'S NOT
A paradox is a statement that seems unbelievable or absurd, but is actually true. In short, it tells us that one thing is its opposite—that love is hate, that generosity is greed, that truth is a lie. Complex characters often embody a number of paradoxes because they thrive on contradictions. One could say, for example, that Macbeth embodies the paradox "success is failure." He shows this to be true by struggling so ruthlessly for success that he destroys himself. His success is his failure.

The title character of David Mamet's play *Edmond* embodies the same paradox in reverse. He shows us that "failure is success." Edmond exits his marriage, enters a seamy underworld, commits murder, and ends up in prison where he is being assaulted by his cell mate, yet in this imprisonment finds his true place and salvation. His failure is his success.

Because it appears to be a self-contradiction, a paradox is a mystery that needs to be untangled in order to be understood. This untangling occurs when we can finally see that the paradox is true in spite of itself—when we understand, for example, the failure of Macbeth's success or the success of Edmond's failure.

ABOUT THE EXERCISE
Try this first with your main character. Then repeat it later with other principal characters, one at a time. For best results, be flexible. Remember that paradox offers new ways to look at your character, and stay open to new possibilities as you explore and untangle the paradox you create. This is primarily an exercise in discovery. Complete each step before moving on to the next one. If you feel stuck, make up a quick answer. Even if it's not the best response, it may trigger valuable new ideas later.

■ STATING THE PARADOX
Create a paradox which your character could conceivably demonstrate to be true:

1. *Dominant characteristics.* A multidimensional character manifests many different traits—both positive and negative—during the course of a story. These characteristics may be physical, psychological, or social. All are in some way important, but not equally so. Some traits dominate the mix so much that they define who the character is. Ideally we discover these defining traits not through explanations but through the inferences we make as we observe the character's behavior, especially in times of stress.

Think about the dominant traits that your character exhibits in the story now. For example, a character may be ambitious, self-destructive, delicate as a flower, or clumsy as an oaf. Identify three of your character's strongest defining traits and try to include at least one positive and one negative among them.

2. *Defining trait.* Think about the three defining traits you named. Choose one of them as the basis for a paradox that your character embodies—or could potentially embody—in your story. As you do this, keep in mind that you will be working with opposites. Circle the trait you want to explore further. For example, a character might be defined as "delicate as a flower in bloom."

3. *Root of the defining trait.* Whether positive or negative, this defining trait is rooted in a general quality, condition, desire, or feeling. Depending on how you see the character, for example, you might trace the defining trait back to a

- quality, such as honesty, cowardice, beauty, evil, or truth;
- condition, such as freedom, injustice, friendship, chaos, or wealth;
- desire, such as ambition, greed, hunger, revenge, or atonement; or
- feeling, such as love, hate, anger, fear, or guilt.

Identify the general root of your character's defining trait, express this root as a noun—try to find an interesting one—and be specific. For example, the trait "delicate as a flower in bloom" might be traced back to a condition of fragility.

4. *Opposite trait.* A paradox shows that opposites are the same. Think about the noun you just chose, identify its opposite, and express it as a second noun. For example, the opposite of fragility is strength. Be sure you have a clear opposite. If you have trouble finding one, you may need to go back and rethink your choices so far.

5. *Paradox.* A paradox is a statement with a subject and contradictory complement linked by "is" or "are." In the paradox "losing is winning," the subject is "losing" and the complement is "winning." Look at the contradictory nouns you chose for your paradox. One will be the subject and one, the complement, but which is which? It makes a difference. For example, "fragility is strength" might produce a Blanche DuBois from *A Streetcar Named Desire*. However, if you reverse it to "strength is fragility," you could end up

with Lennie from *Of Mice and Men,* an oaf who doesn't know his own power and inadvertently kills what he only wants to pet. State your paradox now.

■ **EXPLORING THE PARADOX**

Flesh out the terms of the paradox within the context of the story:

1. *Factors contributing to the defining trait.* Whether it is now the subject or complement of the paradox, the first noun you chose reflects a defining trait of the character that may be inborn (a product of heredity) or acquired (a result of life experience) or both. For example, contributing factors to Blanche's fragility might include

- a wealthy upbringing on a plantation where she may have been routinely pampered and protected from hardship by her parents;
- genteel society of the upper-class 1930s and 1940s South that expected her to act the role of a fragile belle with the grace and beauty of a flower; or
- personal successes she achieved by being indirect and manipulative rather than forthright and honest, especially in the company of men.

Name three factors that have contributed to your character's defining trait. Try to include new material from your character's present or past.

2. *Actions that reveal the defining trait.* We learn who characters are by observing what they do, particularly when they are under stress. In *Streetcar*, Blanche demonstrates her fragility when she

- must gulp down whiskey to steady her nerves after discovering that her married sister's cramped, shabby apartment has little room for a third party;
- takes long, steamy baths in the apartment's only bathroom to help herself recover from the "nervous exhaustion" she claims to suffer from; and
- requires paper lanterns over the lightbulbs to shield herself from their harsh and telling glare.

How does your character reveal the defining trait? Identify three specific actions that demonstrate this dimension of your character. If you can't find three actual examples from your story now, use hypothetical examples that could make sense if added later.

3. *Factors contributing to the opposite trait.* Now look at the contradictory noun in your paradox. This may or may not describe an important aspect of your character so far. Either way, imagine that it does and that certain factors are responsible. For example, strength is the opposite of Blanche's fragility. Three contributing factors might be

- her ability to pick up the pieces and go on with her life after the suicide of her young husband;
- survival skills that she developed from having to fend for herself and endure a life of prostitution after losing her job and her home; and
- the desperation that drives her to seek any refuge at any cost: she is

at the end of her rope and it's a last call for strength in a cold, cruel world.

Drawing from your story as it stands now or as it could become later, identify three factors that have contributed to your character's contradictory dimension.

4. *Actions that reveal the opposite trait.* This other side of your character also can be revealed through behavior. For example, Blanche shows us her strength when she successfully

- convinces Stella to let her move in despite the fact that Blanche will be physically and emotionally imposing on Stella's marriage to Stanley;
- uses a façade of youth, refinement, and innocence to charm Mitch and manipulate him into asking her out on a date; and
- repeatedly defends herself against Stanley's barbs, accusations, and threats instead of cowering before him.

Identify three examples of how your character demonstrates the contradictory dimension. If you can't find three actual examples from your story now, use hypothetical ones that could make sense if added later.

■ UNTANGLING THE PARADOX

Think about the contradictory dimensions you have been exploring in your character. Ideally, the two opposites combine into one and the same thing revealed at one and the same time. In other words, at some point or at any number of points in the dramatic journey, the opposites coexist simultaneously as true, each itself and the other. These are the moments of enlightenment.

In *Streetcar*, Blanche demonstrates that fragility is strength. She does this by using her southern-belle gentility and helplessness to impose herself on others and manipulate them to give her what she wants—whether it's a place to live, a date, a marriage proposal, or a stolen kiss from a young newspaper delivery boy. In each of these moments, Blanche is both weak and powerful at once—her fragility is her strength—and it is in these moments that the paradox is untangled.

Sum up your work in the exercise by explaining how your paradox is—or could be—shown as true through what your character does. This is a simple explanation of how the two opposites could coexist simultaneously in one action.

WRAP-UP

Through this exercise, you may have discovered that your character already embodies a paradox. If so, be sure that your vision of the character is clear and that you have found the best ways to show us the paradox through dramatic action. For example, you may need to develop the character's contradictory side more fully.

On the other hand, you may have learned that your character does not yet embody a paradox. If so, consider using this tool to continue exploring new material. You may create a more complex and fascinating personality, and a character who affects story events in ways we don't expect.

Related tools in *Character, Scene, and Story*. To flesh out a character in more depth, try any exercise in the "Developing Your Character" section, particularly "The Imperfect Character" and "What Is the Character Doing Now?"

THE CHARACTER YOU LIKE LEAST

THE QUICK VERSION
Flesh out your story's least sympathetic character

BEST TIME FOR THIS
When a character seems like nothing more than an evildoer

LEARNING TO LOVE YOUR CHARACTERS, ESPECIALLY THE BAD ONES
To write any character, you need to put yourself in the character's place and see how the world looks and feels from that unique perspective. This approach is especially important when developing a character who has undesirable traits or does terrible things. If you do not fully understand the character's needs and motivations, you may find yourself with a two-dimensional "villain" who fails to emerge from the page in an interesting and believable way.

From Iago in *Othello,* to Nurse Ratched in *One Flew Over the Cuckoo's Nest,* to Hannibal Lecter in *The Silence of the Lambs*, drama is populated by characters whom we love to hate or fear. These often are the ones who engage us most as we observe their misbehavior and wait to see if they get their just deserts.

Stock villains—such as the heartless landlord or evil stepsister—are the stuff of fables, but in a complex dramatic story they are the products of writers who did not know their characters well enough to write them. In the end, the antagonists whom we hate or fear most are often those whom the writer loved most.

Some characters may be wicked, selfish, or ruthlessly bent on power, and their negative traits may rage openly or lie hidden behind a façade of beauty or charm. If you have such characters in your story, you need to get on their side long enough to write them. If you do not understand the problems they have suffered and the good they have in mind, their bad deeds may seem to us only like hollow plot devices orchestrated by the author.

Whom do you like least in your story? How well do you really know this character? How clearly have you experienced life through his or her skin? Use this exercise to find out more about an unlikable character whom you have already begun to develop. This character does not need to be a "villain," but simply one who seems to have no redeeming qualities and has become difficult to write. Exercise examples are from the Alfred Hitchcock film *Psycho* based on a novel by Robert Bloch and screenplay by Joseph Stefano.

■ A DEEPER LOOK AT YOUR CHARACTER'S PAST

Choose a "bad guy" to explore—for example, Norman Bates—and begin to think about the traits and actions that make the character difficult to like. Focus first on the character's past and see if you can uncover any new facts or insights that may lead to a different understanding of the character's present.

1. *Past misfortunes.* Unlikable character traits and deeds often can be traced back to painful life experiences that have affected the character's physical, mental, and/or emotional development. When Norman Bates was only five years old, for example, his father died. After that, his mother became clingy and demanding. Then, after years of letting Norman diligently care for her as if they were the only two people in the world, she betrayed Norman by taking on a lover. Think about the misfortunes your character has suffered. What are the three worst things that have happened to him or her before the story begins?

- *Negative impact.* Painful experiences often leave scars. The loss of his father forced Norman at the age of five to realize that death can strike at any time and take away those we love most. This awareness filled him with an anxiety that has never ceased and still brings a stutter to his speech. His mother's insatiable dependency forced him to lose contact with the outside world and grow up to be a friendless, socially awkward young man trapped inside the walls of his mother's needs. When one day he discovered her in bed with a strange man—a contradiction of all she had taught him—Norman was left with the devastating realization that even your own mother can betray you and that sex can be a dangerous threat to family intimacy.

  Think about your character's three misfortunes and identify a negative impact that each has made on your character.

- *Positive impact.* Painful experiences also can lead to character strengths. The loss of Norman's father made him the "man of the house" at an early age and showed him the importance of responsibility. Caring for his mother and later the Bates Motel taught him the value of hard work and attention to details. The isolation that accompanied these duties has molded him into a resourceful young man who can entertain himself with solitary hobbies such as bird watching and taxidermy. The discovery of his mother's illicit affair helped him finally see the truth behind her hypocrisy and gave him the power briefly to escape her constant control. Think about your character's three misfortunes and identify a positive impact that each has made on your character.

2. **Bad deeds in the past.** Ten years ago, when Norman discovered his mother in bed with a lover, he poisoned them both. Then, instead of giving his mother a proper burial, he hid her body in the house. As time went by, he began secretly to dress, speak, and act like her. Think about your character's backstory. Relatively speaking, what are the three worst things your character has done before the story begins? These actions may or may not be related to the past misfortunes you just identified.

- *Emotional and intellectual viewpoint.* By exploring the emotional life that fuels a character's bad deed, you may gain a better understanding of why and how this deed occurs. It also is important to know what desire the character is trying to satisfy. Whether right or wrong, and regardless of how they may feel about it later, characters act for one basic purpose: to acquire or achieve something that they perceive to be good at the time, just as a liar may be seeking protection. Or a sadist may be seeking pleasure. Or a suicide may be seeking peace.

  Each of Norman's past actions stemmed from a unique emotional and intellectual viewpoint that reflected his life experiences up to that time. The double murder was fueled by jealousy and the need to release the unbearable stress of knowing that he had been betrayed by his closest ally. Hiding his mother's body was an action born in guilt and love, and shaped by a desire to keep her near. His assimilation of her personality mixed the love of his mother with the fear of losing her, and the need to keep her alive in whatever way he could. Try to see the world from your character's unique emotional and intellectual viewpoint. For each of the three bad deeds from the past, how did your character feel? What "good" was he or she pursuing at the time of action?

- *Negative traits.* We get to know who characters really are by observing their behavior—particularly under stress—and making inferences about what we have seen. Ultimately, what characters do is more telling than what they say, especially when their actions contradict their words.

  Bad deeds imply character traits or qualities that are negative. Norman's murder of his mother and her lover shows that Norman has not only a rabid jealous streak but also a violent side. Hiding her corpse suggests that he cannot face her death or his guilt for causing it, and that he has made a habit of living in denial. His assimilation of his mother's personality suggests that he is psychotic. Think about your character's three bad deeds. What negative traits or qualities do they imply?

- *Positive traits.* If bad deeds can be triggered by a desire for good, they also can imply character traits or qualities that are positive. You may need to search deeper to find something positive within the character's negative behavior. Norman's murders were heinous acts, but suggest a good son who has heeded his mother's teachings about justice, family, and traditional sexual mores. Keeping her corpse implies that, despite his transgressions, he can be loving and loyal to the end. His assimilation of her personality shows that he is creative (he has devised a unique way to preserve her) and generous (he is willing to give up half of himself to keep his mother alive). Think about your character's three bad deeds from the past. What positive traits or qualities do they imply?

■ A DEEPER LOOK AT YOUR CHARACTER IN THE STORY

Now think about your same character after the story starts. Continue to look for new facts or insights that may help you find the sympathy or empathy you need to write a believable character who can add power to your script.

1. **Misfortunes in the story.** Dramatic characters tend to find themselves in trying situations that test their limits. In *Psycho,* Norman's mother half viciously scolds him because he found a motel guest attractive and invited her up for supper. Much to his horror, Norman later discovers that the jealous mother has murdered the motel guest in the shower. Later, despite his meticulous disposal of the criminal evidence, Norman finds himself being interrogated by a detective named Arbogast who has come in search of the missing woman. Think about what your character experiences in your story. Relatively speaking, what are the three worst things that happen to him or her?

- *Negative impact.* Besides interfering with Norman's supper plans, the scolding from his mother makes him feel guilty for having betrayed her. It also makes him feel dirty for having had "cheap erotic" thoughts. The discovery later of Marion's body in the shower upsets him on different levels: not only has an innocent person died violently, but her murder, if discovered, could lead to disastrous consequences for his mother. The detective's unexpected arrival is a frightening disruption in Norman's life and a very real confirmation that his relationship with his mother is at risk. Norman ends up confused, stuttering, and lying badly. Think about your character's three worst experiences in the story and identify a negative impact that each makes on your character.

- *Positive impact.* Norman's scolding from "Mother" stirs up a healthy desire to rebel against her oppressive rules and befriend a hungry woman who has come in from the rain. Norman serves supper to her in the privacy of the motel office, where they have a heartfelt exchange about the traps in which they each live. Later, after Norman learns of his mother's crime, his love for her proves to be unconditional. With exacting care, he cleans up the evidence that could incriminate her. The detective's grilling tests Norman's love even further and confirms that he will do anything to preserve the sacred bond with his mother. For each of your character's three worst experiences, identify a positive outcome.

2. **Bad deeds in the story.** The mother in Norman murders Marion Crane while she is taking a shower in her cabin. Next, Mother murders Arbogast, the detective who has come to the Bates Motel searching for Marion. Then Mother attempts to kill Marion's sister Lila who also has come looking for her. What are the three worst things that your character does during your story? These actions may or may not be related to the misfortunes you just identified.

- *Emotional and intellectual viewpoint.* When Norman murders Marion, he is acting as a mother who feels jealous about the "strange young girl" in her motel and wants to protect her son from the woman's "ugly appetite." When Mother kills Arbogast, it is not jealousy but fear that drives a desire to protect herself from harm. When Mother attempts to kill Lila, it is again fear that motivates the attack and the desire to preserve the status quo. For each of your character's three bad deeds, identify the character's unique emotional and intellectual viewpoint.
- *Negative traits.* The murder of Marion Crane shows that Norman cannot handle his own sexual appetite, that his emotions are still dangerously out of control, and that half of him remains capable of extreme brutality. The murder of Arbogast and the attempted murder of Lila reflect these same traits and also show an escalation of Norman's obsessive need to hide and deny the truth. While the murder of Marion is a crime of passion, the subsequent attacks are more the acts of a cold-blooded killer eliminating enemies. Think about your character's three bad deeds from the story. What negative traits or qualities do they imply?
- *Positive traits.* Behind Marion's gruesome death is a loving mother who will do anything to protect her son from sexual depravity, and a devoted son who will do anything to keep his mother happy. Behind Arbogast's murder is a protector determined to guard her home from a dangerous intruder. Behind the attempt on Lila's life is a fighter with the courage and stamina to stand up to two more intruders—

Lila in the house and her accomplice Sam in the motel office. Think about your character's three bad deeds from the story. What positive traits or qualities do they imply?

■ REEVALUATING THE CHARACTER

You've been exploring different sides of your character, past and present, with a focus on finding good among his or her bad traits and behaviors. Continue to look for new character information as you address these summary questions:

1. In Norman's life, perhaps the most unfair thing that happens to him is the death of his father. This early loss is what shapes the rest of Norman's existence and traps him in a symbiotic relationship with his mother. Past or present, what is the most unfair thing that happens to your character?

2. One of Norman's most endearing qualities is the kindness he sometimes shows to others—whether it's a mother in need or a hungry stranger on a rainy night. What is your character's most endearing trait or quality?

3. Perhaps Norman's most admirable trait is his sense of duty. He will do everything it takes to fulfill his responsibilities, from tending to a mother who "goes a little mad sometimes," to changing the unused beds in the motel every week to avoid dampness in the sheets. What is your character's most admirable trait or quality?

4. One of Norman's most fascinating traits is his dual personality. What is your character's most fascinating trait or quality?

5. From a certain angle, Norman's discovery of Marion's murder might be viewed as one of his saddest moments in the story: he has been left alone again in a cruel world with a mother who is out of control. As you look at the world of your story, what do you see as the saddest moment for your character?

6. One of Norman's most forgivable faults is the mental illness that now prevents him from distinguishing between illusion and reality. What is your character's most forgivable weakness or fault?

7. One of Norman's most generous acts in the story is to befriend Marion when she first arrives at the motel in distress. In fact, it is his homespun wisdom that leads to her change of heart about the cash she stole in Phoenix. What is your character's most generous or loving deed?

8. One of Norman's most courageous acts in the story is to stand up to the aggressive private detective and attempt to get rid of him in order to avoid further violence. What is your character's most courageous deed?

9. The greatest good that Norman pursues in the story is the safety of his mother. He is literally selfless in his quest to keep her alive and well. What is the greatest good that your character pursues in your story?

10. What's most at stake for Norman in the story is survival: his mother's and his own. What is personally most at stake for your character?

WRAP-UP

If you cannot see a character as anything but a "bad guy," you have made a judgment that can override many other story possibilities—often important ones—and result in a character who feels flat and predictable. Remember to love your bad characters as much as the good ones, and try to see the world of the story from each character's unique perspective.

Related tools in *Character, Scene, and Story.* To explore character flaws in more depth, go to the "Developing Your Character" section and try "The Imperfect Character." To investigate early influences in a character's life, try "Meet the Parents" in the same section.

IN SO MANY WORDS

THE QUICK VERSION
Identify what matters most about an important character

BEST TIME FOR THIS
After you are well into the story

WHO EXACTLY ARE THESE CHARACTERS?
How are your characters each universal? How are they each unique? What matters most about them? Ideally, the principal characters in your story are both empathetic (they have universal traits that we understand at a gut level) and engaging (they have unique traits that set them apart from the crowd). As you write and particularly as you rewrite, it's important to know which traits best define each character and to show us these traits through the action of the story.

ABOUT THE EXERCISE
Try this exercise with your main character first. You may wish to repeat it later with your other principal characters one at a time so that you can see how they compare. For best results, remember to honor the exercise word limits. Their purpose is to help you gradually sharpen focus on the character. Exercise examples are based on an interpretation of Berniece from *The Piano Lesson* by August Wilson.

■ **KEY CHARACTER FACTS**
To begin, think about these character elements:
   1. *Most important onstage relationship.* In *The Piano Lesson*, Berniece interacts onstage with her uncles Doaker and Wining Boy, her eleven-year-old daughter Maretha, her would-be suitor Avery, her brother Boy Willie, and his friends Lymon and Grace. While Berniece is closest to her daughter, the onstage relationship that commands most of her attention is that of Boy Willie, whose return after three years summons up the ghosts of the past and threatens all that she holds dear. Think about your character's onstage relationships. Identify and describe the most important one.
   2. *Most important offstage relationship.* One of the most important people in Berniece's backstory was her husband Crawley, who was killed by sheriff's men three years ago while he was helping Boy Willie gather some stolen wood. She is still in deep mourning over this loss. Her grief and anger keep her at a distance from almost everyone around her now. Think about

relationships from your character's offstage or past life—such as family members, old friends, or old rivals—who have had a profound influence on your character's development and worldview. Identify and describe one of the most important of these offstage relationships, including how it still affects your character here and now.

3. *Strengths*. In *The Piano Lesson*, we discover that Berniece has the courage to stand up to her brother, who wants to sell the family piano that they both own and that she wants desperately to keep. Identify one of the greatest strengths that your character will demonstrate in action during the story.

4. *Weaknesses*. In *The Piano Lesson*, we also discover that Berniece is afraid of ghosts, whether it's the one who appears to be haunting her upstairs room, or the ancestors whose images have been carved into the family piano and may be conjured up if she were to play it again. Identify one of the greatest weaknesses or vulnerabilities that your character will demonstrate in action during the story.

5. *Universal traits*. How is your character like the rest of us? Most dramatic characters have universal needs. These translate into a core set of physical, psychological, and social traits that define characters as human and enable us to empathize with them—even if we sometimes disagree with them. Among Berniece's universal characteristics is the need to guard the legacy of her family. Identify one of your character's universal traits and look for the most significant and profound example.

6. *Unique traits*. How is your character least like the rest of us? All characters have certain physical, psychological, and social traits that define them as distinct individuals unlike anyone else in their story. Berniece has the power of a priestess who can conjure up the ghosts of her ancestors by playing the family piano. However, she has not touched the piano since her mother died years ago. In a few words, describe one of your character's most unique characteristics.

7. *Most important values*. What matters most to your character in life? Right or wrong, our values are the product of our experiences and often explain why we feel and behave the way we do. In order of importance, for example, here are three things that Berniece values and that often motivate her behavior: (1) her family's past, (2) her daughter's future, and (3) her independence. In order of importance, what are three things that your character most values and that most motivate him or her during the story?

8. *Least important values*. What matters least to your character in life? While many characters manifest common human values, they may have low regard for some of the things that most people tend to hold in esteem. This disinterest or disdain may motivate them to pursue unusual courses of action. Here are three commonly valued things that are not valued by Berniece: (1) brotherly ties, (2) what other people think, and (3) marriage. What are three things that your character least values during the story?

9. *Backstory experiences.* How does the past influence the way your character thinks, feels, and behaves in the present? Many of the character's decisions and actions during the story, especially during times of stress, can be traced back to significant experiences that he or she had before the story begins. Whether positive or negative, these experiences were key turning points that helped shape who the character is now. One of the most significant experiences from Berniece's past is the loss of her husband three years ago. This has redefined her relationship with her brother Boy Willie, whom she holds responsible for her husband's death. It was Boy Willie who orchestrated the robbery that led to the fatal shooting. Briefly identify one of the most significant turning points from your character's past and its impact on your character in the present.

10. *Contradiction.* Great characters often embody contradictions. Here they seem one way. There they seem the opposite. For example, Berniece treasures family, yet does not hesitate to threaten her brother's life. Name two contradictory traits or behaviors that your character manifests—or could manifest—during the story.

11. *Comparison.* Similes and metaphors are poetic comparisons that enable us to communicate a lot in only a few words. For example, Berniece is like a sacred piano that has not played music in many years. Write a poetic comparison—either simile or metaphor—that captures the essence of your character.

12. *Change.* If a dramatic journey matters, it has a significant impact: it changes something fundamental about the character who drives it. Berniece starts out as one who can guard her family's past, but not build upon it. She ends up as one who has accepted the role handed down to her long ago by her mother: to carry the family legacy into the future. Briefly describe how your character changes because of what happens or doesn't happen in the story.

■ SIX NARRATIVE PORTRAITS OF YOUR CHARACTER

You have now explored your character in some detail. This has been a warm-up to help you write a few narrative descriptions of the character. Keep in mind that these will be personal portraits and not plot summaries.

First portrait. Describe your character in about 100 words. As you do this, you can repeat any of the details you found during the first part of this exercise and add whatever new information feels appropriate. Remember to honor the word limits. They are designed to pull focus on what matters most.

Second portrait. Some of the traits and facts in the first portrait are more important than others. Sharpen your focus on the character by revising your description down to a length of about 50 words. As you do this, you may simply eliminate half of the words in the first portrait or use new ones, but honor the limit.

Third portrait. Review your shortened summary and cut it in half again. Try to retain the most important parts of the description, within a length of about 25 words. As before, you may simply eliminate words or use new ones.

Fourth portrait. Continue to sharpen focus on the character as before by revising the portrait down to a sentence of exactly 10 words—no more and no less.

Fifth portrait. Revise the portrait down to exactly three words—no more and no less. You may use new words if you wish. They may either work together as a phrase or read separately like items on a list.

Sixth portrait. Revise the portrait down to one word. You may simply choose one of the three words from the fifth portrait or find a new word that best sums up the character.

WRAP-UP

What is the most interesting discovery that you made about your character? How is he or she universal? How is he or she unique? Use what you have learned about the character to guide your scene and story decisions as you develop your script.

Related tools in *Character, Scene, and Story*. To flesh out a character in more depth, try any exercise in the "Developing Your Character" section, particularly "Character Interview," "Character Fact Sheet," or "Nothing but the Truth."

Causing a Scene

Scenes are the steps of a dramatic journey. Ideally, each scene centers on one main event that reveals new information about the characters, changes the world of the story, and brings the dramatic journey closer to its destination. Use these scene development exercises during writing or revision to flesh out the elements of dramatic action, add power and depth to scenic events, and refine your dialogue.

While any number of characters may be present in a scene, each exercise focuses on the two most important ones to help you get started. Character 1 in any scene is the character who most actively makes it happen. This role is usually filled by the main character of the whole story, but others may serve as Character 1 in a scene if the main character is absent or not driving most of the scenic action. Character 2 is the second most important character in the scene.

BASIC SCENE STARTER

THE QUICK VERSION
Integrate a basic set of questions into your process for developing a scene

BEST TIME FOR THIS
During scene planning

THE SCENE: A BASIC BUILDING BLOCK OF DRAMA
Every dramatic story is a quest of some kind. No matter how complex the quest may be, it traditionally boils down to one main character trying to achieve one overriding, all-important goal. This goal may be tangible—such as a pot of gold, secret formula, or kingdom—or intangible—such as truth, love, justice, or freedom. Either way, a series of dramatic events occurs as the character pursues the goal and encounters obstacles that make it difficult to attain.

If enough is at stake, the character tries different strategies to overcome these obstacles, and sometimes succeeds and sometimes fails. This action continues under increasing pressure until a crisis is reached and the character must make a decision that triggers climactic action, reveals important truths about the character, and often changes him or her in a meaningful way. In the end, the quest succeeds or fails as a result of everything that has happened along the way.

These story dynamics reflect the three most basic principles of dramatic action: desire (what the character wants), motivation (why the character wants it), and obstacle (anything that might prevent the character from achieving the objective). The same principles are at work on a smaller scale in each scene of the story.

A scene is a unit of dramatic action caused by a character who wants something, has an important reason to pursue it here and now, and must deal with whatever problems stand in the way. The action typically takes place in one setting in real time, and adds up to a dramatic event. For example, something is begun or ended. Or, something is accomplished or fails to be accomplished. Whether positive or negative, the main event of the scene changes the world of the story in a significant way, and moves the character closer to, or further from, completing the quest.

From a technical point of view, each scene breaks down into smaller units of action called beats. Each beat has a single focus, such as a certain character need, behavior, or topic. Some beats may reflect the inner workings of the character's heart and mind, but most represent strategies, or tactics, that the character tries in order to achieve an objective. For a detailed look at beats, see "Thinking in Beats" later in this guide.

As you develop the main event of a scene, you need to think about how this event fits into the larger sequence of events that add up to the story. You also need to think about how this event breaks down into the smaller components of moment-to-moment dramatic action. Each scene thus requires an eye on the big picture as well as the details of the ever-changing here and now.

ABOUT THE EXERCISE

There is no "correct" way to develop a scene, and it's important to find a process that works best for you. More likely than not, you will gain much from taking the time to warm up before you leap into the scene and begin making discoveries in the moment. By doing some preparation first and getting a feel for the scene dynamics, your writing process may be faster, easier, and more productive.

■ TWELVE QUESTIONS FOR YOUR CHARACTER

The main character of a scene is the one who drives most of the dramatic action and makes the scene happen. In most cases, the main character of the scene is also the main character of the story, but not always. Use the following questions to flesh out the main character of any scene you are about to write. If you wish, you can adapt these same questions to the other characters in the scene as well.

1. *Who are you? (character)*. This is the most important question because the character is the story. In any scene, the lines of dialogue and beats of action all flow from who the character is. To create a dramatic event, you need to know your character inside out. If he or she has changed since the story began, you also need to know what specific changes have occurred and how this redefines the character here and now.

2. *Where are you? (setting)*. You can find a lot of story action by making specific choices about the physical setting for a scene. To say only that it takes place in the character's "home," for example, is to miss the creative opportunities that might arise from knowing exactly where in the home your characters will interact, whether they are in the kitchen, bedroom, attic, or backyard. Take the time to know what's in the setting as well. Think visually, and look for the truth in objects. Is there an object here, common or uncommon, that could be pivotal to the dramatic action of the scene?

3. *When are you? (time and given circumstances)*. The hour of the day, time of the week, and season of the year can all influence how a scene unfolds. Sometimes the time frame includes special circumstances—such as a holiday, birthday, or funeral—that can heighten this influence. Know exactly

when the scene takes place and whether this time includes any immediate circumstances that may affect the character's entrance or behavior.

4. *What's your situation here and now? (social, political, economic life)*. The world of the story is in constant flux. If there are any important social, political, or economic dynamics currently at work, make sure you know what they are and how they could affect your character in the scene.

5. *How do you feel? (physical and emotional life)*. It's easier to put yourself into your character's shoes when you know how the character feels both physically and emotionally, especially when the scene begins.

6. *What are you thinking about? (intellectual life)*. What is not said in a scene can be just as important as what is said. Know what's on the character's mind at this time in the story. Stay aware of what the character cannot say during the scene. Look for opportunities to suggest, not explain, any important conclusions that the character has reached.

7. *What do you want from the other character? (desire or objective)*. This is another key question because the character's scenic objective is what makes the scene happen. In some cases, the character enters with this objective in mind. In other cases, the character enters with something else in mind and the scenic objective is aroused because of what happens early on. Know what your character wants and what triggered this need. Know, too, that once the scenic objective is achieved or fails to be achieved, the scene is over.

8. *Why do you want that? (motivation)*. Dramatic characters tend to be driven by high stakes which make it increasingly important in the story to achieve their scenic objectives. If properly motivated, characters will fight hard to get what they want. Who characters are and aren't, what they believe and don't believe, what they have experienced and not experienced—all contribute to their motivations in the scene. Make sure the stakes are high enough to make the scene happen.

9. *What's the problem? (obstacle or conflict)*. The character's pursuit of a goal begins to generate dramatic action when the character meets obstacles or conflicts that make the objective difficult to achieve. There is always a problem to be solved. The size of such problems tends to grow as the story continues, with life getting worse and worse as the action unfolds.

10. *How will you deal with the problem? (strategy or tactics)*. If the scenic objective is important enough and if the central conflict is big enough, the character will probably need to try different strategies in order to tackle the objective. These changes of behavior show different sides of the character and create the beats, or units of action, of the scene.

11. *How will the past influence you now? (exposition or backstory)*. Every scene fits into a continuum of experience that began long before the story did and will continue after it ends. Drama shows us the "here and now" and suggests the "there and then." Know how the recent and distant past will affect your character in the present tense of the scene.

12. *What will happen as a result of all this? (main event)*. Though much may be discussed and much may occur, each scene adds up to one main event. This is a stepping stone in the main character's dramatic journey: a turning point—positive or negative—that moves the character closer to the final destination of the story. Know what happens in the scene.

WRAP-UP

This basic set of questions can be applied not only to your scenes but also to your whole story. As you prepare to write or rewrite, keep your primary focus on who your characters are (question 1). Then make sure you know what they want (question 7), why they will do everything possible to achieve that objective here and now (question 8), and what specific obstacles stand in the way (question 9).

Related tools in *Character, Scene, and Story*. For another look at basic scene development tools, go to the "Causing a Scene" section and try any stage 1 exercise, from "The Real World" to "The Scenes within the Scene."

WHERE IN THE WORLD ARE WE?

THE QUICK VERSION
Explore the physical life of a setting and use it to find new story ideas

BEST TIME FOR THIS
During scene planning

FINDING YOUR STORY IN THE PHYSICAL LIFE OF THE SCENE
No matter what your story is about, and no matter where your characters happen to be now, they are rooted in a physical life that reflects certain truths about them, their world, and the dramatic journey that is unfolding. At any given moment, physical life includes the setting and time of a scene, the objects in this setting, and the physical elements that define or govern this place. You can often discover exciting new story ideas by taking the time to explore a scene's physical context.

For example, imagine a desk drawer stuffed with papers. What do they suggest? Are they unpaid bills? Old love letters? Pages of an unfinished novel? Each answer leads to a different story. Or imagine the drawer not full of papers, but hiding a gold key. What does that suggest? Who put it there? And why? In either scenario, knowing what's in the desk drawer might be integral to scene planning. In other cases, the contents of the drawer may be totally irrelevant. So may the desk.

Physical life helps paint a picture of who your characters are, where they live, how they live, and what's happening—with little or no dialogue. Think of the upright piano in *The Piano Lesson* hand carved with mask-like figures resembling ancient African totems. Sitting in a parlor in Pittsburgh in the 1930s, the piano becomes not only a focal point of dramatic action but also the symbol of an African American family's past that stretches back to the days of slavery and personal family tragedies.

Or, think of Babe in *Crimes of the Heart* wandering the house with a loose noose around her neck, or Lieutenant Colonel Kilgore in *Apocalypse Now* standing fearlessly among battlefield explosions to enjoy the smell of napalm in Nam while others flee. Physical life images like these instantly reveal a lot about the characters, bring visual power to the story, and reduce the need for words of explanation.

ABOUT THE EXERCISE
Use this exercise to flesh out the physical life of a scene, and find objects and elements that can trigger or influence dramatic action. To do the exer-

cise, you need to know who will be in the scene and have at least a rough idea of what will happen.

You also need to know where and when the scene will take place. Remember that setting and time *do* matter. Interaction in a bedroom is different from interaction at a bus station. Outdoors is different from indoors. Day is different from night. Be sure to make the most appropriate choices for your characters and action. If you have used this setting before in your story, focus on how the place has changed.

Exercise examples are from my play *Hotel Desperado*. Character 1 is Max, a drifter in his twenties who is haunted by a violent past and has now ended up by chance in a strange and sleazy residence hotel. Character 2 is Bolton, an elderly ex-con, who is a permanent resident here. Their relationship: they met recently in the hotel lobby. What happens in the scene: Bolton comes to believe that Max is a criminal. Setting and time: Max's hotel room just before midnight.

■ EXPLORING THE SETTING OF YOUR SCENE

A quick way to understand the physical life of a scene is to put your characters in a specific place that you yourself have actually been—for example, it's not just a hotel room. It's a real hotel room where you once stayed. This approach lets you know automatically what's it like there and where things are. If it's not possible or appropriate to use a setting you have experienced firsthand, your writing will be easiest if you can picture the place clearly in your mind's eye.

For either approach, think about the setting you chose to explore and how this location is unique. Try to be as specific as possible as you answer the following questions. Remember that big discoveries can evolve from small details.

1. *Which physical elements here might affect the scene?* It may be important to know, for example, that there are two locked doors, that the room is overheated, that it has a foul smell, or that fireworks are exploding in the distance. Explore the setting through your senses:

- *See it.* Visualize the setting. Look around carefully. Find three interesting images and describe them briefly—such as a broken alarm clock on the bedside table, an old Bible in the drawer with a phone number written in blue ink on the inside cover, and a small blood stain in the carpet.
- *Listen to it.* Name at least two sounds that you can hear in this place, however faintly, and describe them—such as a scratching sound inside the wall, and the muffled sound of a TV from the room below.
- *Smell it.* Name at least one smell, pleasant or unpleasant, in this place—such as a hint of lilac bubble bath or a strong whiff of dirty socks.
- *Taste it.* Is there anything here to be tasted? If so, find it, identify it,

and describe its taste—such as cold, acidic coffee with too much sugar.

- *Touch it.* Imagine running your hand over parts of this place or the things in it. You might focus on texture, or surface temperature, or other sensations of touch. Describe an interesting one—such as the sheet of the bed gritty with sand and damp with perspiration.
- *Feel it.* Now try to feel the place again with your whole self. Focus this time on the general atmosphere, mood, temperature, or feeling of the place from either a physical or intuitive point of view and describe what it feels like—for example, cold and drafty, or gloomy, or claustrophobic.

> **For an in-depth sense study of a scene, try "In the Realm of the Senses" later in this guide.**

2. **What objects matter most?** Whether it's a lottery ticket in a coat pocket or a mostly empty takeout box of fried chicken, objects are real, they're concrete, and they help root your story in the here and now. They become most important when they motivate character behavior, influence the course of dramatic action, and help turn the story in unexpected directions. In your setting, think about the following:

- *Objects we can see.* Some of the objects in your setting will be clearly visible when the scene begins. Without repeating a previous response, look around again. Identify two or three objects that could play a key role in the dramatic action, and tell where these things are located when the scene begins—for example, an opened bottle of bourbon on the floor beside the bed, a leather belt draped across the back of a chair, and an old seascape calendar on the wall with all of the pages ripped off.
- *Objects we can't see.* Some objects are not in view when the scene begins. They may be simply out of sight or intentionally hidden. Look at the room again, but this time with X-ray vision. Find one interesting thing in the room that cannot be readily seen because it is either intentionally or unintentionally out of view. Tell what and where it is—for example, a gun hidden under the pillow of the bed.

3. **What lies beyond?** There is always more world beyond what we can see in front of us during a scene. Knowing what's out there may help you find more story. If there are two doors in a bedroom, for example, it may be important to know that one leads to a bathroom where someone is hiding. It also may be important to know that beyond these walls lies a Chicago ghetto, or an African jungle, or a beach leading to the Mediterranean. If the setting is outside, look around in every direction. If the setting is inside, go

to the windows or doors and look out. Describe what lies beyond the immediate setting of the scene.

4. *How does the time now affect this place?* Think again about when your characters will be in this setting and make more specific choices about the hour, day, month, and season. Even if you don't identify this precise time in the scene, it may affect the lighting, temperature, weather, and other physical elements as well as the atmosphere and mood that we will experience. Identify specifically when the scene occurs and how this time might affect the dramatic action. For example, it's approaching midnight on a cold rainy Easter Sunday in April. The mood is dark and lonely. The characters are tired, uncomfortable, on edge.

■ **ANALYZING THE SETTING OF YOUR SCENE**

You've begun to flesh out the physical life of a place that your characters will inhabit during a scene. Now look again at your findings:

1. *From any character's point of view, what is the most pleasant physical feature of this place?* Interpret "pleasant" any way you wish, and either repeat a previous response or find a new one. From Max's point of view, for example, the most pleasant thing about this hotel room is the deadbolt lock on the door.

2. *From any character's point of view, what is the most unpleasant physical feature of this place?* Interpret "unpleasant" any way you wish, and either repeat a previous response or find a new one. From Max's point of view, the most unpleasant thing here is the blood stain in the carpet.

3. *From an objective point of view, what is the most striking physical feature of this place?* Interpret "striking" any way you wish, and either repeat a previous response or find a new one. To an objective outsider, the most striking feature of the hotel room might be the scratching sound inside the wall.

4. *What are the three most intriguing physical elements?* As a way of summing up your work or perhaps still adding new ideas, identify the three most interesting physical elements of your setting—for example, the gun under the pillow, the blood stain in the carpet, and the scratching sound in the wall.

5. *How might each of these elements affect the scene?* Physical life can trigger a scene (perhaps the scratching sound inside the wall has prompted Max to ask for Bolton's help) or affect the emotional landscape (the sight of the blood stain has put Max on edge) or turn the action in unexpected directions (Bolton finds the gun, thinks that Max is the one who hid it under the pillow, and threatens to have him thrown out of the hotel). Think about the three most intriguing physical elements you identified and briefly describe how each could play an important role in your scene. Look for possibilities that go beyond incidental stage business to the realm of what is essential to the dramatic action.

6. *What is the most important physical element here?* This is a summary of your findings. Of the three physical elements you explored, which one could be pivotal to the scene because of how it affects your characters or motivates their behavior? For example, the scene might center on the hidden gun, and who did or did not hide it under Max's pillow. Briefly describe how the most important physical element in your setting will be pivotal to your scene.

> *When writing physical life into a scene, be selective and precise. In the end, one good physical element will serve you better than a truckload.*

WRAP-UP

Physical life is an important and often overlooked source of story. Here are some physical life tips to keep in mind when you are looking for new story ideas or feel stuck in the middle of a scene:

- Try changing one important physical element in the setting: alter something, add something, or take something away.
- Find an object that has been hidden there without your realizing it. Let your characters surprise you. Make the object pivotal to the story action.
- Take an important object away from one character and give it to another character.
- Make a radical change in where or when the scene takes place.

> **Related tools in *Character, Scene, and Story.*** To continue tapping the power of physical life, go to the "Developing Your Character" section and try "Objects of Interest." Or go to the "Causing a Scene" section and try "The Real World" or "The Color of Drama."

THE ROOTS OF ACTION

THE QUICK VERSION
Explore the immediate given circumstances for a scene

BEST TIME FOR THIS
During scene planning

UNDERSTANDING THE UNIQUE CONTEXT OF EACH SCENE
The immediate given circumstances for a scene reflect what has happened so far in the world of the story and what exists here and now as a result of that history. Some circumstances trace back to the distant past. Some stem from what just happened in the last scene, or since the last scene, or—if this is the first scene—in the recent backstory. The given circumstances for each scene differ from those for every other scene because they keep changing as, event by event, the story unfolds.

To know the immediate given circumstances is to know the roots of action for the scene. It is to know how the world of the story at the beginning of this scene differs from how it was at the beginning of the last scene. It is to know how the characters will enter the scene because of what they were just doing. It is to know what other positive or negative factors from the past will influence their behavior here and now.

ABOUT THE EXERCISE
Think about your characters just before they enter the scene. What have they each been doing? What do they each know or believe now? How do they feel? Use this exercise to address questions like these as you prepare to write a scene. Before you can begin, you need to know who will be in your scene, what their relationship is, and what will happen between them. As you explore the scenic context, stay open to possibilities you haven't considered before. Try to discover something new.

Exercise examples are from the opening scene of Joe Orton's classic black comedy *Loot*. Character 1 is Fay, a practical, emotionally distant home nurse. Character 2 is McLeavy, an elderly Catholic whose wife died three days ago while under Fay's care. The scenic event: Fay launches a plan to seduce McLeavy by persuading him to put his deceased wife behind him and marry again as soon as possible.

■ CURRENT SITUATION IN THE WORLD OF YOUR STORY

What circumstances are at work in the lives of the characters when your scene begins? There may be any number of interesting developments, but the only ones that currently matter are those which could be roots of action for this particular scene.

  1. *Physical circumstances.* In any story, characters exist in a specific reality where certain physical laws, conditions, and events may influence their behavior. In the opening of *Loot,* one of the most important physical circumstances—indeed the circumstance on which the whole scene rests—is the death of Mrs. McLeavy. Other related physical circumstances are the presence in the room of Mrs. McLeavy's coffin, Mrs. McLeavy's clothing, particularly her fluffy slippers, and a large wardrobe cabinet which is normally open but now, for reasons unknown to the characters, is locked. Each of these physical elements will influence the dramatic action of the scene. For example, Fay will try three times to open the cabinet. Its lock will finally motivate her to summon McLeavy's son for the key. Think about the current situation in the world of your story. Describe any immediate physical circumstances—personal or environmental—that could affect what will happen between the characters in your scene.

  2. *Psychological circumstances.* The character's inner world is another key influence on dramatic action. This is the realm of emotions, perceptions, beliefs, thoughts, desires, strengths, and weaknesses. In the opening of *Loot,* certain psychological circumstances will be critical to the scene. Mr. McLeavy is suffering from the loss of his wife. He has been a widower for only three days and must now face the harsh reality of the funeral today. All this has left him sad, confused, and vulnerable. Fay, on the other hand, feels no sorrow or remorse over the death of Mrs. McLeavy. (In fact, we will find out later that Fay was responsible for the old woman's hasty departure.) Fay is now psychologically at the top of her game with an eye on Mrs. McLeavy's fluffy slippers and her husband's estate. Briefly identify any psychological circumstances that could influence your scene.

  3. *Social circumstances.* Social dynamics—how people interact, what rules they live by, how they fit or don't fit into a community—are another key influence. Social values, customs, and expectations can play a defining role in how and why dramatic events occur. Important social factors are woven throughout the opening of *Loot* and define the relationship between the characters in different ways: lower class and middle class, employee and employer, hunter and prey. It is the social realm that brings Fay to the McLeavy household as a nurse, dictates that the death of the patient terminates her contract, and brings a sense of urgency to the launch of her swindle. It is also the social realm that makes it initially unthinkable for McLeavy to marry so soon after his wife's death. He is described as "the leading Catholic layman within a radius of forty miles," and it would trigger

a scandal if he were to give in to Fay's charms. Briefly describe any social circumstances that could influence what happens in your scene.

4. *Economic circumstances.* Economics—who has spending power and who doesn't—is the focus of many dramatic stories, and *Loot* is no exception. As its title suggests, money is what makes the world of *Loot* go round. The most significant economic factors in the opening scene are Mr. McLeavy's access to wealth and Fay's lack of access to it. Are there any important economic circumstances at work when your scene begins? If so, briefly describe them.

5. *Political circumstances.* Politics—who has power and who doesn't—is often a significant ingredient in character relationships and interactions. The opening of *Loot* presents a mix of power dynamics. Fay controls the situation at hand—she has no problem putting on Mrs. McLeavy's slippers and claiming them for herself—and she drives most of the dialogue and action. Fay is in charge of the here and now. McLeavy, on the other hand, has the power in the long term. He may be malleable now due to sorrow and confusion, and unable to stop Fay from saying and doing whatever she wants, but, in the end, he is the one with the money. It is McLeavy—not Fay—who will ultimately decide Fay's fate by saying yes or no to her proposal. Think about the power structure of your world. What are the most important political circumstances at work when your scene begins?

■ **A CLOSER LOOK AT CHARACTER 1'S PAST**

The main character of a scene is the one who drives most of the action and makes the scene happen. In the opening scene of *Loot*, Character 1 is Fay. Who is the main character of your scene? Begin to focus more on this character as you continue to explore how the recent and distant past may affect him or her during the scene.

1. *Recent past.* Just before *Loot* begins, Fay has been working for the last six months in the McLeavy household as a nurse in charge of Mrs. McLeavy's home care. During this time, she secretly convinced Mrs. McLeavy to change her will and direct her half of the family estate to Fay. The other half of the estate, however, is still in the hands of Mr. McLeavy. Three days ago, in an effort to get that fortune out of Mr. McLeavy's hands, Fay turned him into an eligible bachelor by secretly killing his wife with a generous dose of poison.

Think about what has happened just before your scene begins and find the last significant event in the character's dramatic journey. This may have occurred in the last scene, since the last scene, or in the recent backstory. Briefly identify Character 1's last significant experience.

- *Information acquired.* Fay's nursing experience has given her the chance to observe the McLeavy household closely, get the lay of the land, and obtain personal information from family members, including Mrs. McLeavy on her deathbed. Fay has learned, for example, that Mr. McLeavy is a devout Catholic and prominent member of St. Kilda's parish. This information will shape the seduction she launches: she will portray herself as a devout Catholic and Mrs. McLeavy as a false Catholic not worth mourning for more than a fortnight. Fay's presence in the home also has enabled her to evaluate Mr. McLeavy's bank accounts, his vulnerability as an aging man about to lose his wife, and his unspoken attraction to Fay.

Think some more about the last significant experience in your character's dramatic journey. Whether correct or incorrect, what new information did the character acquire from this experience? Briefly identify any new "facts" that the character learned from the last experience—for example, from the last scene—and that will influence his or her behavior in this scene.

- *Conclusions reached.* The knowledge that Fay gained during her time in the McLeavy household has led her to conclude that her plan to get Mr. McLeavy's money will succeed. This belief motivates her to launch her plan now and steer Mr. McLeavy's thoughts to the subject of remarrying someone like herself as soon as possible.

Think about what your character learned from the last significant experience. Identify one new conclusion that the character has reached as a result of that information: a belief—right or wrong—that may influence him or her in the scene.

2. **Distant past.** The immediate given circumstances for a scene are often laced with threads that stretch back to the distant past. In *Loot*, Fay has a history of marrying and murdering for money. This profession began years ago when marriage to her first husband failed and she decided not to divorce him but to shoot him. Her success in getting away with murder and inheriting a windfall set the stage for a life of crime. With seven successful murders behind her, Fay is cold-blooded and confident in the here and now of the scene.

Think about what happens in your scene. See if you can find an experience from the distant past—from years or even decades ago—that could influence your character now, even if he or she is not aware of this influence. Identify the past experience and how it might affect your character in the scene.

■ A CLOSER LOOK AT CHARACTER 2'S PAST

Every character in a scene is influenced, to some degree, by the recent and distant past. In the opening of *Loot*, the second most important—and, in this case, the only other—character is Mr. McLeavy. Who is the second most important character in your scene? Focus next on this character as you continue to explore how the past may affect him or her during the scene. If there are other characters in your scene and if it feels appropriate, you can use the following steps to flesh them out later as well.

1. *Recent past.* Three days before the opening of *Loot*, McLeavy's ailing wife of many years, the mother of his son, died. Think about what has happened just before your scene begins and briefly identify the last significant onstage or offstage event in this character's dramatic journey.

- *Information acquired.* McLeavy has been told by Fay that his wife's death was due to natural causes. This information will dissuade him from suspecting anything unusual about the death. As a result, he is now primarily concerned about the funeral arrangements, particularly the floral displays. In fact, as an enthusiast of roses, his only comment on his wife's death is that he's "glad she died in the right season for roses."

     Think some more about the last significant experience in your character's dramatic journey. Identify any new "facts"—right or wrong—that the character learned and that may influence him or her in the scene.

- *Conclusions reached.* The discovery of his wife's death and the information that it was due to natural causes has led McLeavy to believe that the matter of his wife is over and done with, and that he will live out the rest of his life as a lonely widower. This belief adds to the resistance he displays in the opening scene when Fay suggests a different type of future for him—as her husband.

     Think about what your character learned from his or her last significant experience. Identify one new conclusion that the character has reached as a result of that information: a belief—right or wrong—that may influence him or her in the scene.

2. *Distant past.* Long ago in the world of *Loot*, McLeavy once met and kissed the pope. This experience sealed his commitment to the Catholic church and triggered his quest to be a lay Catholic leader in his community. His religious background will make him strongly resistant to Fay's advances and scheming in the opening scene.

Think about what happens in your scene. See if you can find an experience from the distant past that could influence your character now—even if he or she is not aware of this influence. Identify the past experience and how it might affect your character in the scene.

■ THE SCENIC CONTEXT: WHAT MATTERS MOST

In *Loot*, the given circumstances that most affect the opening scene are: (1) Fay is a cold-blooded killer driven by greed; (2) McLeavy is a wealthy Catholic mourning the recent loss of his beloved wife; and (3) Fay secretly murdered his wife and is planning to murder McLeavy as well after marrying him and inheriting his half of the estate.

These three facts woven together create a scenic context from which character objectives, problems, motivations, and actions will grow. It is important to note, however, that not all of these critical facts are revealed to the audience at this time. By the end of the scene, we know only that McLeavy is a wealthy Catholic mourning the loss of his wife and that Fay has a desire to marry McLeavy. It will not be until later in the story that we discover that Fay is a cold-blooded killer with McLeavy's life and loot on her mind. The importance of the immediate given circumstances is not measured, therefore, by how much time is devoted to them in the dialogue of the scene. Rather, their importance is measured by how much they affect the characters here and now.

Think about the context for your scene. Regardless of whether or not they are revealed during the scene, what are the most important given circumstances?

WRAP-UP

To write a scene, you need to know the circumstances that will fuel the dramatic action. It is especially important to know the most immediate of these circumstances—what happened just prior to the scene—so that you know what the characters have most recently experienced, and how they are thinking and feeling as a result of this. By taking the time to explore the scenic context, you also may find it easier to determine the scene's point of attack: when exactly it should begin.

> **Related tools in** *Character, Scene, and Story.* To learn more about the given circumstances of a scene, go to the "Causing a Scene" section and try "What's New? What's Still True?" or "Why This? Why Now?"

WHAT DOES THE CHARACTER WANT?

THE QUICK VERSION
Flesh out the main objective of the character who drives a scene

BEST TIME FOR THIS
When you are planning, writing, or rewriting a scene

DESIRE AS A KEY TO UNDERSTANDING CHARACTER
Like people, characters do not act or even speak unless they want something. This desire may be conscious or unconscious, physical or psychological, healthy or unhealthy. Know what your main character wants most in
life and you will have a better understanding of what your story is about.
Know what the character wants in each scene and you will have a better
understanding of who the character is. Know what the character wants in
each beat and you will have a better understanding of how the character
will behave next.

A *"beat"* is a unit of dramatic action in a
scene. If you are not familiar with beats, see
"Thinking in Beats" later in this guide

Character desires come in different sizes and operate at different levels.
Whether they are driving a whole story (*story goal*), a whole scene (*scenic
objective*), or only a beat of a scene (*beat action*), these dramatic needs are
what make the character active and cause things to happen. Most character objectives, particularly at the scenic and beat level, are behavioral. They
reflect the desire to affect another character in an important way. While
countless behavioral objectives are possible, all fall into four basic categories: to make the other character feel good, to make the other character
feel bad, to find out something important from the other character, or to
convince the other character of something important.

Some objectives are physical. They focus on not another character but a
physical task, such as getting the room ready for the start of the day (*Endgame*) or trying to stick a birthday candle onto a cookie so you can secretly
celebrate your birthday (*Crimes of the Heart*).

The only time that the story is not driven by objectives is during those moments, if any, when a character retreats in monologue to a world of imagery in order to explore innermost thoughts and feelings, or to relive a memory, as Edmund does in *Long Day's Journey into Night* when he recalls his exhilarating life at sea.

ABOUT THE EXERCISE

Choose a scene to develop and use this exercise to figure out the main objective that will drive it. Exercise examples are from scene 5 of *Betrayal* by Harold Pinter.

■ **YOUR CHARACTER'S SCENIC OBJECTIVE**

Answer these questions about the scene you are focused on now:

1. *Main character of the scene*. This is who drives most of the action and makes something important happen. The main character of the scene is usually also the main character of the story. In some scenes, however, the main character of the story may not be present or may be the object of action rather than the cause of it. In such cases, the main character of the scene is someone other than the main character of the story. In scene 5 of *Betrayal*, the main character of the scene is Robert. Who is the main character of your scene?

2. *Key influences*. Each scene centers around one main event that changes the world of the story and is caused by the main character in pursuit of a scenic objective. To choose this objective and write the scene, you need to know what's happening in the world of the story at this precise and unique point in time, particularly for the main character of the scene. Consider such factors as:

- *Backstory*. Think about what's happened in the character's life before the story begins. Are there any significant events from the past that might affect what your character wants now?
- *Immediate given circumstances*. Think about what's happened in the story so far and particularly in the last scene. What is the character's current situation as this scene begins. Are there any key circumstances—positive or negative—that will affect what your character wants now?
- *Character relationship*. Unless the characters here are strangers, they know each other to some degree and have been together before. Is there anything from their shared history—especially from the last time they were together—that will affect what your character wants in this scene?
- *Setting*. Think about where the scene takes place and what important objects and other physical elements may be present. Is there anything about this environment that might affect your character's scenic objective?

- *Physical and emotional life.* How does your character feel when the scene begins and how might this affect your character's scenic objective?
- *Intellectual life.* Focus on what your character knows and believes at this time in the story. What is the character thinking about when the scene begins and how might this affect your character's scenic objective?

3. **Specific stimulus**. While many influences combine to shape the character's needs, each scene is triggered by a specific turning point—a decision, discovery, idea, emotion, interaction, or external event—that occurs either before the scene or during it. If the stimulus occurs prior to the scene, the character enters knowing what he or she wants to accomplish. If the stimulus occurs during the scene, the character acquires the objective as a result of what happens early on.

In the world of *Betrayal*, while Robert and Emma are on vacation, for example, Robert goes to an American Express office to cash travelers checks, accidentally discovers a letter addressed in his best friend's handwriting to his wife, and suspects that they are having an affair. This discovery occurs offstage and triggers the scene which takes place the next day in Robert and Emma's hotel room. What specific turning-point experience triggers your scene? Does this stimulus occur before the scene or during it?

4. **Possible character needs**. Regardless of when it is aroused, the scenic objective remains intact until it is either achieved or thwarted, and this success or failure signals the scene's end. The scenic objective not only drives the scene, therefore, but holds it together. This does not imply that the character may act only one way during the scene. One scenic objective can produce many different strategies, which, in turn, create different beats of action.

To find your character's scenic objective, think about the specific stimulus for your scene and how it might affect your character's needs here and now. Take a few moments to explore different possibilities. Imagine that what will drive most of the scenic action is your character's need for one of the following:
- *To make the other character feel good*—for example, to flatter, seduce, impress, comfort, or cheer up. If Robert has begun to suspect that his wife Emma is having an affair with his best friend Jerry, he might want to try to win her back. This could be the scenic objective for a tender love scene in which the affair is never mentioned. Suppose that your character had a "feel good" objective in your scene. What would it be?
- *To make the other character feel bad*—for example, to threaten, warn, frighten, scold, or make feel guilty. Robert's reaction to the possibility of being betrayed could trigger a more vengeful reaction. Instead of

trying to win Emma back, he might want to punish her and make her feel rotten and ashamed for what she has done. Suppose that your character had a "feel bad" objective in your scene. What would it be?

- *To find out something important from the other character*—for example, to ask questions directly, probe indirectly, or inspire confession. If Robert suspects that Emma and Jerry have betrayed him, he might want to learn if it's true and, if so, how long the affair has been going on and how serious it has become. Suppose your character had a "find out" objective in your scene. What would it be?
- *To convince the other character of something important*—for example, to prove a point beyond all doubt. This is not the same as "explaining" things. Like the other three behavioral objectives, it is an emotionally charged need to achieve an important end. Robert's reaction to his discovery might be to convince Emma that, for the sake of their children, she must end the affair. Suppose your character had a "convince" objective in your scene. What would it be?
- *To complete a significant physical task*—for example, to obtain an object of importance or make a meaningful change in the physical life of the character or environment. Unlike the four behavioral objectives, this physical goal may or may not demand a specific response from the other character. Perhaps Robert knows that his wife now has the suspicious letter he noticed at American Express. His physical objective might be to get the letter from her so that he can read it for himself. Suppose your character has a physical objective in your scene. What would it be?

5. **Conscious need**. To act with intent, characters must know what they want—or at least think so. In the *Betrayal* scene, Robert's conscious objective is to find out if Emma is having the affair and, if so, how serious it has become. Now that you have explored different possibilities for your scene, choose the conscious objective that makes the most sense for your character at this time in your story.

6. **Subconscious need (if any)**. Some characters also have a more powerful subconscious need that is different from the conscious objective and rules the action. While Robert wants to find out how badly he has been betrayed, he may also have a subconscious desire to punish his wife for her infidelity. This deeper desire drives him to play a cruel cat-and-mouse game with her throughout the scene. Is there any subconscious objective at work in your scene? If so, what?

7. **Motivation**. Dramatic action will result when your character takes steps to pursue the scenic objective and encounters obstacles that make it difficult to achieve. To deal with these conflicts, the character must be properly motivated, with stakes important enough and urgent enough to make

compromise or surrender unthinkable. What's at stake for Robert are his two most important relationships: with his wife and his best friend. He will do everything he can to learn the full truth about them. In your scene, what is at stake for your character?

8. *First action.* The character's first action in the scene may or may not be driven by the scenic objective, depending on when this need is aroused:

- *If the scenic objective was triggered prior to the scene*, the character's first action is driven by this need whether we realize it or not. When the Robert and Emma scene begins, Robert knows exactly what he wants to find out. His first action is not to ask her about the affair, however, but only to bring up the subject of Jerry in a seemingly innocent way. He is laying the groundwork for a trap which will later force Emma to confess.

- *If the scenic objective is triggered during the scene*, the character's first action is driven by a different need—usually of lesser importance. This keeps the character active until the scenic objective is sparked and begins to drive the action. Suppose that Robert were to discover the suspicious letter not at American Express the day before, but in the hotel room during the scene. His first action might be simply to find a misplaced tourist map. This lesser objective could initiate his interaction with Emma and lead to the unexpected discovery of the letter.

Whether your character's scenic objective is triggered before the scene or during it, what is your character's first action?

As you write, let your character's scenic objective lead you to spontaneous discoveries about each new beat rather than try to plot out the beats in advance.

9. *Character information.* We learn who dramatic characters are by observing them in action and making inferences about what they do. What they want tells us a lot about who they are. Robert's conscious need to learn the truth about the affair shows the importance he places on his marriage to Emma and his friendship with Jerry. His subconscious desire to torment Emma in the process shows how much he has been hurt by the betrayal. Think about what your character wants in your scene. What does this reveal about the character?

WRAP-UP

You can use these steps to figure out any character's scenic objective. Over time, you can adapt this process to your own needs and do it more instinctively. Once you know the scenic objective, keep your character focused on it. Remember that one goal can produce many different behaviors, and that

the other characters and audience may not always know what the character is really doing. Allow the other characters to change objectives as often
as makes sense in their responses to your main character's actions. Be sure
to stop the scene when it ends, that is, when the scenic objective has been
achieved or utterly failed.

Related tools in *Character, Scene, and Story*.
To explore how character objectives can
drive a story, scene, or beat of action, go
to the "Causing a Scene" section and try
"Levels of Desire." To focus on the main
character's primary goal in the story, go to
the "Building Your Story" section and try
"Character on a Mission."

WHAT'S THE PROBLEM?

THE QUICK VERSION
Flesh out the conflict of a scene

BEST TIME FOR THIS
When you are planning, writing, or rewriting a scene

CONFLICT: A TOOL TO TEST AND REVEAL CHARACTER

Conflict in drama is anything that makes a character's objective difficult to achieve. Simply put, conflict is obstacle. It's whatever the character must overcome in order to succeed. Conflict is often equated with argument—which is indeed a common and obvious type of conflict—but obstacles can take many other forms as well. In fact, anything, even love, can be a problem if it gets in the way of what a character wants. For example, after learning that her boyfriend is married, she wants to leave him, but she can't because, even though he lied to her, she still loves him.

Conflict reveals and heightens the character's objective. Without obstacles, we don't feel the importance of the character's needs. You can explain these needs in a speech, but it won't mean much dramatically, because we are getting the information intellectually rather than emotionally. For example, a man wants to pay his taxes. He writes a check to the IRS and puts it in the mail. No problem. And no drama. Suppose, however, that he owes much more than he can pay, that he's facing a prison sentence if he doesn't settle up within thirty days, and that no one will lend him money because of his bad credit. This is what incites the play *Search and Destroy* by Howard Korder. As we watch the character deal with these obstacles and go to increasingly unscrupulous means to get cash, no explanations are necessary. We can see what he's after and how important it is to him.

We often find out who people really are by observing their behavior under stress. Conflict has a way of exposing our true values and testing our commitment to what we claim is important to us. In drama, slowly rising conflict puts more and more pressure on the character and strips away superficialities. It tests the character and forces him or her to take bigger risks. This helps us see who the character really is.

When push comes to shove, for example, we discover that one who exuded bravado is really a coward, or that one who has cowered often is really a hero. Meanwhile the characters are affected by what they do and how the world responds to them. They change—for better or for worse—because of what they've been through.

Choose a scene to develop and use this exercise to flesh out the conflict of the scene. Exercise examples are from scene 2 of *Glengarry Glen Ross* by David Mamet.

■ YOUR CHARACTER IN CONFLICT

To explore possibilities for scenic conflict, consider elements like these:

1. *Main character's scenic objective.* A dramatic scene typically centers on one character pursuing one overriding scenic objective and encountering obstacles that make it difficult to achieve. Before you can define the conflict in your scene, you need to know what the main character's scenic objective is. This spine of action will determine what is and isn't a problem here and now. In *Glengarry Glen Ross*, the main character of the scene is Moss. His main objective is to convince his coworker Aaronow to steal important files from their real estate office and sell them to a competitor. Who drives most of your scene and what does this main character want most?

2. *Another character's needs.* In a dramatic story, the forces of conflict tend to be complex and challenging. They can arise from many different sources. The most common source of conflict is the other character: one who wants something contrary or contradictory to what the main character wants. Suppose Moss wants to convince Aaronow to rob the office. Aaronow becomes an obstacle to that objective if he wants instead to stay out of trouble. His desire for safety poses a major threat to Moss's success in the scene. In your scene, how might another character's needs pose obstacles to the scenic objective?

3. *Another character's traits.* The main character's scenic objective also may be threatened by the physical, psychological, or social traits of the other character. These obstacles may be inherent in the other character, such as defining personality traits, or temporary, such as current physical or emotional states. Since Aaronow is far from genius level, for example, it will be difficult for Moss to instruct him in the plan. Aaronow is also depressed— he has just lost a real estate sale—and this will make him unresponsive to anything but his own gloom. At the same time, Aaronow is fearful. Though he will be attracted to the prospects of instant wealth, he also will be overly cautious about even discussing—let alone pulling off—a betrayal of the bosses who rule his life. In your scene, how might the other character's traits get in the way of the scenic objective?

4. *Main character's inner world.* Conflict also may rise from within the character who is pursuing the objective. Personal characteristics (such as self-delusion, altered state of consciousness, or physical weakness) and emotional states (such as fear, guilt, doubt, or confusion) can make characters their own worst enemy. For example, Moss's view of the world is steeped in a bigotry and anger that can distract him from his goal. He also has problems articulating his thoughts clearly. Think about the main char-

acter of your scene. What inner conflicts might make the objective difficult to achieve?

5. *External situation.* Characters often find themselves in situations with social, economic, political, physical, or other dimensions that make their objectives difficult to achieve. For example, Moss and Aaronow live in a cut-throat sales world which has turned them into desperate and ruthless men. To convince Aaronow to rob the office, Moss must overcome the legal risk of proposing a crime and the professional risk of stirring up mutiny. Moss's objective is also made difficult by the plan itself, which asks Aaronow to do all of the dirty work and assume most of the risk while Moss is elsewhere having dinner. How might the circumstances of the scene pose obstacles to the scenic objective?

THE CENTRAL CONFLICT OF THE SCENE
In drama, problems tend to travel in packs and multiply like mad. Conflict is often a combination of obstacles that arise on many different levels all at the same time. Together, they represent the opposing forces that the character must face, with one force central to the struggle. The main problem for Moss, for example, is Aaronow's resistance to the plan. Think about the possible conflicts you have identified for your scene. Which of these would you pick—or how would you combine any of them—to identify the central conflict? This is the biggest problem that must be overcome in order to achieve the scenic objective.

THE OPENING PROBLEM
In drama, there is always trouble afoot—even when the scene is just beginning. The opening problem is usually large enough to put something at stake for someone, and yet small enough to allow room for the conflict to grow. The opening problem for Moss is not Aaronow's resistance to the robbery scheme, but rather Aaronow's depression over missing a sale. Before the scheme can even be presented, Moss must figure out a way to fire up Aaronow and make him receptive to betraying their bosses. Think about the possible conflicts you have explored so far and identify the opening problem of your scene. This will begin to define the jumping-off point for action.

WRAP-UP
As you write the scene, keep conflict ever present. Let it grow and change as the action develops and turns the story into new and unexpected directions. Some conflicts will be resolved. Some won't. Either way, new problems and obstacles will emerge and make life increasingly difficult for the main character. If conflict drops out, the story will begin to feel talky and wooden. Scenes tend to work best:

- *When conflict equals the objective.* If the problem is too small or too large, we predict the outcome and lose interest in the story because we're way ahead of the character. We know that a simple problem will be easily solved and that an impossible problem will never be solved. However, if there is a slight chance that a difficult problem might be solved, we remain engaged to see what will happen.

To create strong character objectives, create strong conflicts. If a character objective seems weak, you may need to strengthen the problem.

- *When conflict slowly rises rather than leaps to a crisis.* In drama, things build—from small to large, from ordinary to extraordinary. If the drama starts in crisis or peaks too early, it will have nowhere to go after that and will have to keep repeating the same dynamic. We will lose interest in the story because it's more and more of the same. By starting small and letting the forces of conflict rise slowly, you can allow plenty of room to build tension and to keep moving the character—and us—into new territory. Often a story will begin with a minor problem of the main character or a major problem of a minor character.

  In addition, we can't read the character's mind unless you explain it to us. But drama is not the realm of explanation. Ideally, we observe the character's behavior and make inferences about what the character feels and thinks. We need time to watch the character in action and understand his or her motivations. This lets us participate emotionally in the transition to crisis. Ideally, conflict does not leap to crisis so quickly that we don't understand what happened. Instead, it slowly builds, step by step, so that we can stay with the character the whole way.

- *When conflict leads to action, not inaction.* Dramatic characters, particularly main characters of stories, know what they want and have high stakes behind that need. Conflicts are stimuli that cause these characters to take new and often unexpected courses of action. To keep us emotionally engaged, dramatic characters do not compromise or give up their objectives. They do not become passive—at least not for long. The most interesting person in the story is usually the one who is most active.

- *When conflict generates a variety of behavior.* It is often conflict that forces a character's strategies to change. Conflict becomes static when characters stay too long with a strategy that clearly doesn't work. Obstacles give characters a reason to keep changing strategies, and this creates different units of action. In combination with the scenic objective, conflict creates the beats, or units of action, of the scene.

Related tools in *Character, Scene, and Story*. To identify other obstacles that your character might face at a certain time in the story, go to the "Causing a Scene" section and try "Mother Conflict."

GOOD INTENTIONS

THE QUICK VERSION
Give your characters compelling reasons to pursue their objectives

BEST TIME FOR THIS
When you want to heighten the conflict of a scene

BATTLE OF THE GOOD GUYS
In drama, one of the most common sources of conflict is the other character. When that character wants something contrary or contradictory to what this character wants, and when they both have something vital at stake, conflict is inevitable. In myths, fables, action stories, and other genres that present the world in simple, larger-than-life terms, one of these characters is often a hero and the other a villain. Their interaction becomes a battle between a "good guy" and a "bad guy."

However, two characters with opposing needs do not necessarily have to fit this mold. In fact, the most dynamic and complex conflict often results when both characters see themselves as right, and act with the best of intentions. Their interaction becomes a battle between a "good guy" and a "good guy." While the characters may not agree on what "good" is, the desire to achieve their version of it can fuel a conflict of dramatic proportions.

ABOUT THE EXERCISE
Use this exercise to write or revise any scene where two or more characters face a common problem, but have opposing views about how to solve it. For example, a family has outgrown its home. The father wants to sell the house and buy a larger one, but the mother wants to stay and build an addition.

The goal is to create a confrontation between the characters by making sure that each one's objective is not only important and urgent, but also—from the character's perspective—good and right. If their motivations are strong enough and noble enough, the characters will find themselves locked together in the problem. Neither will be willing to compromise or give up, and the conflict will rise to a dramatic level.

To begin, choose a scene to write or edit. In order to explore character motivations in the scene, you need to know who the characters are, what problem they face here and now, and what each character wants from the other as a result of the problem.

■ UNDERSTANDING CHARACTER MOTIVATIONS

To create the strongest conflict, give each character something good to fight for—or at least something each perceives as good at this particular time in the story. Use these questions to help you explore your character motivations.

1. *Review character objectives.* Look at how you stated the objective for each character. For best results, be sure that each goal is positive. Suppose a man wants to convince his wife to move to a new house, but she does not want to leave this one. The latter objective is stated as a negative—"does not want"—and becomes dramatically stronger when restated as a positive that gives the character something to work toward: she wants to convince her husband of what a wonderful home they already have. If either of your characters has a negative objective, restate it as a positive.

Imagine a man in the ocean being hunted by a shark and swimming frantically toward land. If the man is a dramatic character, he will gain the most power not from a negative objective—to get away from the shark—but from a positive objective—to reach the shore.

2. *Look at the situation again through Character 1's eyes:*
- Think about Character 1's objective. Why is this a good thing to fight for at this time? Define the logic that leads Character 1 to perceive the objective as a positive goal.
- Think about what's at stake for Character 1. Why is the objective not only good, but also important? In other words, what will make compromise or surrender seem impossible?

3. *Look at the situation again through Character 2's eyes:*
- Think about Character 2's objective. Why is this a good thing to fight for at this time? Define the logic that leads Character 2 to perceive the objective as a positive goal.
- Think about what's at stake for Character 2. Why is the objective not only good, but also important? In other words, what will make the character want to fight to the finish to achieve this objective?

4. *Establish urgency.* To create a battle of "good guys," you need to make sure that your characters cannot avoid the conflict. Why must this scene driven by these characters with these objectives and these motivations take place here and now? In other words, why is the situation urgent? Why can't the characters avoid each other or put this whole thing off until later?

5. *Create a three-word summary of the scene*. For each character, find one word to identify the "good" that he or she will fight for in the scene. Then add the word "versus" between the two "goods" so that you have a three-word summary of the scene—for example, "Comfort versus stability," or "Freedom versus security," or "Pleasure versus health."

6. *Write the scene*. Use your summary as a guide to develop the scene around opposing characters who each have good intentions. If the situation is important and urgent, the characters will now fight to the finish for what they see as right.

WRAP-UP

Even the most heinous of acts can be driven by a good intention. For some, an act of destruction may be seen as an act of justice. An act of deception may be seen as an act of protection. An act of punishment may be seen as an act of salvation. No matter what they do, characters always move toward what they perceive as good at the time—even if they later change their minds and regret what they have done.

> *Find the right balance between motivation and objective. If the motivation feels too small to justify the objective, the character's actions may seem silly or melodramatic: "He had no real reason to go to all that trouble." If the motivation feels too big, the character's actions may seem illogical or unbelievable: "With so much at stake, she would have tried harder."*

To understand the good your character is after, try to see the situation truly and fully through the character's eyes. Know what deep needs are driving the struggle to achieve that good, and make sure that the stakes are high enough. If you find that you need to raise the stakes in a scene, try one of the following:

- *Reach for a higher good*. In great drama, high stakes are at risk, such as friendship or health. When the stakes don't feel high enough, you can up the ante by endangering a higher good. For example, instead of friendship, try putting love at risk. Or, instead of health, try putting survival at risk.
- *Make a good more valuable*. Stakes that are great in quality, scarce in quantity, unique in nature, first of a kind, or last of a kind tend to be extra valuable and give characters more steadfast reasons to fight for them. In *Romeo and Juliet*, what's at stake is not only love but great

love. In *Raiders of the Lost Ark*, what's at stake is not only a sacred artifact but the one and only Ark of the Covenant that housed the tablets of the Ten Commandments.

• *Broaden the impact.* Motivation often increases when more people may be affected by the gain or loss in question. In *Cape Fear,* a man fighting against a maniac for survival is engaged in an important struggle, but it is even more critical since the lives of his family are at risk as well. In *Erin Brockovich*, a legal clerk works to expose a big corporation as the cause of contaminated water in the area. Her fight is valiant, but its importance soars when it means justice for hundreds of people whose health has been affected.

Related tools in *Character, Scene, and Story*. To explore character motivation in more depth, go to the "Causing a Scene" section and try "Why Did the Character Cross the Road?"

HOW IT HAPPENS

THE QUICK VERSION
Begin to develop appropriate strategies for a character pursuing a scenic objective

BEST TIME FOR THIS
During scene planning, writing, or revision

ONE OBJECTIVE, MULTIPLE STRATEGIES
Once you know a character's objective, conflict, and motivation for a scene, you are ready to explore the strategies that he or she will employ in this particular situation. The result is a dramatic action plan that the character may try to work out in advance but is mostly improvised as certain strategies fail or produce unexpected results. The need to keep revising the plan is fueled by the character's commitment to achieve the objective as well as any subconscious desires at work.

Because different strategies are usually needed to achieve an objective that is important and difficult, the "how" of action is dynamic: it keeps changing as the character is forced to manage the unexpected and try something new. One scenic objective, therefore, does not confine a character to one subject or one type of behavior. Instead, it can be the fountainhead for a complex variety of topics and actions. In the end, these changing strategies are the very stuff of the story itself: the behavior we observe and dialogue we hear.

For example, in scene 15 of *The Elephant Man*, a play by Bernard Pomerance later made into a film by David Lynch, Merrick—the physically disfigured title character—is visited by Ross, who once employed him in a sideshow. Since their last encounter, Merrick has become a celebrated figure in London and friend of the rich and famous, while Ross has sunk into oblivion. The main character of the scene is Ross. His objective is to strike up a new business relationship with Merrick. This will not be easy, however, since Ross has proven to be a despicable person who kept Merrick in a cage, treated him like an animal, and then robbed him and left him to die when the sideshow failed. What's at stake for Ross now is his own well-being.

This combination of elements produces a series of different strategies for Ross: he asks for Merrick's forgiveness, proposes the idea of being his manager with a 10 percent commission, tries to make Merrick feel sorry for him, goes back to selling the deal, offers to help Merrick find a prostitute, grovels in a more desperate attempt to win Merrick's sympathy, and finally offers to reduce the commission to 5 percent. Though his action plan fails, it creates a rich, multibeat scene that shows much about both characters and the different worlds they have come to inhabit.

Ross's action plan is unique to him but illustrates a structure that is typical in dramatic stories. The first action is what the character sees as either the least demanding or most timely step. For Ross, a desperate man who has behaved badly, the most timely step is to bridge the divide between Merrick and himself. Until Ross can put the past behind them, he will have no chance to even pitch his idea, let alone convince Merrick to accept it. Ross must begin by apologizing. This is also his easiest job in the scene, since his apology consists only of words, not real remorse, and since, as it turns out unexpectedly, Merrick has already forgiven him.

The second step of action is what the character perceives to be the next easiest or next most timely thing to do after the success or failure of the first step. For Ross, this means dropping the subject of the past and getting to the reason for his visit: the great deal he has to offer. This step is more difficult than the apology, because the stakes have gone up: this is something that Ross really cares about.

As Ross steps from trying to promote his business scheme, to admitting that he's old and sickly, to offering himself as a pimp, to confessing his fear of dying in the poorhouse, his strategies continue to become increasingly difficult. Each new step is a greater personal challenge with more at stake. By the time he reaches the final step—the offer to shrink his commission to 5 percent—he has exposed the full, humiliating truth about himself: he is not a shrewd businessman with a profitable deal but a lost soul willing to settle for any crumb that anyone will throw his way.

We learn a lot about characters by how they try to achieve their objectives: what strategies they choose and don't choose, how well they execute these strategies, how they manage the unexpected, and how they think and act under rising pressure. Ideally, if you give two characters the same objective and put them into the same situation, you will end up with two different action plans, because each will draw from—and reflect—a unique set of values, beliefs, and life experience. Think about what your character wants in the scene you are working on now. How will your character attempt to get that? What will this process reveal about him or her?

ABOUT THE EXERCISE

To do this exercise, you need to have made some basic choices about the main character of your scene. You should know this character's objective and motivation, and have a sense of the conflict that will make the objective difficult to achieve.

Use the following steps to brainstorm possible strategies your character might try in pursuit of the objective. It can be helpful to think about such strategies in advance, but don't plan them in too much detail or attempt to impose your plan on characters who don't want to cooperate after the scene has begun. If you make compelling new discoveries while writing the scene, trust your instinct and see where they lead you instead of forcing yourself to conform to a scenic plan.

As you step through the exercise, remember that a "beat" is a unit of dramatic action in a scene and that a change of beat often reflects a change of strategy. If you are not familiar with beats, see "Thinking in Beats" later in this guide.

■ YOUR CHARACTER'S FIRST STRATEGY

1. *Action.* Start to think about how your character will try to achieve the scenic objective in this particular situation. To figure out the first step of action, you need to consider who the character is and what he or she would perceive as the least demanding or most timely thing to do here and now. Try to look beyond the generic to find a choice that says something telling about your character.

- Briefly identify the first strategy—for example, to patch things up by asking for forgiveness.
- What does this strategy reveal about your character?
- Can the first strategy be refined or revised to show something more interesting about your character? If so, how?
- Consider your character's unique perspective. What results would this character logically expect from taking this first action in this situation?

2. *Reaction.* Imagine different possible outcomes of the character's first step. A second strategy will be needed if either of the following happens:

- The first strategy succeeds but is not a final step in achieving the objective. There is more to do.
- The first strategy fails. If this is the case, identify at least one unexpected result of the strategy and why it occurred.

A second strategy is not needed if your character achieved the objective as a result of the first step. The scene is over and consists of only one beat. Choose the outcome that feels right for your scene and, if appropriate, begin to think about the next step of action.

■ YOUR CHARACTER'S SECOND STRATEGY

1. *Action.* Your character's second strategy is what your character now sees as the least demanding or most timely step after the success or failure of the first step.

- Briefly identify the second step of your character's action plan.
- How is this strategy different from the first strategy?
- For your unique character here and now, what makes the second step more challenging than the first step? How have the stakes gone up?

- What new information does the second strategy reveal about your character?
- Can the second strategy be refined or revised to show something more interesting about your character? If so, how?
- Consider your character's unique perspective. What results would this character logically expect from taking this second action in this situation?

2. *Reaction.* Imagine different possible outcomes of the character's second strategy. A third strategy will be needed if either of the following happens:

- The second strategy succeeds but is not a final step in achieving the objective. There is still more to do.
- The second strategy fails to produce the desired outcome. If this is the case, identify the actual outcome and why it occurred.

A third strategy is not needed if your character has achieved the objective as a result of the second step. The scene is over and consists of only two beats.

■ DISCOVERING ADDITIONAL STRATEGIES AS YOU WRITE

You have now fleshed out ideas for two beats of action. This has given you a jumping-off point for the scene and a sense of what the first beat change will be. After you begin writing the scene, work in the moment with your character to find any additional strategies that he or she might try in pursuit of the objective. Remember that this changing plan of action will continue until the character finally succeeds or reaches a point of utter failure.

As you switch to new strategies, keep looking for the next easiest or next most timely step for this unique character and aim to make each new step more difficult than the one before so that the stakes keep slowing rising.

WRAP-UP

In the realm of character strategies, the term "easiest" is relative to the character and the situation. If you are thirsty and need water, for example, the easiest course of action would probably not be to climb into a spaceship and fly light-years away to a distant planet. Instead, you would probably just go into your kitchen and pour a glass of water at the sink. If you are the title character from *The Man Who Fell to Earth*, however, you would have to reevaluate, because you would be living on a planet where water is in short supply. For you, the easiest course of action would be the spaceship and the long journey—and that would only be the first step.

As you develop your script, keep looking for strategic choices that reveal important information about your character. Try to avoid generic responses and remember that character strategies are the stuff of each scene. They determine how the action unfolds, what types of behavior your characters manifest, what topics they discuss, and what sides of their unique personalities are revealed in the process. Most importantly, character strategies help you show, not tell, the story. What can we learn about your characters by observing the pursuit of their objectives?

> **Related tools in** *Character, Scene, and Story.* To flesh out character strategies and tactics further, go to the "Causing a Scene" section and try "Levels of Desire" or "The Strategics of the Scene."

CHARACTER ADJUSTMENTS

THE QUICK VERSION
Explore character feelings and attitudes that influence scenic action

BEST TIME FOR THIS
During scene planning, writing, or revision

HOW CHARACTERS BEHAVE: A QUESTION OF ATTITUDE
Dramatic characters are emotional beings who care enough about their dramatic journeys to make us care about them, too. As they try different strategies to achieve their objectives, they have to keep making personal adjustments to the various positive and negative ways that the world responds to their efforts.

For example, a college graduate starting an important new job may be awed by her colleagues at first. She may grow cold toward a group who snubs her and then hostile to one who tries to get her fired. The adjustments from "awed" to "cold" to "hostile" reflect an emotional dynamic that changes as the character makes new discoveries about the situation at hand.

In drama, an "adjustment" is the feeling or attitude that a character visibly manifests at any given time in a scene. Some character adjustments are involuntary: the new employee's initial awe and later hostility are emotional responses that she cannot suppress. Other adjustments are voluntary: she chooses to act cold toward those who snub her. In some cases, what we observe is the true state of the character: a boy acts excited because he is excited. In other cases, what we see is only a façade used to implement a strategy: a girl acts friendly to someone she dislikes in order to obtain information. Or a man acts cocky to mask his insecurity.

Adjustments often tie to the discoveries that characters make as they pursue their scenic objectives. Whether large or small, positive or negative, each new discovery is a moment of evaluation that either reinforces the current adjustment or leads to a new one.

By focusing on adjustments, particularly the opening adjustment of each character in a scene, you can gain a clearer sense of how each will maneuver the action. Suppose that the character's objective is to convince his sister to lend him money, and that his first strategy is to tout the importance of family. If he is used to getting what he wants from his sister, his opening adjustment might be confident. Or, if he and his sister tend to disagree on money matters, he might instead be cautious. Or, if he is stressed out by financial pressures, his opening adjustment might be anxious. Whether voluntary or involuntary, true or false, each adjustment suggests a different way to use family relationships as a step toward asking for a loan.

ABOUT THE EXERCISE

Choose a scene that you want to write or revise. Focus on one character at a time, and use the following steps to find his or her adjustment at the start of the scene. You also can use this exercise to explore emotional and attitudinal changes that might occur as the scene unfolds. However, it is usually best not to plan such changes too much in advance, but to discover them in the moment as you write.

To do this exercise, you need to know what the character wants and what problem he or she faces as the scene starts. You also need to know how the character will begin to work toward his or her objective in spite of the problem. In other words, you need to know the character's opening strategy.

As you step through the exercise, remember that a "beat" is a unit of dramatic action in a scene and that a change of beat often reflects a change of adjustment. If you are not familiar with beats, see "Thinking in Beats" later in this guide.

■ EACH CHARACTER'S OPENING ADJUSTMENT IN THE SCENE

Focus first on Character 1, the main character of the scene. Then repeat the steps as indicated for anyone else present when the scene begins.

COMMON CHARACTER ADJUSTMENTS

Apologetic ↔ Unapologetic	Cooperative ↔ Combative	Loving ↔ Hostile
Aspiring ↔ Smug	Courageous ↔ Cowering	Loyal ↔ Rebellious
Awed ↔ Irreverent	Curious ↔ Indifferent	Lucid ↔ Bewildered
Bold ↔ Timid	Excited ↔ Bored	Mature ↔ Childish
Calm ↔ Anxious	Forgiving ↔ Unforgiving	Sexual ↔ Asexual
Candid ↔ Guarded	Friendly ↔ Aloof	Shy ↔ Cocky
Caring ↔ Callous	Gallant ↔ Rude	Sober ↔ Intoxicated
Cautious ↔ Rash	Grateful ↔ Ungrateful	Solemn ↔ Silly
Cheerful ↔ Depressed	Happy ↔ Sad	Tender ↔ Cold
Confident ↔ Insecure	Innocent ↔ Guilty	Trusting ↔ Suspicious

1. *Choose an opening adjustment.* Think about the character's objective, problem, and strategy when the scene starts. Use the table to help you find an opening adjustment that best fits this character here and now in the story.

2. *Analyze the adjustment:*

- Is the adjustment a conscious choice that the character has made or an involuntary emotional or personal response to the circumstances at hand?
- Is the adjustment a true state of the character here and now, or a false front to carry out a strategy or hide vulnerability? If the adjustment is a true state, why does the character feel that way? If the adjustment is a false front, why is the character projecting it and how does the character really feel?

3. *Explore new possibilities:*

- To learn something new about the scene and how it might unfold, repeat step 1 with a different answer. Then repeat step 2 and respond appropriately.
- You now have two sets of answers for step 1 and possibly also for step 2. Repeat step 1 again with yet another answer. As you do this, push yourself to find a third adjustment as different as possible from your original choice. Remember that this is only an exercise to explore story possibilities. Then repeat step 2 again and respond appropriately.

4. *Explore the adjustment of whoever else is in the scene.* For each of the other characters in the scene, repeat steps 1 and 2.

■ THE FIRST BEAT OF THE SCENE

Use the best of what you found to imagine what happens in the opening beat of the scene. Try to see it in your mind's eye. Remember that this beat will be driven by one character's strategy to achieve an objective and that the dramatic action will be influenced by each character's adjustment. The beat will end when the first strategy succeeds, reaches the failure point, or gets interrupted. When you have a working sense of what happens in this first unit of action, go to the next part of the exercise.

■ THE SECOND BEAT

Answer these questions after you have thought through the first beat of the scene:

1. Did the character's first strategy succeed or fail, and why?

2. What has the character discovered as a result of this success or failure?

3. How does the character feel as a result of this discovery?

4. Does the character still have the same problem or has a new obstacle emerged? If a new conflict is present, what is it?

5. What is the character's second strategy after the success or failure of the first strategy?

6. What is the character's adjustment now? Use the table again to find an adjustment that best fits your character. If the adjustment will stay the same, think about changing another character's adjustment so that the dynamics of the next beat will be different.

7. Is the new adjustment a conscious choice that the character has made or an involuntary emotional or personal response to the current situation?

8. Is the new adjustment a true state of the character or a false front to carry out a strategy or hide vulnerability? If the adjustment is a true state, why does the character feel that way? If the adjustment is a false front, why is the character projecting it and how does the character really feel?

■ LAUNCHING THE SCENE

By taking the time to explore character adjustments, you have a working sense of how the first two beats of the scene might unfold. Use the best of what you found to write these beats and the dramatic action that ensues. Remember that the scene will end when the character driving it finally achieves or fails to achieve the scenic objective. Until then, look at each new character strategy as an opportunity to explore new adjustments and find new story material. Try to find these emotional and attitudinal changes instinctively without leaving the moment of the scene. Go back to the table of adjustments only if you get stuck.

WRAP-UP

Adjustments show how characters feel—or appear to feel—as they try to overcome obstacles and get what they want. These emotionally based attitudes keep shifting as the character continues to make new discoveries about the world of the story beat by beat, scene by scene. Adjustments often determine the outcome of a scene. Positive adjustments may help some characters succeed. Negative adjustments may cause some characters to fail.

For the dramatic writer, adjustments are tools to bring variety to character behavior at the scenic level and to show, not tell, the story. As you develop scenes, try to stay aware of each character's ever-changing adjustment to the here and now, and be particularly mindful of each character's opening adjustment. Whether it is a true display of the character's inner life or a posture tied to a character strategy, this jumping-off place can help you leap into the action and make something specific happen from the time the scene begins.

Related tools in *Character, Scene, and Story*. To continue exploring character emotions, go to the "Developing Your Character" section and try "The Emotional Character." Or go to the "Causing a Scene" section and try "The Emotional Onion."

SCENE IN A SENTENCE

THE QUICK VERSION
Define and explore the main event of a scene

BEST TIME FOR THIS
During scene planning, writing, or revision

CENTERING A SCENE ON ONE MAIN EVENT
The scene you are developing now will be one of the events in your character's dramatic journey. Ideally, though many actions may be taken and many topics discussed, the scene will center around one turning-point experience that changes the world of the story in a significant way, reveals something new about the characters, and moves the story forward. What will be the main event of the scene? How will this grow out of past events? How will it pave the way for future events?

ABOUT THE EXERCISE
To do this exercise, you need to have a rough idea of what might happen in your scene. From this starting point, you can explore new possibilities and determine how to shape the event in a way that works best for your story. Stay open to new ideas and feel free to keep revising your core description of the scene.

Exercise examples are from scene 25 of *Frozen* by Bryony Lavery. The scene takes place in the visiting room of a prison. Character 1 is Nancy, a middle-aged, middle-class woman whose daughter was murdered twenty years ago during a series of brutal killings in London. Character 2 is Ralph, the killer, who has since been arrested and jailed. Though Nancy and Ralph have had a horrific connection for two decades, this is the first time they have ever met face to face. What happens in the scene: Nancy forgives Ralph for the murder of her daughter.

■ THE MAIN EVENT OF THE SCENE
Think about what's happened in your story so far: who your characters are, where they are now in the dramatic journey, and where they might be heading from here. Then flesh out the following:

1. *Core description.* In one simple sentence, as short as possible, describe the main event of the scene as best you can. Think of this as a high-level, bare-bones, core description of what happens—for example, "Nancy for-

gives Ralph." That's a three-word synopsis. How economically can you sum up your scenic event? Try it now and remember that this is only a starting point.

- *Reality check*. If you used more than twelve words in your core description, you are getting way too complicated. Reduce it now to twelve words or fewer. What really matters most?

2. **Prior event.** The events of your story have a cause-and-effect relationship that strengthens the throughline and holds the dramatic journey together. Think about the scenic event you described as the result of at least one previous event—something that happened earlier in the story or backstory. Then try this:

- Copy your core description—for example, "Nancy forgives Ralph." If you wish to edit your summary, keep it to twelve words or fewer.
- Add a clause that taps the power of the word "because" and describes a prior event that caused or contributed to the current event—for example, "Nancy forgives Ralph . . . *because* her daughter Ingrid convinced her that it's the only way Nancy can move on with her life after twenty years of emotional paralysis."

3. **Character trait.** Dramatic events are caused not only by what happened earlier but also by who the characters are now. Think about the traits of your characters and their physical, intellectual, and emotional states at this particular time in the story. Focus on one personal factor that could contribute to what happens in the current scene. Then try this:

- Recopy your core description—for example, "Nancy forgives Ralph." If you wish to edit your summary, keep it to twelve words or fewer.
- Add a clause that taps the power of the word "because" and describes a character trait or condition that contributes to what happens in the scene—for example, "Nancy forgives Ralph . . . *because* she is desperate enough to try anything that might free her from her anger and grief."

4. **Something more.** Try to shake up your thinking about the scene and see it in a new way. Imagine that there is actually more to it than you first envisioned. Perhaps the action goes further, or something greater happens, or something new is revealed. As you look for new ideas, don't be afraid to take creative leaps—big ones—but stay true to your characters. Then try this:

- Recopy your core description—for example, "Nancy forgives Ralph." If you wish to edit your summary, keep it to twelve words or fewer.
- Add a clause that taps the power of the word "and" and describes a new possibility for the scene, something greater or more that could happen—for example, "Nancy forgives Ralph . . . *and* he strikes back at her with an uncontrollable burst of hostility and rage."

5. **Something different**. What if your scene had a different truth and perhaps a different focus from what you first envisioned? As an exercise, imag-

ine that your core description needs to be qualified in some way so that the true meaning or true impact of the scene becomes clear. Then try this:

- Recopy your core description—for example, "Nancy forgives Ralph" If you wish to edit your summary, keep it to twelve words or fewer.
- Add a clause that taps the power of the word "but" and qualifies or brings new meaning to the dramatic action of the scene—for example, "Nancy forgives Ralph . . . *but* only after she has forced him to see the reality of his crimes and suffer unbearable anguish."

6. *Future impact on Character* 1. In the chain of events that add up to a dramatic story, each event is not only the effect of a previous event, but also the cause of a new one. Because that happened then, this is happening now. And, because this is happening now, something else will happen later. The events connect. As you write a scene, therefore, it can be helpful to know where it will lead. Consider possible results of the scenic event: how it might affect Character 1, change the world of the story, and move the dramatic journey forward. Then try this:

- Recopy your core description—for example, "Nancy forgives Ralph." If you wish to edit your summary, keep it to twelve words or fewer.
- Add a clause that taps the power of the word "consequently" and describes one important future impact of the scene on Character 1: an effect that we will see in the next scene or later on—for example, "Nancy forgives Ralph. . . . *Consequently*, she will be freed from the anger and grief that has frozen her for twenty years."

7. *Future impact on Character* 2. If a scenic event matters, it will affect everyone present. Think some more about the possible consequences of your scenic event and how it might affect the second most important character here. Then try this:

- Recopy your core description—for example, "Nancy forgives Ralph." If you wish to edit this summary, keep it to twelve words or fewer.
- Add a clause that again taps the power of the word "consequently" but this time describes an important future impact of the scene on Character 2: an effect we will see in the next scene or later on—for example, "Nancy forgives Ralph. . . . *Consequently*, he will experience such remorse that he will hang himself in his prison cell."

ONE-SENTENCE SUMMARY OF THE SCENE

You've now developed seven different summaries of the scene you want to develop. Summary 1 is a core description of the main event. Summaries 2 and 3 focus on why this event occurs. Number 4 explores the possibility of adding more content; 5 suggests unexpected meaning; and 6 and 7 identify important results of the event. By looking at the scene from these different high-level angles, you may have learned something new about it or clarified your thinking about what happens.

To complete the exercise, write a one-sentence synopsis of the scene as you see it now. You can repeat or combine any part of the first seven summaries or write a brand new synopsis. Focus on what matters most. Be sure to keep the synopsis short so that it can serve as an at-a-glance guide while you write the scene—for example, "Nancy forces Ralph to experience unbearable remorse for his crimes and then forgives him for the murder of her daughter."

WRAP-UP

The goal of this exercise has been to get a clear, big-picture view of the scene you will write next and to explore possibilities for how it might unfold and where it might lead. Nothing is set in stone, and you may wish to change this synopsis as you go along, but for now you have a working context for the scene: a guide to steer you through the blank page ahead.

Related tools in *Character, Scene, and Story.* To identify the importance and urgency of a dramatic event, go to the "Causing a Scene" section and try "Why This? Why Now?" To use a character relationship to map out how an event unfolds, try "Relationship Storyboard" in the same section.

SEEING THE SCENE

THE QUICK VERSION
Develop a simple visual storyboard of a scene

BEST TIME FOR THIS
During scene planning, writing, or revision

A PICTURE IS WORTH A THOUSAND WORDS — OR MORE
We receive most of our information about the world through our eyes. Whether the images around us seem positive or negative, familiar or new, they tell us a lot, affect us deeply, and leave lasting impressions. Visual imagery is a key tool of the dramatic writer because it taps into the power of sight and offers an economical and emotionally charged way to show, not tell, a story. What we often leave the theater with are not the brilliant lines of dialogue we heard, but the images we saw, such as:

- A magnificent angel dangling in the air over a bedridden young man in *Angels in America, Part One: Millennium Approaches*
- A woman raising her fist in a defiant pose of survival with the smoking ruins of her home behind her in *Gone with the Wind*
- A retired chauffeur spoon-feeding his aged ex-employer in *Driving Miss Daisy*
- A young boy paralyzed in fear as he watches his brother drowning in a backyard washtub in *Ray*
- A woman holding her mother's hand to a steaming hot stovetop in *The Beauty Queen of Leenane*
- A man waking up in a forest and discovering that donkey ears have sprouted from his head in *A Midsummer Night's Dream*
- A woman sobbing over the dead body of her son while picking up stolen money strewn about the room in *The Grifters*

Images like these speak a thousand words about the characters we see and the dramatic situations in which they find themselves. What memorable images have you created in your story? How can you make your script more visual?

ABOUT THE EXERCISE
Use this discovery exercise to find new visual material for a scene that you have written or mostly written. For best results, look for something new in each exercise response and avoid rehashing what you already know. Keep

exploring the scene from different angles so that, in the end, you will have a variety of images from which to choose.

Exercise examples are from scene 4 of *Angels in America, Part One: Millennium Approaches* by Tony Kushner. Character 1 is Prior, a young man who "occasionally works as a club designer or caterer, otherwise lives very modestly but with great style off a small trust fund." Character 2 is Louis, also known as Lou, "a word processor for the Second Circuit Court of Appeals." Their relationship: lovers of four years. What happens in the scene: Prior reveals that he has KS, or Kaposi's sarcoma, an AIDS-related disease that, in the mid-1980s, was usually fatal.

■ **TRANSLATING YOUR SCENE INTO**
A SIMPLE VISUAL STORYBOARD

1. *Divide the scene into three parts.* Break the scene down into a beginning, middle, and end. These parts do not have to be of equal length or importance, but each is different from the other two: the end is different from the beginning because of what happens in the middle. Think of each part as a scene within the scene and briefly describe what's happening in it. For example:
   • Beginning: Two lovers, Louis and Prior, gossip about Louis's family—they have just left the funeral of his grandmother—and end up in a spat.
   • Middle: Prior reveals that he has KS.
   • End: Louis rushes off to rejoin his family for his grandmother's burial and leaves the frightened Prior behind.

2. *Name each part.* As a focusing exercise, give each part of the scene a title that highlights what's going on. For example:
   • Beginning: "Two Guys at a Funeral"
   • Middle: "I'm Going to Die"
   • End: "Am I Going to Die Alone?"

3. *Find an image for each part.* Imagine each of your three titles as the caption for an image that depicts a key moment of action in your scene. Describe each image briefly. For example:
   • Title: "Two Guys at a Funeral." Image: Louis and Prior sit on a bench outside a funeral home both dressed in funereal finery, talking.
   • Title: "I'm Going to Die." Image: Prior with his jacket off and a rolled-up sleeve shows Louis a dark purple spot on the underside of his arm near the shoulder.
   • Title: "Am I Going to Die Alone?" Image: Louis races off in a panic while Prior, looking terrified, sits alone on the bench with his hand over the mark on his arm.

4. *Evaluate the storyboard so far.* Think about the three images in sequence and the story that they show. For example, the visual story of Louis and Prior depicts two guys who start out together and end up apart because of

something that one reveals. Without dialogue, we may not know that the two men are lovers, that the purple mark on one's arm is the symptom of a fatal disease, or that one is left with the fear of dying alone. Nevertheless, we can "see" that this is a scene where a physical revelation changes the dynamics of a relationship from positive to negative. In your scene, consider the following:

- What story do your three images show without dialogue? Try to look at your sequence with fresh eyes and see what is really being depicted. If the sequence consists of "talking heads," for example, it shows only that people are engaged in conversation. The visuals are not serving the story.
- In some scenes, characters end up exactly where they started, and that is itself the point: they're stuck. In most scenes, however, something important changes. Compare your third image to your first image. As you do this, compare where the characters are, how they appear, and what they are doing. Is the third image clearly different from the first? If not, how can you create a greater visual contrast between them?
- Ideally, the second image shows what causes the change that takes place in the scene and links the other two images. Suppose Prior had simply told Louis about his diagnosis. The dialogue would have moved the story forward, but the picture of this critical moment would have consisted only of two people talking. By not only telling Louis about the disease but also showing it to him, the scene presents instead the powerful image of Prior unveiling the lesion on his arm. Look again at what's happening in the second image of your sequence. Does it present a dramatic picture of what changes the dynamics of the scene? If not, how can you create a more telling middle image that links the first and third images?

5. *Find three new images*. Look again at the three captions you wrote for your scenes within the scene. As an exercise, take a creative leap and imagine that each caption describes a totally different image of the same characters engaged in the same scenic event. For example, another image for "Two Guys at a Funeral" might be Prior hugging Louis tenderly, and Louis looking back to see if anyone from the family can see this display of affection. Briefly describe a brand-new image for each of your three captions. Try to surprise yourself, but stay true to your characters and story.

6. *Evaluate the new images.* Think about the three new images and the story they show. How does it differ from the story shown by the first set of images? For example:

- Do the new images create a different focus in the dramatic action, change the meaning of what's happening, or reveal new character information?
- Do the new images suggest any new ideas for how the scene unfolds?

- Do you see the opportunity to strengthen any image so that it is more dramatic or shows the story more clearly? If so, take a moment to revise your work now.

7. **Pick the best image for each part.** You have now created six possible images for your scene: two for the beginning, two for the middle, and two for the end. Pick the best image in each pair so that you end up with three images again in sequence.

8. **Reevaluate the captions.** Look again at the captions you have written. If you have found a new emphasis for the dramatic action or learned something new about your characters or story, you may want to revise the captions to reflect these discoveries. If so, revise the captions now so that they work better with the current sequence of visuals. You now have a simple storyboard of your scene.

9. **Find an unexpected detail in each image.** Each of these three images offers many details—some of which you've already discovered and some of which you haven't. If you were to zoom in on the image of Prior showing Louis the sore on his arm, you might suddenly notice that the purple lesion has the shape of a mouth print. For each of your three images, zoom in and find an interesting visual detail that you did not see until now. Briefly describe it. Try to surprise yourself, but stay true to your characters and story.

10. **Title the visual details.** The close-up of the deadly purple lesion on Prior's arm suggests a caption: "The Wine-Dark Kiss of the Angel of Death." These words actually end up in the dialogue of the scene. It's one of the ways that Prior communicates the seriousness of his condition. Look again at your three new visual details and give each a caption that highlights what's most interesting or dramatic about it.

11. **Identify the most important moment.** As you've explored your scene visually at different levels of detail, you've been thinking about your characters and what they do. In the Louis and Prior scene, the moment when Prior reveals his KS is tragic and memorable. Even more important to the story, however, is the moment afterward when Prior confesses his reason for not revealing the deadly diagnosis sooner: he was afraid that Louis would leave him. What is the single most important moment in your scene?

12. **Convert the most important moment into an image.** When Prior finally lets down his guard and confesses his fear, he is a man standing helplessly outside a funeral parlor with his suit jacket off, shirt sleeve undone, and arm stained with a kiss of death. The lover to whom he has turned for comfort is now walking away so that the space between them is widening. The lover looks as angry as Prior looks scared. Find a visual image that embodies the single most important moment in your scene and describe it in detail. This picture will most likely be near the end of the scene. If it overlaps with the ending image you already have, try to find something new about it.

WRAP-UP

The pictures you create in your story can go a long way toward revealing character and moving the dramatic journey forward. Use the best of the imagery you found to strengthen the visual power of your scene. As you continue working on your script, keep looking for opportunities to show, not tell, your story, especially at those times when your characters find themselves in extreme situations. These are the bold strokes of the story and will have the most impact on us in the audience if we can literally "see" them happen.

Related tools in *Character, Scene, and Story.* To continue translating scenic information into dramatic imagery, go to the "Building Your Story" section and try "Living Images."

THERE AND THEN

THE QUICK VERSION
Reveal background information without stopping the story

BEST TIME FOR THIS
During scene revision

UNLEASHING THE POWER OF EXPOSITION

While drama shows us the "here and now" of the characters, exposition tells us about the "there and then." It explains anything we cannot observe directly, such as what happened before the story began, what happened between this scene and the last one, or what's happening elsewhere now in the world of the story. Exposition also encompasses the inner lives of the characters: their deepest thoughts, memories, and feelings. In short, it's anything that has to be explained to the audience.

Exposition is essential to any story—the past shapes who the characters are and what they want now—but it can be a challenge to explain things without stripping away the emotional life of the story and bringing it to a halt. The goal is to weave facts from the past into the story so seamlessly that we receive this background information without realizing it. Here are a few tips for managing exposition:

Start with action in progress, not explanation. Get the lines of action into motion and establish the opening problem, even if it's a small one. Don't begin the scene with a bunch of exposition that feels like a setup.

Raise questions first. Use the "here and now" of the characters to stir up curiosity about the "there and then." If we are wondering about a character's past, for example, we'll be happy when something about it is finally explained. Make the exposition a payoff instead of an intrusion.

Stay in the present. Exposition tends to works best when it is not the main topic at hand. Instead of dwelling on information for its own sake, focus instead on the character's objective and use the exposition to support it. As a result, we will learn about the past or offstage world only because of what the character is trying to accomplish in the present.

Imply, don't explain. The best way to reveal exposition is often through implication. Give us hints and clues that suggest rather than explain the information you want us to know. If we are trying to piece these clues together and figure things out, you've got us where you want us: leaning forward and involved in your story.

Say less. Parcel out exposition in bits and pieces, and weave it into the action when it is appropriate to do so. Remember that we are smart enough to piece these fragments together even when they are not fully and logically articulated in chronological order. Less is more.

Use subtext. Much can be revealed by what is *not* said during a scene. A character's silence, evasiveness, or refusal to deal with a certain issue can tell us a lot. Think about what's going on between the lines.

Let images say it for you. Remember that a picture is worth a thousand words and that much can be conveyed through the physical life of the story: the setting, the objects that reside or don't reside in it, even the clothing that the characters wear. Whenever possible, try to "show, not tell," the story.

Beware of foils. A "foil" is a character who exists only to ask the right questions so that the other character can conveniently dish out all the information that the author wants us to know. You may have a foil on your hands if a character does little but ask question after question.

Beware of characters who speak only for the sake of the audience. Such characters love to sit around and discuss what everyone already knows. They dwell on the obvious, relive memories—often in great detail—and brilliantly analyze themselves and each other. Their retrospective elucidation is information-packed, but often feels so phony and contrived that we don't care about what we learn.

Keep the characters up to speed with the audience. Don't make us wait while one character reports to another character what the rest of us saw happen in an earlier scene. An easy way to avoid such repetition is to start the new scene later—after the uninformed character has been brought up to speed. The only time such rehashing works is when there is something new about it—for example, the teller misrepresents the facts because he is lying, mistaken, or deluded about what happened.

Force out the facts. Information that has to be forced out of a character can be more interesting than information freely given. By suggesting that the character has something to hide, you can create dramatic tension that makes us want to get in on the secret.

Avoid clichés. Watch out for overused methods of inserting exposition into the story. A classic exposition cliché is the "feather duster" scene in which an old-fashioned play would open with servants dusting the room and gossiping in great detail about the family they serve, thus setting up the story for everyone in the audience. Today, the term "feather duster" applies to any scene in which characters talk to each other only to impart plot details. Other exposition devices that have become shopworn include letters, telegrams, television and radio news broadcasts, and telephone answering machine messages. If you feel it necessary to use one of these devices, try to find a unique way of handling it.

Dramatic writers sometimes view exposition as a necessary evil. When managed well, however, exposition can be a powerful tool to motivate present-tense action and turn the story in new directions. Properly motivated, a sudden revelation can heighten drama and set action on an unexpected course for both the characters and the audience. In short, exposition is not to be avoided: it is to be unleashed.

Dramatic action implies that, however fascinating the past may have been, the present is even more fascinating. That's why the story takes place here and now—not there and then.

ABOUT THE EXERCISE

Use this exercise to revise a scene that feels expositional—for example, it reveals important information about the past but does so in a way that drags down the action. You can also adapt this exercise to any new scene you are planning.

■ THE EXPOSITIONAL FACTS IN THE SCENE

To begin, read through the scene you want to revise and identify the expositional information revealed in it. This includes facts about the past, the offstage world of the story, or the deepest inner workings of the characters. For example, here are a few expositional facts that come to light during the opening scene of *The Real Thing* by Tom Stoppard. Each of these occurred before the scene begins:

- Max and Charlotte are an English couple whose marriage is in trouble. Charlotte has been traveling a lot lately and claims it's for business, but Max suspects her of having an affair.
- Charlotte is due back any moment from her latest trip, which, she claimed, was to Switzerland. While she was gone, however, Max found her passport—proof that she could not really be visiting a foreign country.
- After returning home from each of her phony trips, Charlotte has tried to forestall suspicion by presenting Max with a "souvenir" from the country she supposedly visited.

List the expositional facts that you want to reveal in your scene and focus particularly on those that seem to be getting in the way of what's happening here and now.

THE FACTS THAT MATTER MOST

Look at the list of expositional facts from your scene:

1. Is all of this background information absolutely necessary for your story to be understood and experienced by an audience? See if you can eliminate any of your expositional facts without damaging the story throughline. Remember that less is more.

2. Of the facts that remain, are all of them really and truly needed in this particular scene? See if any might work better in an earlier or later part of the story.

3. In the opening scene of *The Real Thing*, Max's discovery of Charlotte's passport is among the most important background information revealed. Look at the list of expositional facts that still remain for your scene. Which are the most important? Number them in order of their significance to the story and use the next part of this exercise to analyze them with the appropriate level of attention.

■ WEAVING EXPOSITION INTO THE DRAMATIC ACTION

Use these steps to evaluate each of your most important expositional facts. Analyze one fact at a time.

1. Before Max's discovery of his wife's passport is revealed, the curiosity of both Charlotte and the audience is stirred when she returns home and Max greets her with an erratic rush of questions about her trip. Why is he acting so strangely? The news about his discovery answers this question and thus works as payoff which we welcome. Think about your expositional fact. What question might this answer? How might you raise this question in our minds before you pay it off?

2. Max reveals his discovery because he wants to find out whether or not his wife is actually having an affair—a scenic objective which he ultimately fails to achieve. Nevertheless, the objective gives him a reason to bring up the passport and make news of its discovery pivotal to what's happening here and now. Think about the character in your scene who reveals the expositional fact. What does this character want? How can exposition be used to support this objective?

3. After Charlotte is grilled about her trip abroad, the simple announcement about the forgotten passport speaks volumes about her deception. Consider the amount of information that your expositional fact entails. Can you reduce it to fewer words by focusing on what matters most? Can you explain less and imply more about it? Are there any new clues you can add to the scene so that this fact can be presented in a more streamlined way? If it is a major or complicated fact that requires detail, can you boil it down to bits and pieces that are revealed here and there throughout the scene instead of all at once?

4. Max's discovery is embodied in the passport itself—a physical object—which he produces at the appropriate time as evidence of his find. This creates a telling image that is rooted in the physical life of the story and makes it unnecessary to debate whether or not he is telling the truth. Think about your characters in the unique physical life of your scene. Can you translate your expositional fact into an interesting image that speaks for itself and reduces the need for dialogue?

5. Look again at how your exposition is being revealed. Is one of the char-

acters acting as a foil—asking question after question—so that the other character can conveniently deliver this information? If so, how can you turn the foil into an active character with an objective and problem?

6. Is your exposition a rehashing of something the characters already know, such as a "remember when" retelling of a memory they share? In other words, are they discussing this information only for the benefit of the audience? If so, how else can you reveal the fact so that something new is happening here and now? Is this really the best time in the story to bring out this information?

7. Does the expositional fact include any information that the audience already knows? If so, can you start the scene later so that the audience doesn't have to sit and wait while your characters update each other? Can the scene start later so that this repetition can occur offstage?

8. Can any of this information be suggested by what the characters don't say? Look for opportunities to convert explanations into silences and implications. Keep in mind the emotional life of the actors, which later may make many of your lines feel redundant and unnecessary.

9. If one character is explaining something to another, what might motivate the teller to try to conceal this fact or at least part of it? What might force the character to reveal this information anyway? See if you can use conflict to make the revelation of the fact more dramatic.

10. If you are using a letter, telegram, television or radio broadcast, telephone answering machine message, or other cliché to reveal this fact, is the device really necessary? How else might you reveal this information?

11. Take a creative leap and see if you can find any new, interesting ways to reveal your information—for example, through the physical life of the scene, the needs and behaviors of the characters, or the nature and course of the dramatic event unfolding here and now.

WRAP-UP

How you handle exposition is a sign of your skill and experience as a dramatic writer. When presenting information about the "there and then," try to show, not tell, as much as possible, and remember that less is more when explanations absolutely must be made.

Related tools in *Character, Scene, and Story*. To explore the offstage world of the story further, go to the "Developing Your Character" section and try "The Invisible Character." Or go to the "Causing a Scene" section and try "The Past Barges In."

THE AHA!S OF THE STORY

THE QUICK VERSION
Explore scene dynamics by fleshing out three types of character discovery

BEST TIME FOR THIS
During scene planning, writing, or revision

CHARACTER DISCOVERY: A LINK TO WHAT WILL HAPPEN NEXT
Most of the turns in a dramatic story are the effects of important discoveries that the characters make about themselves, each other, or the world at large. Such discoveries may translate into good news or bad news, and may prove to be accurate or inaccurate over time. In each case, the character experiences an *aha!*—a new realization, insight, or conclusion—that leads to a change in behavior and a shift, large or small, in the dramatic journey.

At the story level, *aha!*s are often turning-point experiences that can trigger a new scene or, if extraordinary enough in impact, a new act. It is often a character discovery that launches a dramatic journey or brings it to its close, or both. At the scenic level, *aha!*s can result in new beats: new units of dramatic action in which a different topic, emotion, or character strategy comes into play because of what the character has just learned. As you develop your script, it is important to understand the *aha!*s of the story: to know what they are, where they came from, and where they might lead.

ABOUT THE EXERCISE
Use this exercise to explore your characters as discoverers who cause a dramatic event to unfold. Choose a scene to develop, and focus on one character at a time. Imagine what he or she might learn as the scene unfolds, and how these discoveries might influence the dramatic action. As you do this, stay true to the character, but be willing to surprise yourself.

Exercise examples are from *Proof* by David Auburn. The main character is Catherine, twenty-five, a mathematics student who gave up college and social life to stay at home and be the sole caregiver of her father. He is Robert, in his fifties, a world-renowned genius in mathematics who became mentally disturbed years ago and has since spent most of his time writing in notebooks.

■ A KEY SELF-DISCOVERY
Throughout any dramatic story, characters make certain discoveries about themselves. Whether positive or negative, accurate or inaccurate, these

*aha!*s may be triggered internally or externally, and may center on something physiological (*I've had too much too drink*), psychological (*I'm falling in love*), or sociological (*I can't pay the rent*).

In *Proof*, the opening scene takes place late at night on Catherine's twenty-fifth birthday. Robert tries to convince his depressed daughter to stop moping around and get on with her life. One of the most important discoveries that Catherine makes in this scene is a self-discovery: she realizes that, like her father, she may be going mad. Think about what happens in your scene. Identify one of the most important self-discoveries that your character makes—or could possibly make—at any time during the dramatic action. Whether true or false, this is a realization, insight, or conclusion that could have significant consequences. What is it?

1. *Trigger.* Catherine's discovery of her potential madness arises near the end of the exchange with her father when, in a stunning dramatic moment, she—and we in the audience—realize that Robert isn't really there. In fact, he died a week ago of heart failure, his funeral is tomorrow, and she's been alone this whole time. Yet here she has been seemingly talking with him and drinking the champagne he brought for her birthday. As she pieces the clues together, Robert spells out the conclusion for her: having late chats with your dead father is a "bad sign." What triggers your character's self-discovery?

- *Emotional impact.* The realization of her mental instability leaves Catherine feeling confused, frightened, and alone. What is the immediate emotional impact of your character's self-discovery?
- *Behavioral impact.* As a result of questioning her sanity, Catherine has begun to mistrust herself and, by extension, everyone around her. When Hal, one of her father's former students, enters, she turns on him with suspicion. Hal has been here for the past three days reviewing her father's notebooks to see if there is any important information that should be published for posterity. Catherine accuses Hal of wanting to steal her father's work. What action does your character take as a result of his or her self-discovery?

2. *Later consequence.* Catherine's self-discovery stirs up an insecurity and mistrust that she will have to battle for the rest of the play. Even after she later opens her heart to Hal, she will retreat to mistrust when he and her sister are both skeptical of the revelation she makes at the end of the first act: the most extraordinary proof of a math theorem in her father's notebooks was actually written by Catherine. Think about the self-discovery you are exploring. What possible later impact might it have on the character's dramatic journey?

3. *Analysis.* Is Catherine really going mad? While she does exhibit signs of mental instability, she also learns to manage her personal relationships, and to come to terms with her mathematical genius. The accuracy of her

self-discovery, therefore, remains unresolved. When it first occurs, it seems like a negative turn in her life. Yet, over time, the questioning of her sanity leads to positive outcomes, such the ability to use her vulnerability to trust and love Hal. Think about the self-discovery you are exploring. How true or false is it, and why? How positive or negative is it, and why? Could it lead to more unforeseen results and have a greater impact on the character's dramatic journey?

■ **A KEY DISCOVERY ABOUT THE WORLD OF THE STORY**
Characters also learn things about the specific world around them. These discoveries may center on other people (*my next door neighbor is a drug dealer*), organizations (*the company plans to downsize the staff*), places (*this condominium site was once a sacred burial ground*), or things (*that lottery ticket in my pocket is worth five million dollars*).

In *Proof,* Catherine's worst fear about Hal appears to be true when she learns that he was trying to smuggle one of her father's notebooks out of the house. Identify an important discovery that any of your characters makes—or could possibly make—at any time in the scene about a person, place, or thing in the world of the story.

1. **Trigger.** Catherine learns about the smuggled notebook when it accidentally falls out of Hal's jacket as he is leaving the house. What triggers the discovery that your character makes about someone or something in the world of your story?

2. **Emotional impact.** Catherine's belief that Hal may have betrayed both her father and herself makes her angry. What is the immediate emotional impact of your character's discovery?

3. **Behavioral impact.** After seeing the notebook fall out of Hal's jacket, Catherine overreacts and calls the police to have him arrested. What action does your character take as a result of his or her discovery?

4. **Later consequence.** Catherine's rash reaction to the hidden notebook leads her not only to apologize to Hal the next night but also to seduce him. In effect, she swings from one extreme to another in her relationship with him. Think about the discovery you are exploring. What possible later impact might it have on your character's dramatic journey?

5. **Analysis.** The discovery of Hal's theft proves later to be false. Though he was, in fact, secretly removing the notebook, his purpose was to have it wrapped as a birthday present for Catherine, since it contains a birthday inscription from her father long ago. At first, the discovery seems negative and creates a hassle for Hal with the police, but it leads inadvertently to a positive result: the connection that Catherine and Hal make when she acknowledges her error and apologizes to him. How true or false is your character's discovery, and why? How positive or negative is it, and why? Could it lead to more unforeseen results and have a greater impact on the character's dramatic journey?

■ A KEY UNIVERSAL DISCOVERY

Sometimes characters acquire knowledge that leads them to discoveries that are universal in scope. Whether positive or negative, true or false, these realizations, insights, and conclusions reflect what the character believes about such big topics as human nature (*like father, like son*), society (*power corrupts*), or spirituality (*death is only a transition to another type of life*).

When *Proof* opens, Catherine has been doing nothing for the past few years except take care of her father. Over the past month, she has wasted her time, often sleeping past noon and getting up only to eat junk food and read magazines. When her father confronts her with this reality, Catherine is forced to see a universal truth about the value of time: "When you throw days away, you never know what else you throw away with them—the work you lost, the ideas you didn't have, the discoveries you never made." Identify an important universal discovery that your character makes—or could possibly make—at any time in the scene: a truth or belief that transcends the specific world of the character to include the world we all inhabit.

1. *Trigger.* In *Proof,* Catherine comes to realize that each day matters and must be well lived. This discovery is triggered by her father's reprimand after observing her unproductive and melancholy behavior over the past month. What triggers the universal discovery that your character makes?

2. *Emotional impact.* Catherine's insight about the importance of time makes her feel regretful about the "thirty-three and a quarter days" that she has virtually thrown away with her idleness. What is the immediate emotional impact of your character's discovery?

3. *Behavioral impact.* Shaken by the failure of doing nothing, Catherine will feel compelled to act—and to do so decisively—when she discovers Hal trying to smuggle out one of her father's notebooks. Her universal discovery thus fuels her phone call to the police. What action does your character take as a result of his or her universal discovery?

4. *Later consequence.* Catherine's discovery about the importance of living life fully contributes to her decision later to pursue Hal romantically and to trust him with an extraordinary proof of a mathematical theorem she has written. Think about the discovery you are exploring. What possible later impact might it have on the character's dramatic journey?

5. *Analysis.* Catherine's universal discovery is one which many of us might see as true. For her, it provides an accurate assessment of her current situation and an upturn in her personal growth, since it stimulates her to start making changes that will lead to more meaningful relationships with others. How true or false is your character's universal discovery, and why? How positive or negative is it, and why? Could it lead to more unforeseen results and have a greater impact on the character's dramatic journey?

WRAP-UP

As they pursue their objectives and deal with the conflicts that stand in the way, characters are continually experiencing *aha!*s that lead them to new visions of themselves, others, and the world at large. Such discoveries often overlap, with one leading to another, just as a discovery about someone else (*my father is a mad genius*) can lead to a self-discovery (*I may be a mad genius as well*) and ultimately a universal discovery (*genius and madness may both be hereditary*). As you enter any new scene, keep track of what your characters know and believe now, how they acquired this knowledge, and, most importantly, what they will do as a result of it.

> **Related tools in *Character, Scene, and Story*.** To uncover what else your character may be hiding, go to the "Causing a Scene" section and try "Classified Information."

HEATING THINGS UP

THE QUICK VERSION
Explore different ways to force a character confrontation

BEST TIME FOR THIS
When you want to heighten conflict in a scene

WHAT'S BAD FOR THE CHARACTER MAY BE GOOD FOR THE STORY
Drama is the art of showdown. To make conflict grow, you need not only to present your characters with problems, but also to create unavoidable reasons for them to confront each other in search of solutions. If a conflict can be easily ignored or delayed, or if it can be diffused through compromise, your characters will have little reason to trouble themselves. It is when they are stuck in a conflict with opposing needs and something vital at stake that they rise to the level of dramatic action.

We know that a simple problem will be easily solved and that an impossible problem will never be solved. If a problem is too small or too large, therefore, we predict the outcome and lose interest in the story. However, if there is a slight chance that a difficult problem might be solved, we remain engaged to see what happens.

ABOUT THE EXERCISE
Use any of the following conflict techniques to add dramatic tension to a scene. For best results, approach each technique as an opportunity to look at your story from a different angle and brainstorm new ideas. Even if you end up not using the technique in this particular scene, you may uncover valuable character and story material that you want to keep.

■ **BINDING DISAGREEMENT:**
A PROBLEM THAT CAN'T BE IGNORED
A sure way to trigger a confrontation between your characters is to join them in a "binding disagreement." Such unions are made up not of legal terms, but of needs, obstacles, and motivations. To create a disagreement,

give your characters contrary or contradictory objectives. And, to make the disagreement binding, make sure that the motivations to achieve these objectives are so compelling that neither character can walk away from the fight. The mutual determination to overcome an opposing force will bind the characters not only to the conflict, but also to each other, and a show-down will inevitably occur.

In Sam Shepard's *True West*, for example, two brothers each want to be best. Since only one can by definition be "best," however, each brother's objective becomes an obstacle that the other must try to overcome. This begins a competitive series of challenges that escalates into a deadly face-off because each brother has high stakes at risk—survival—and cannot give up the fight.

To heat up a scene, start with the basic step of joining your characters through a conflict that neither can ignore. If you have already attempted this and it didn't work, try changing something about the binding disagreement. For example:

1. Give the characters irreconcilable needs so that one character's objective cannot succeed unless the other character's objective fails. Think about what your characters want now. If their needs are not irreconcilable, how can you change them so that they are?

2. Make sure that strong obstacles are in place. If you have created truly opposing needs, you have automatically given each character the most common conflict in drama: the other character. Review the objectives you just chose. How does each pose an obstacle to the other character? What other conflicts might add to each character's struggle here and now?

3. Motivate a fight to the finish. When the going gets tough, even the tough don't get going—unless they have a reason to do so. Think about what's at stake in your scene. In a binding disagreement, the stakes must be high enough to make compromise or surrender seem impossible to both characters. What is at stake for each of your characters now? How might you raise these stakes even higher?

A number of scenic elements—such as setting, time, circumstances, character traits, and character actions—offer other opportunities to heighten conflict. Consider using any of the following techniques in combination with a binding disagreement.

■ THE LOCKED CAGE: NO ONE CAN LEAVE NOW

It's hard for characters to avoid each other's needs when they are physically confined in the same space. This "locked cage" may come in many forms, such as a prison cell (*Kiss of the Spider Woman*), concentration camp (*Bent*), sinking ocean liner (*Titanic*), spaceship (*Alien*), deserted island (*Swept Away*), the afterlife (*No Exit*), phone booth (*Phone Booth*), or even just an old house in the country (*Night of the Living Dead*). Whether the confinement is due to iron bars, endless sea, or hungry zombies wandering around outside, a cage can be dramatically helpful because it prevents the characters from fleeing when conflict begins.

To heat things up in your scene, imagine putting your characters into a locked cage:

1. Look at the current setting. If your characters are not physically confined, how might this place be changed—at least temporarily—so they cannot escape? Remember that, with a few creative alterations, just about anywhere can become a cage. In *It Had to Be You*, for example, a man suddenly finds himself trapped in his date's apartment because of a blizzard outside.

2. Think about the unique world of your story. If you wanted to cage your characters for this scene, is there a better setting available? If so, what is it and how would this change of setting affect the dramatic action?

■ A TICKING CLOCK: TIME IS RUNNING OUT

Sometimes what heats up conflict is not the confinement of a cage but the ticking of a clock. The looming deadline works wonders in such films as *Run, Lola, Run!* where a woman must beat the clock to save the day, and *Waiting for Guffman*, where the director of a small-town pageant must get the show ready by performance time.

Imagine using a "ticking clock" to heat things up in your scene:

1. If your characters face a deadline, how might you increase the urgency or importance of it? For example, can you make the deadline closer or the consequences more dire if the characters fail to meet it?

2. If the characters do not face a looming deadline, how might you change the story so they do? What would be the consequences of not beating the clock?

■ THE VISE: THE WALLS ARE CLOSING IN

Pressing situations can cause confrontations between characters who might otherwise try to avoid their differences. Circumstances close in like a vise and build pressure that becomes unbearable. In *Waiting for Lefty*, a Depression-era taxi driver returns home to find himself in a vise: his furniture has been repossessed, his kids have gone to bed without supper, and there isn't even enough cash to resole his daughter's shoes. These pressures pit him against his wife, who wants him to stop making excuses for years of hardship and start demanding a decent wage from the taxi owners and union racketeers. The vise has closed in: he must organize a labor strike or lose his family.

Imagine heating up your scene by putting your characters into a vise:

1. Think about the given circumstances for the scene. What facts might you add or change to make this situation more urgent for each character?

2. Brainstorm one new thing that each character might do, say, or reveal during the scene to put even greater pressure on the other character.

3. What is the breaking point that will make confrontation unavoidable?

■ A PROVOKING QUALITY: YOU SHOULDN'T BE THIS WAY

A character may have a personal trait, quality, state, or condition that is perceived by another character—correctly or not—as an unavoidable reason for confrontation. In *Angels in America*, a deadly lesion appears on a young man's arm. This physical condition provokes a showdown with his lover, who cannot handle the demands of being a caretaker or the horror of becoming a witness to death.

In *Long Day's Journey into Night*, a father is so cheap that he would rather send his ill son to a third-rate doctor than pay the cost for a good one. This psychological trait—his obsession with saving money—provokes a showdown with the oldest son, who fears for his brother's life.

In the film *Monster*, a woman suddenly finds herself in a deadly battle with a stranger because of her profession: she is a prostitute. This sociological trait is perceived by the man—a psychopath—as a license for violence and murder.

Imagine using a character attribute to heat things up in your scene:

1. From personal appearance to health to sobriety or lack of it, your characters have physical qualities that affect how they look, act, and feel. These attributes may be inherited or acquired, permanent or temporary. For any character in the scene, what physical trait, quality, state, or condition could trigger an unavoidable confrontation here and now?

2. Your characters each have psychological traits that affect their attitudes, temperament, interests, ambitions, morality, sex life, and emotions. For any character in the scene, what psychological trait—positive or negative—could trigger an unavoidable confrontation?

3. The sociology of your characters includes their home life, work life, social life, economics, politics, religion, and role or lack of role in society. For any character in the scene, what sociological trait could trigger an unavoidable confrontation?

4. Whether physical, psychological, or social, what new personal attribute could you give to any character to make confrontation unavoidable here and now?

■ THE UNFORGIVABLE SIN: YOU SHOULD NEVER DO THAT

Sometimes it is not who characters are but what they do that causes trouble. They break a moral, legal, or personal law that has been defined as sacred. In some cases, this law is widely recognized and honored in the world of the story, and any violation of it makes confrontation legally or morally necessary. In *Hamlet*, for example, a man who wants to rule a country secretly murders the king and marries his wife. This crime is an "unforgivable sin" that raises the king's ghost from the dead and ultimately leads to an unavoidable and deadly showdown with the king's son.

Alternatively, the law in question may be a personal one that most people would not honor or perhaps even recognize as a serious limit. In

The Beauty Queen of Leenane, a plain, lonely woman attempts to leave home and get married. This breaks a personal law that has been defined by her manipulative mother and which makes it wrong for the daughter to be anywhere other than at her mother's side. The result of this unforgivable sin is an inescapable and frightening power struggle between them.

In some stories, it is not an unforgivable sin but only the perception of one that causes problems. Either through error, deception, or self-delusion, one character wrongly believes that another character has crossed a legal, moral, or personal boundary and must be confronted. In *Othello,* a man bent on revenge misleads another man to believe that his wife has been unfaithful. This perceived transgression forces the husband to confront and kill the blameless wife.

Imagine using an unforgivable sin to heat things up in your scene:

1. What is a legal or moral law that could be broken by one of your characters just before the scene or during it? How and why would this unforgivable sin make confrontation unavoidable now?

2. What is a personal law that could be defined by one character as important and broken by the other just before the scene or during it? How and why would this unforgivable sin make confrontation unavoidable now?

3. What is a perceived unforgivable sin that could force your characters into a showdown? Would this misconception be the result of error, deceit, or self-delusion and how would it make confrontation unavoidable now?

WRAP-UP

When conflict arises, characters need reasons to deal with each other and fight for what they want, especially if they find themselves in trying circumstances that may push them to emotional extremes. As you develop your script, keep the "binding disagreement" in mind and consider other conflict techniques—such as the locked cage, ticking clock, vise, provoking quality, or unforgivable sin—to heat up the dramatic action when tension has begun to falter.

Related tools in *Character, Scene, and Story.* To explore new sources of conflict for a scene, go to the "Causing a Scene" section and try "Mother Conflict." To add importance and urgency to a scene, try "Why This? Why Now?" in the same section.

THE EMOTIONAL STORYBOARD

THE QUICK VERSION
Use the emotional life of your characters to flesh out a dramatic event

BEST TIME FOR THIS
During scene planning

CHARACTER EMOTIONS: INTEGRAL THREADS OF DRAMATIC STORY
The emotions of the character are integral to story structure because they ground the character in the present, and tie it to the past and future—all at once and at a gut level. By exploring character emotion, therefore, you can learn a lot about not only the character but also the story. Use simple questions like these to guide you:

- *How does the character feel now?* This critical and often overlooked question focuses on the ever-changing present moment of the character. Whatever the character says or does at this moment is being influenced, to some degree, by the character's emotional life—or lack of it.
- *Why does the character feel that way?* This question reflects the character's past. The stimulus for the emotion may have been recent (something that just happened in this scene) or distant (something that happened before the scene or even long ago in the backstory). The stimulus may have been internal (a character perception or memory) or external (something that someone else said or did). To know your character is to know what triggered the character's emotion, and why.
- *What will character do as a result of this feeling?* This question shifts the focus to the future: what will happen in this scene or later in the story as a result of the character's feelings now? If the emotion is strong enough, it can produce physical and psychological responses that affect the character's needs, speech, and behavior. From a dramatic viewpoint, character emotion is of little use until it leads to observable character action of some kind.

If a scene is of any length, and if it has more than one beat, and if it rises above the level of monotony, the character will experience different emotions during the course of the scene. Some of these feelings will be more important than others.

Suppose that a scene has three parts—beginning, middle, and end—and that the character's primary emotion in the scene is hate. For beginning, middle, and end, you could show hate, hate, and hate. That sounds pretty dramatic. However, the emotional redundancy may make the scene stale and predictable. Imagine how much more dynamic the scene might be if it showed emotional variety, perhaps an escalation of feeling, such as irritation, anger, and hate, or a dramatic change, such as hate, surprise, and sympathy, or—in less happy circumstances—tenderness, surprise, and hate.

Emotions are complex phenomena that can be interpreted different ways. You may learn more about the character and the scene if you look beyond the surface of each emotion for deeper meaning. Some say that all human emotions can be viewed ultimately as a form of anger, fear, or love. Whether or not you agree with this theory psychologically, it provides a useful tool for exploring emotions dramatically.

For example, your character's primary emotion in a scene might be hate. If you were writing *Mississippi Burning*, you might see this hate as a form of anger. If you were writing *The Laramie Project*, however, you might add a different depth to the gay bashers' hate by seeing it as a form of fear. Or, if you were writing *Who's Afraid of Virginia Woolf?* you might even see hate as a form of love.

ABOUT THE EXERCISE

This exercise can help you explore the emotional lives of your characters and use these feelings to create a simple storyboard for a scene. The storyboard in this case will not be a sequence of images, but rather a sequence of emotions that suggest the scenic movement.

While characters may experience any number of feelings in a scene, this exercise asks you to focus on the most important emotion that the character feels during each of three scene parts: beginning, middle, and end. These parts may not be of equal length or importance, but each differs from the other two: the end is different from the beginning because of what happens in the middle. This simple breakdown can help you find the broad strokes of a dramatic event and how it happens. Before you begin, you need to know who will be in the scene, what their relationship is, and what the main event of the scene will be. Your concept of the main event may change as you work through the exercise.

Examples are based on an interpretation of the opening scene of act 2 of *The Pillowman* by Martin McDonagh. The play takes place in an unnamed totalitarian state where a writer is being interrogated by police about the gruesome content of his short stories and their similarities to a series of local child murders. The second act begins in the police holding cell.

Character 1 is Katurian, who is, by day, a cleaner in a slaughterhouse and, by night, a passionate writer of children's stories about torture, murder, and other abuse. He has written over four hundred of these twisted tales and, so far, published one of them. Character 2 is Michal, his mentally impaired brother whom Katurian has cared for since they were teenagers. The main event of the scene: Katurian discovers that three of the fictional murders in his stories have inspired the childlike Michal to commit three real-life copycat murders.

■ **EMOTIONAL STORYBOARD OF CHARACTER I**

Focus first on the main character of the scene—for example, Katurian—and answer these questions to help you explore his or her emotional life in the scene:

I. *Primary emotion.* Characters experience different emotions at different times, and these feelings vary in intensity, impact, and importance. In the McDonagh scene, the primary emotion that Katurian feels is horror, which, for him, is a form of fear. He is in danger of losing everything he values. Interpret "primary" any way you wish and identify your character's primary emotion in the scene. Then interpret the emotion by imagining it as a form of anger, fear, or love. Which would it be? What would this tell you about the character?

- *Storyboard.* Katurian's horror occurs mostly in the middle of the scene. Where in your scene—beginning, middle, or end—does your character's primary feeling mostly occur? By making a choice now, you will begin to define a focus for the scene and how it unfolds.
- *Stimulus.* A key cause of Katurian's horror is Michal's revelation that he has reenacted three murders from Katurian's stories. The stimulus for Katurian's horror is thus immense: not only has his brother killed innocent children, but the deaths were inspired by Katurian's own writing. Identify the stimulus for your character's primary emotion.
- *Behavioral impact.* One of the most immediate results of Katurian's horror is the need to know what exactly happened and why. The emotion thus triggers a new beat action: to find out from Michal the full and horrible truth. Think about your character's primary emotion. Identify at least one important effect of this emotion on your character's behavior later in this scene or, if appropriate, later in the story.

2. *Second emotion.* Katurian's second most important emotion in the scene is protectiveness, which, for him, might be a form of love—and a big shift from the horror he feels elsewhere in the scene. What is the second most important emotion that your character experiences in your scene? If you were to view this as a form of anger, fear, or love, which would it be? What would this suggest?

- *Storyboard.* Katurian's protectiveness is aroused near the scene's end when he is able to forgive his brother for his crimes. Where in your scene does the character's second emotion occur? Choose one of the two remaining blanks in the character's emotional storyboard.

- *Stimulus.* One cause of Katurian's protectiveness is his relationship with Michal: Katurian has always been his brother's keeper. This responsibility stems from Katurian's understanding that Michal has a diminished mental capacity and is not fully responsible for his actions. Briefly identify an important cause of your character's second emotion.
- *Behavioral impact.* One effect of Katurian's protectiveness is the need to save Michal from the sadistic police who will soon return, and, in a gesture that echoes *Of Mice and Men*, to protect him by smothering him to death with a pillow. The scene ends with Katurian tenderly kissing his dead brother. The feeling of protectiveness will also lead into the next scene, when Katurian will sacrifice his own life—he will confess to murders he did not commit—in order to bargain with the police and protect his stories from being destroyed. Briefly identify at least one way that your character's second emotion will affect his or her behavior.

3. **Third emotion.** This exercise asks you to fill in three blanks of a character's emotional storyboard: beginning, middle, and end. If Katurian feels horror in the middle and protectiveness in the end, the remaining blank in his emotional storyboard is the beginning. Katurian's primary emotion here is relief which, for him, might be a form of love.

- *Storyboard.* Fill in the remaining blank in your character's emotional storyboard by identifying the emotion that your character feels here. If this feeling were a form of fear, anger, or love, which would it be?
- *Stimulus.* When the scene begins, Katurian and Michal are reunited in a cell while the police go elsewhere. This gives Katurian the chance to confront his worst fear: he asks Michal to swear that he did not kill any children. Michal obliges by swearing that he did not. This response is the cause of Katurian's relief. It will be undone later when Katurian learns the truth. Identify the stimulus for your character's third emotion.
- *Behavioral impact.* Katurian's relief fosters the hope that he and Michal can still find a way out of this bad situation. This hope, in turn, leads to a plan which begins with Katurian's instruction to Michal to not sign any papers. Briefly identify at least one way that your character's third emotion will affect his or her behavior.

Among the different feelings he experiences in the scene, Katurian moves from relief in the beginning, to horror in the middle, to protectiveness in the end. This sequence suggests an emotional arc which reveals that Katurian is under incredible stress, that in spite of his macabre stories his moral compass is still intact, and that he loves and understands his brother. Think about the emotional arc that you found for your character in your scene. What does this arc reveal to you now about your character?

■ EMOTIONAL STORYBOARD OF CHARACTER 2

Now focus on the emotional arc of the second most important character in the scene—for example, Michal. If there are more than two characters in your scene, and if it feels appropriate, you can try this exercise with the other characters as well.

1. **Primary emotion.** In a strong contrast to Katurian's primary emotion of horror, Michal's primary emotion in the scene is amusement, which, for him, might be a form of love. What is the primary emotion that your second character feels in the scene? If this feeling were a form of fear, anger, or love, which would it be?

   - *Storyboard.* Michal's amusement occurs mostly in the beginning of the scene. In which part of your scene—beginning, middle, or end— does your character most feel the primary emotion?
   - *Stimulus.* What triggers Michal's amusement is the reunion with his brother after being separated, and the sight of Katurian hugging his leg. Michal's amusement also stems from his childlike view of the world. Here he is a murder suspect being imprisoned in a totalitarian state by sadistic police, and his main concern is that they put lettuce on his ham sandwich. What is the stimulus for your character's primary emotion?
   - *Behavioral impact.* One effect of Michal's amusement is the desire to play a trick on his brother. This is why Michal at first denies being the child killer. What is an important behavioral effect of your character's primary emotion?

2. **Second Emotion.** Michal's second most important emotion is anger, which, for him, might be a form of fear. What is your character's second most important emotion in the scene and might this be a form of fear, anger, or love?

   - *Storyboard.* Michal's anger occurs mostly in the middle of the scene. In which part of your scene—beginning, middle, or end—does your character most feel the second emotion?
   - *Stimulus.* When Katurian learns the truth, he smashes Michal's head against the stone floor of the cell. More than the physical pain, the realization that his brother would turn against him—and possibly leave him—is what triggers Michal's anger. What is one important cause of your character's second emotion?
   - *Behavioral impact.* One effect of Michal's anger is to attack Katurian where it hurts most: Michal says that Katurian is not only mean like their vicious parents, but also a bad writer. What is an important effect of your character's second emotion?

3. **Third Emotion.** Michal is amused in the beginning of the scene and angry in the middle. The remaining blank in his emotional storyboard is the end. Here Michal feels contentment, which, for him, might be a form of love.

- *Storyboard.* Fill in the remaining blank in your character's emotional storyboard by identifying the emotion that your character feels here. If this feeling were a form of fear, anger, or love, which would it be?
- *Stimulus.* The cause of Michal's contentment is the story that his brother is telling him. It's written by Katurian and one of Michal's favorites: "The Little Green Pig." What is the stimulus for your character's third emotion?
- *Behavioral impact.* One effect of Michal's contentment is that, oblivious to his hopeless situation, he falls asleep like a child listening to a bedtime story. This enables Katurian to save him from the police by smothering him to death with a pillow. What is an important effect of your character's third emotion?

Michal moves from amusement in the beginning of the scene, to anger in the middle, to contentment in the end. This emotional arc reveals him as one who has limited ways of understanding the world, is not fully responsible for his actions, and loves his brother. What does your second character's emotional arc reveal to you now?

■ COMBINING THE TWO EMOTIONAL STORYBOARDS

If the McDonagh scene were broken down into a simple emotional storyboard with three parts, it might show the following:

1. In the beginning, Katurian is relieved and Michal is amused. After the trials of act 1, life for the two brothers now seems to be looking up. As a focusing exercise, this part might be subtitled "A Light at the End of the Tunnel."

2. In the middle, Katurian is wracked with horror and Michal is having a tantrum. In contrast to the first part, things have taken a dramatic turn for the worse. This section might be subtitled "The Horrible Truth."

3. In the end, Katurian feels protective and Michal feels content. Their turmoil has now settled into a final resolution as the brothers return to their traditional roles with each other. This part might be called "Goodnight, Sweet Prince."

In effect, the emotional lives of the characters both create—and evolve from—the scene's throughline. Look at how the emotional arcs of your characters connect and don't connect as they move from the beginning, to the middle, to the end of your scene. Think about the throughline that this suggests. As a focusing exercise, write a telling subtitle for each of the scene's three parts. Then write the scene.

WRAP-UP

Great dramatic works are often filled with provocative ideas—they make us think—yet great dramatic works are not primarily intellectual in nature.

They are woven from human emotion and designed to create experience: to make us feel. It is through our emotional responses that we discover the intellectual content of the story. A key to stirring these responses in the audience later is to make character emotion an integral and organic part of scene development now.

Related tools in *Character, Scene, and Story*. To explore a character's emotional life in more depth, go to the "Developing Your Character" section and try "The Emotional Character." Or go to the "Causing a Scene" section and try "The Emotional Onion." To map out the action of a scene through the filter of a character relationship, try "Relationship Storyboard" in the same section.

IN THE REALM OF THE SENSES

THE QUICK VERSION
Do an in-depth sense study of a scene

BEST TIME FOR THIS
During scene planning, writing, or revision

DRAMA AS SENSORY EXPERIENCE
In a play or film, we literally see and hear the story. Our senses of sight and hearing are active. In some cases, other senses are stirred as well—even if only in our minds. Through sense memory and emotional involvement with the characters, we may smell, taste, or feel what's happening in a scene. Whether it is real or vicarious, sense experience is a powerful component of any dramatic scene and, like most other components, can be shaped and composed to heighten the story's impact.

ABOUT THE EXERCISE
Use this exercise to plan a new scene or revise an old one by exploring the setting, characters, and dramatic action viscerally. For best results, you need to decide who is in the scene and have at least a rough idea of what will happen. Even if your decisions later change, they will give you a starting point for an in-depth sense study.

Exercise examples are based on an interpretation of the opening scene of Sarah Kane's visceral play *Blasted*, which explores the relationship between a rape in a hotel room and the destruction of a city during war. Character 1 in this scene is Ian, a middle-aged man from Wales who works as hack reporter for a tabloid newspaper. Ian is a cancer-riddled cynic who has already lost one lung, and is smoking and drinking himself to death. Character 2 is Cate, in her twenties, an innocent lower-middle-class woman from South London who stutters under stress and is subject to epileptic seizures. She is unemployed and lives with her mother. Their relationship: Ian and Cate were once lovers. This is the first time they've been alone since he ditched her without an explanation. What happens in the scene: Ian tries unsuccessfully to seduce Cate.

■ **SKETCHING OUT THE SCENIC CONTEXT**
To pave the way for your sense study, think about your scene and briefly identify the following:

1. *Given circumstances.* In the world of *Blasted*, a number of given circumstances are at work when the opening scene begins:

- Ian's miserable health and cynicism have left him feeling depressed, lonely, and sexually frustrated. This circumstance contributes to why he has suddenly invited Cate to a hotel and now wants to seduce her.
- Cate agreed to meet Ian because he sounded so happy and because she is by nature a caretaker. However, she no longer loves him. This fact will fuel her resistance to his sexual advances and later put her in danger.

Think about how the past affects the present. Identify a few of the most important given circumstances for your scene. Try to see how each circumstance will be relevant to the scenic action—for example, how it might affect character objectives, problems, motivations, or strategies.

2. *Setting.* The play *Blasted* takes place in one setting: a hotel room which will undergo significant changes when, in scene 3, a bomb from the street demolishes the premises. For now, it is simply an expensive hotel room in the city of Leeds. Briefly define the setting for your scene. Ideally, this is a place which—because of what it is and how it is—will help you show, not tell, your story.

3. *Time.* Scene 1 of *Blasted* takes place in the evening. It is springtime just before a civil war. Briefly describe when your scene takes place.

■ WHAT DO YOU SEE?

We typically receive most of our information about the world through sight. Imagine your scene unfolding as a visual experience. Use what you see in your mind's eye to create the following portraits:

1. *Still life.* Imagine that, if you could freeze your scene at any time and study any of its visual details, you would find an interesting still-life image that reveals something important about what's going on. It's a "still life" because it focuses on things, not characters. In the opening of *Blasted*, for example, one might find a still life of roses perfectly arranged in a crystal glass vase on a table. Next to the vase is a bottle of gin from a hotel minibar and a pile of tabloid newspapers with salacious headlines, such as "British Tourist Slaughtered in Sick Murder Ritual." For this scene of sleazy seduction, a still life of roses, gin, and tabloids might be titled "Tools of the Trade." For your scene, find one telling still life from any time in the dramatic action. Describe the image and give it a title that adds meaning.

2. *Portrait of Character* 1. Imagine next that you could freeze your scene at any time to find a portrait image of your Character 1. It is a "portrait" because it paints a telling picture of who this character is. A portrait of Ian from the scene might show him with a glass of gin in his hand staring out the window of the hotel room. His face and posture suggest one who

has given up on himself. Only his eyes still seem alive. They are burning with hatred and disgust because he despises what he sees outside. This portrait might be titled "I Hate the World." As you continue to explore your scene visually, find a telling portrait of your Character 1 from any time in the scene. Describe the image and give it a title.

3. *Portrait of Character 2.* A portrait of Cate from the same scene would be quite different from that of Ian. She is a young woman, full of life, bouncing up and down on a big bed. Her face is lit up with joy as if she has never seen a bed like this before. She is giggling and having a wonderful time. This portrait might be titled "Joy Is an Island." As you continue to explore your scene visually, find a telling portrait of your Character 2 from any time in the scene. Describe the image and give it a title.

4. *Double Portrait.* A portrait of two characters can reveal something interesting about not only each character but also their relationship. A double portrait of Ian and Cate might show him standing at the bathroom door with only a white towel wrapped around his waist. He is holding a revolver at his side and looking at Cate. She is sitting on the edge of the bed sucking her thumb and looking uncertainly at the gun. This double portrait might be titled "Ian and Cate Suddenly See Each Other." Find a telling portrait of your Characters 1 and 2 at any time in the scene. Whether they are interacting or each in his or her own world, they are both in the same image. Describe it and give it a title.

■ WHAT DO YOU HEAR?

Most places are full of sounds. Some come from the place itself and the people who occupy it; some come from the world beyond. In the opening of *Blasted*, we might hear such sounds as traffic from the street outside, the glug-glug-glug of gin pouring out of a bottle, the gulping down of the gin, the ringing of the telephone, the running of the bathroom shower, terrible coughing and spitting, the pop of a champagne cork, a knock at the door, the thud of Cate's body hitting the carpet in an epileptic faint, the sound of spring rain. Other than the voices of the characters speaking, what might you hear in your scene? Listen for sounds near and far, loud and quiet, and identify them.

To explore the dramatic potential of sound in more detail, try "The Voice of the Setting" later in this guide.

■ WHAT DO YOU SMELL?

If you could smell the opening of *Blasted*, two aromas would stand out. One is pleasant: a perfume from the flowers so delightful that it brings a smile to Cate's face as she sniffs the bouquet. The other smell is unpleasant: the odor of Ian's body, which is strong and vile because of the toxins he excretes through his ever-sweating pores—even after he takes a shower. He cannot escape his own stink. In your scene, are there any smells—pleasant or unpleasant—coming from the characters, the setting, or the world beyond? See if you can find at least one or two interesting smells here.

■ WHAT DO YOU TASTE?

In *Blasted*, the dominant taste is that of gin. In fact, so much gin is tasted in the scene that Ian has to call room service and order more. Other tastes include the sweetness of champagne, the hearty flavor of ham and cheese sandwiches, the rancid taste of phlegm, the salty taste of skin, the burnt flavor of tobacco, the bitter, stale taste of old cigarettes and gin from Ian's mouth when he tries to kiss Cate. In your scene, are there any tastes—pleasant or unpleasant—that we might experience through the characters? See if you can find at least one or two interesting tastes here.

■ WHAT DO YOU FEEL?

Through the sense of touch, we can experience tangible sensations, such as texture and surface temperature, and atmospheric sensations, such as area temperature and moisture. In *Blasted*, there is much to experience through touch. When Cate first arrives in the classy hotel room and sees its expensive furnishings, she goes around excitedly touching everything in sight. As the scene progresses, touch experiences include the smooth, soft bedspread, the hot water and steam of a shower, the cold steel of a revolver, the dripping of sweat, the warmth of human flesh, the wetness of a tongue, and the dabbing of cold gin on a warm forehead. For your scene, are there any touches—pleasant or unpleasant—that we might experience through the characters? See if you can identify and describe at least one or two interesting things to touch or feel.

■ THE SENSE EXPERIENCES THAT MATTER MOST

By exploring your scene viscerally, you have found a number of different sights, sounds, smells, tastes, and touches. Some of these sense experiences matter more than others. In *Blasted*, the three most dramatically interesting sense experiences might be (1) the double portrait: Ian in only a white towel holding a revolver and Cate sucking her thumb and looking uncertainly at the gun; (2) the portrait of Cate bouncing on the bed; and, (3) the bitter, stale taste of tobacco and gin in Ian's kiss.

Identify the three sense experiences that you find most interesting of all, but with one limitation. As an exercise, your choices cannot all be from the same sense category. For example, they cannot all be visual images or all be sounds. At least two different sense categories must be represented. With this limitation in mind, trust your instinct and list the three most interesting sense experiences in your scene.

A DEEPER LOOK AT THE MOST INTERESTING SENSE EXPERIENCES

You may find new character and story ideas by building on your most important sense experiences and thinking about how they might affect us in terms of the following:

1. *Conclusions.* Sense experience and intellect are intrinsically linked. What we see, hear, smell, taste, and feel triggers thought that leads us to certain conclusions—right or wrong—about ourselves and the world around us. For example, the double portrait of Ian and Cate—him in a towel with a revolver and her on the bed sucking her thumb—might lead us to conclude, "These two people should not be alone together in a hotel room." The portrait of Cate bouncing on the bed might lead to the conclusion "She seems young for her age: innocent and childlike." The taste of Ian's repulsive kiss might lead to the conclusion "This guy is really disgusting." Think about each of your three most important sense experiences from an observer's point of view. For each one, identify a conclusion—right or wrong—that this experience might trigger.

2. *Questions.* Sense experience can lead us intellectually to questions as well as conclusions. The double portrait of Ian with a revolver and Cate sucking her thumb might stir the question "Is he going to do something bad to her?" The portrait of Cate bouncing on the bed might lead us to ask, "Does she really have any idea what she's gotten herself into?" The taste of Ian's repulsive kiss might make us wonder, "How much uglier will this get?" Think about each of your three most important sense experiences from an observer's point of view. For each, identify an important question that this experience might raise.

3. *Emotions.* As we process information through our senses, a wide range of feelings may be triggered. For us in the audience, the double portrait of Ian and Cate might stir up an emotional response of dread. The portrait of Cate bouncing on the bed might trigger a fleeting moment of joy. The taste of Ian's kiss might produce a feeling of disgust. Look at each of your three most important sense experiences from an observer's point of view. For each one, identify an emotional response.

WRAP-UP

By creating sense experiences and evoking sense memories, you can bring us into the world of your story in a specific, immediate, and visceral way. Think about the sensory information you have discovered so far and the types of conclusions, questions, and emotions that it triggers. How might you translate these discoveries into dramatic action for your scene? What new character and story ideas do they suggest?

Related tools in *Character, Scene, and Story.*
To continue tapping the power of physical
life, go to the "Developing Your Character"
section and try "Sensing the Character" or
"Objects of Interest." Or go to the "Causing
a Scene" section and try "The Real World"
or "The Color of Drama."

THE VOICE OF THE SETTING

THE QUICK VERSION
Use nonverbal sound to explore character and story ideas

BEST TIME FOR THIS
During scene planning, writing, or revision

A SOUND IS WORTH A THOUSAND WORDS
While most dramatic writers are aware of the impact that music can add to a scene, and sometimes write specific music requests into their scripts, many overlook the power of other nonverbal sounds. Whether live or pre-recorded, nonverbal sounds can be as important to a scene as any other dramatic element. These "sound effects" are born in the stage directions and, when composed effectively, can not only help set the scene and create a mood, but also add visceral force to story events. Many classic moments in theater owe part of their legacy to a sound effect:

- In *A Doll's House* by Henrik Ibsen, the echoing slam of the door as Nora walks out of her house and her marriage
- In *The Cherry Orchard* by Anton Chekhov, the mournful twang, like the breaking of a harp string, that leads to stillness and then the strokes of an ax far away in the doomed orchard
- In the blackout that ends *Of Mice and Men* by John Steinbeck, the gunshot that signals George's mercy killing of Lennie at the river bank

These are three examples of how sound adds dramatic punch to a story's end, but this is not to imply that sound matters only in final moments. Throughout the dramatic action of *The Caretaker* by Harold Pinter, for example, we hear the sound of water dripping from the ceiling into a bucket hanging overhead. In a world where no one is able to achieve anything of importance, the drip is an ever-present reminder of the failure and trouble that looms over the heads of the characters.

In *True West* by Sam Shepard, the duel of two brothers is launched with the gentle chirping of crickets and accented later by the yapping of coyotes gathering beyond the walls of the house. The stage directions describe the coyote sounds this way: "This yapping grows more intense and maniacal as the pack grows in numbers, which is usually the case when they lure and kill pets from suburban yards."

The sound of a man urinating into a toilet is an important and recurring story element of *Audience* by Václav Havel. A political satire set in a Czech brewery, the play explores class struggle as a lowly and oppressed brewery worker meets with his boss. The boss is a fat cat who drinks beer all day at his desk and has to keep leaving the meeting to relieve himself offstage. During each exit, the only dramatic action on stage is the sound of passing water which grows louder and longer as the boss gets drunker and literally pisses away the profits of the workers.

Nonverbal sound comes in many forms and can be used by dramatic writers in many ways. Ideally, if a sound effect is specified in the stage directions, it is not an arbitrary enhancement, but rather a judiciously chosen building block of the scene. Like each line of dialogue, each sound effect is an essential part of the action.

> *Nonverbal sound can be a powerful tool for dramatic storytelling, but use it sparingly. Too many sound effects can steal focus away from the story and slow the action.*

ABOUT THE EXERCISE

Imagine that each of the settings in your story, like each of your characters, has a unique voice. This "voice of the setting" includes everything we hear beyond the spoken dialogue of the characters and beyond any music that might be added externally as a background to the scenic action. The voice of the setting may be urban or rural, loud or quiet, friendly or unfriendly. It may have an influence on the characters that is big or small, positive or negative. It is a dynamic force affected by whoever and whatever is present as well as the time of day, the time of year, and any other circumstances at work in the world of the story. If we have visited this setting in an earlier scene, its voice now may be significantly different.

What is the voice of the setting for the scene you are developing now? Use this exercise to explore this voice and how it might contribute to the dramatic action. To do the exercise, you need to know exactly where and when the scene takes place and have at least a rough idea of what happens. As you imagine sounds from a variety of angles, feel free to repeat responses. The goal is not to list as many sounds as possible, but rather to find the sounds with the greatest dramatic value.

■ THE UNIQUE SOUNDS OF THIS SETTING

Think about the where and when of your scene. Begin to imagine different sounds that one might conceivably hear in this particular place at this particular time. Whether the setting is interior or exterior, its voice may include a number of sounds made not only in this place but also all around it and in the distance. These sounds may come from weather, environment, living creatures large and small, other elements of nature, people, places, and things of all kinds as well as from the unknown. As you explore different sound categories, remember that they are not mutually exclusive and that it's okay to choose the same sound more than once—even several times—if that feels right.

1. First impressions are often the strongest. What is the first interesting sound you hear as you imagine yourself in this setting at this time?

2. Like the ringing of a telephone or cackling of chickens, some sounds are realistic and recognizable. Identify a few recognizable sounds that you could conceivably hear in this setting at this time.

3. Other sounds, such as an electronic ripple or eerie thump, may be abstract or mysterious. Imagine hearing at least one such sound in this setting at this time and briefly describe what you hear.

4. Whether it comes from near or far, some sound may be continuous and contribute to a setting's ambience—for example, the drumming of rain or the sound of children playing in the distance. If the voice of your setting were to include an ongoing sound, what would it be?

5. Other nonverbal sounds may be sudden and isolated, such as the crash of breaking dishes or the shrieking and flapping of startled birds. What is a sudden, isolated sound that you might hear in this setting at this time?

6. Like the wail of a fire engine siren or the explosion of a firecracker, some sounds may be most striking because of their volume. What is a loud sound that you might hear in this setting at this time?

7. Other sounds, like the tinkle of wind chimes or the moan of a distant foghorn, may be soft. What is a quiet sound that could conceivably be heard in this setting at this time? (It may be quiet only because it's from far away.)

8. Like the applause of an audience or the soothing rush of a waterfall, some sounds may be pleasant. Interpret "pleasant" any way you wish and identify a pleasant sound that could conceivably be heard in this setting at this time.

9. Other sounds, like the grinding of a dentist's drill or the screech of an alley cat, may be unpleasant. Interpret "unpleasant" as you wish and identify an unpleasant sound that could conceivably be heard in this setting at this time.

10. Some sounds, like the ring of a doorbell or the rattle of a rattlesnake, are calls to action. They demand a response of some kind. Among the sounds that might be heard in this setting at this time, what is a sound—positive or negative—that would require someone to do something?

■ THE DRAMATIC POTENTIAL OF THIS SETTING'S VOICE

Think about what you've heard so far in your setting. Use the following steps to see if any of these nonverbal sounds can help you set the scene, create a certain mood, or dramatize the story. For example, nonverbal sound may help you do any of the following:

1. *Establish location.* Sound can help identify the setting for a scene quickly and easily, and can be an especially useful tool on stage if the story occurs in so many different locations that realistic set changes are not feasible. For example, the sounds of lapping waves and squawking gulls immediately put us at a seaside, even though we never actually see water or a shore. Consider how easily certain locales—such as an airport, bowling alley, or gymnasium—can be evoked by the right sound clues. Think about where your scene takes place. If you were to use a sound to establish this location, what sound would it be?

2. *Establish time.* Sound also can help define the time or circumstance of a scene, just the crow of a rooster announces that it's dawn, the blast of a factory whistle signals that the workday has ended, or the ringing of church bells suggests that it's Sunday morning. Is there a sound that could help establish when your scene takes place? If so, what sound would it be?

3. *Create mood.* Just as the ticking of a clock or pounding at a door may heighten a scene's tension, or the warbling of a songbird or gurgling of a brook may add to its peacefulness, sound can contribute much to a scene's atmosphere. Think about the emotional feel of your scene. Is there a sound that could help create the right mood? If so, what sound would it be?

> *One the loudest sounds in drama is utter silence, such as that which precedes the wife's confession of infidelity to her waiting husband in* Betrayal *by Harold Pinter. The emotional weight of the silence makes the confession one of the most dramatic moments in the play.*

4. *Make something happen.* Sound often helps transcend the physical and financial limitations of a production by making it possible to stage just about anything, such as a major battle at sea in *Antony and Cleopatra* by William Shakespeare, or rioting on the streets of Watts in *Twilight: Los Angeles, 1992* by Anna Deavere Smith. Because sound has the power to evoke images, it can work magic on stage, just as the rise and sputtering halt of an engine sound can make a car pull up outside, or the sounds of drums, bugles, and marching feet can make a parade pass by. Through sound effects, lions and tigers can be prowling outside the tent, picture windows can be shattered, and a witch's cauldron brought to a boil—all without animals, glass, or fire. In your scene, is there any sound that could help create an important story element that would otherwise be impractical or impossible to stage?

5. *Create metaphor.* Like words in a poem, nonverbal sounds can create metaphors that help reveal character or add meaning to the story action.

In one of the garden scenes in *Doubt* by John Patrick Shanley, the principal of a Catholic elementary school learns that the new priest on the faculty may be having an inappropriate relationship with a student. The scene ends with the "sound of wind" ushering in a storm: a metaphor for the emotional tempest that the principal will unleash when she confronts the priest. Think about what happens in your scene. Is there a sound that could work on a metaphorical level as well as a realistic one? If so, what sound and what metaphor would it be?

6. *Reduce the need for exposition.* Sound offers opportunities to show, not tell, the story. If we hear the rumbling of thunder, for example, we do not need to be told that a storm is coming. If we hear the firing of a pistol and sudden cheering of a crowd, no one needs to explain that the race has begun. Think about what happens in your scene. Is there a sound that could replace an explanation? If so, what sound and what explanation would it be?

WRAP-UP

Keep exploring the power of sound as you make character and story choices, and use the best of what you find to write or edit your scene. Since you are developing a dramatic script and not a sound design, be selective with the effects that you include in the final stage directions. Focus on those nonverbal sounds that go beyond clever enhancements to become integral units of the dramatic action.

Related tools in *Character, Scene, and Story*. To learn more about the physical realm of your character's world, go to the "Developing Your Character" section and try "Sensing the Character." Or go to the "Causing a Scene" section and try "The Real World" or "The Color of Drama."

THINKING IN BEATS

THE QUICK VERSION
Do a beat analysis of a scene

BEST TIME FOR THIS
When editing a completed scene

THE BEAT: A BASIC BUILDING BLOCK OF A SCENE
Just as a full-length dramatic story is made up of acts, and each act is made up of scenes, each scene is made up of beats. Beats are simply the smallest units of dramatic action. They may come in different sizes and have different functions, but most have a similar structure which mirrors the structure of both the scene and the story.

To write a dramatic story is to think not in lines of dialogue but in beats of action. Each beat is about one thing: a certain topic or activity. Once a beat is introduced, it must be developed to its natural conclusion before a new beat begins. However, there are no rules to dictate what a certain beat's natural conclusion should be or how long it should take to reach it. In some cases, the natural conclusion may even be the lack of a conclusion: an interruption that leaves the matter at hand unresolved. Ideally, you will find, shape, and end each beat instinctively as you focus on your unique characters and the larger scenic elements—such as objective, conflict, and motivation—which the beat will serve.

Though fundamental to the development of dramatic stories, the beat is a concept that many dramatic writers either never learn or too often forget. In the end, scene problems often boil down to beat problems. If a scene is difficult to follow on an emotional level, for example, some beats may be underdeveloped. If a scene feels static, some beats may be overdeveloped.

Thinking in beats is a subjective process that tends to work best when it is also a subconscious process guiding writing decisions. At some point, however, such as revision, you may learn something new about a scene by focusing on a beat analysis of the dramatic action. This analysis can help you not only to evaluate your work, but also to strengthen your deeper understanding of beats as the essential building blocks of a dramatic story.

ABOUT THE EXERCISE
Use this exercise to review the concept of beats and to do a detailed beat analysis of an important or difficult scene that you wish to revise.

■ THREE TYPES OF BEATS

As you break down your script, you may find any of these three basic types of beats:

1. *Behavioral.* The beat is driven by a character's desire to affect another character in some way—for example, to make the other character feel good, to make the other character feel bad, to convince the other character of something, or to find out something. This is, by far, the most common type of beat. The next part of this exercise features a sample behavioral beat from *Hamlet.*

2. *Physical.* The beat is driven by a character's need to complete a specific physical task. This type of beat often unfolds without dialogue and is more common on screen than on stage. Samuel Beckett's play *Endgame* begins with a physical beat in which Clov prepares the sheet-covered room for a new day.

3. *Inner-life.* The beat centers on a character's thoughts, feelings, or memories, and unfolds as an interior monologue. This monologue may be driven by a self objective—such as an inner need to figure something out—or by sheer imagery—such as a poetic description that brings a past experience back to life. In *Long Day's Journey into Night*, for example, Edmund's memory of his life at sea is an inner-life beat driven by imagery.

■ A SAMPLE BEAT AND HOW IT'S STRUCTURED

The following example is from the first scene of Shakespeare's classic play *Hamlet* and illustrates principles common in dramatic stories today. The opening beats of the scene have established that, at this particular time of night for the past two nights, soldiers standing guard here at the castle have seen a ghost. Horatio has heard about the ghost but doesn't believe it exists. Marcellus has brought him here to prove otherwise.

> *Enter Ghost.*
> MARCELLUS. Peace, break thee off; look, where it comes again!
> BERNARDO. In the same figure, like the king that's dead!
> MARCELLUS. Thou art a scholar; speak to it, Horatio.
> BERNARDO. Looks it not like the king? mark it, Horatio.
> HORATIO. Most like: it harrows me with fear and wonder.
> BERNARDO. It would be spoke to.
> MARCELLUS.   Question it, Horatio.
> HORATIO. What art thou that usurp'st this time of night,
>   Together with that fair and warlike form
>   In which the majesty of buried Denmark
>   Did sometimes march? by heaven, I charge thee, speak!
> MARCELLUS. It is offended.
> BERNARDO.   See, it stalks away!

HORATIO. Stay! Speak, speak! I charge thee, speak!
    Exit Ghost.
MARCELLUS. 'Tis gone, and will not answer.

This is a behavioral beat about one thing: the appearance of a ghost. From a broader technical angle, this beat lays the groundwork for the problem of the play—something is rotten in Denmark—and raises questions that draw us into the story. Has the king really returned from the dead? And, if so, why? This beat also establishes an important "rule of the game": this is a world where ghosts can appear. A closer look at this single unit of action reveals that it has a typical beat structure which includes the following elements:

1. *Stimulus.* Something sets a beat into motion. The most common stimulus for a new beat is a previous beat in the scene, so that this beat is the direct result of that beat. In some cases, however, it is inner life—a character need, emotion, idea, or memory—that sparks a new topic or activity. Sometimes the stimulus for a new beat is something that happens by chance—for example, someone new enters the scene and changes the subject. The stimulus for the sample beat from *Hamlet* is the entrance of the ghost.

2. *Action.* Once the beat is set into motion, the basic principles of dramatic action drive it forward. In other words, someone wants something (objective) that is difficult to achieve (obstacle), but has a reason for trying to achieve it anyway (motivation). As with the larger units of scene and story, these dynamics work together to make the conflict slowly rise, though the "event" taking place, at the beat level, may be a relatively small one. All of this implies that a beat has a "main character": someone who makes the beat happen. If the main character of the beat is also the main character of the scene, the beat is often one step of an attempt to achieve the scenic objective.

In the sample beat from *Hamlet,* the role of main character is shared by a group: Horatio, Marcellus, and Bernardo. Acting as one, they have a clear objective: to find out why the ghost is here. Their biggest obstacle is the ghost's silence. Their motivation is the fear that this eerie occurrence may be a bad omen for the kingdom.

3. *Climax.* This is the point beyond which the conflict can rise no further. Finding that point is a subjective process that flows from the unique characters and their current situation. At the beat level, the climax is often relatively simple: a line of dialogue or a physical action which indicates that something has now been achieved or has now failed to be achieved. In the sample beat from *Hamlet,* the climax—the highest point of action—is the exit of the ghost.

4. *Resolution (optional).* In many cases, the beat doesn't come to a complete ending because its climax triggers the next beat, which then inter-

rupts the action to begin something new. In some cases, however, the climax of the beat may be followed by a line or two of dialogue or physical action that wraps things up. The sample beat from *Hamlet* includes a resolution: the acknowledgment from Marcellus that their attempts to communicate with the ghost have failed.

A beat is about one thing. This may be the simplest feature of a beat and also the most difficult to remember during the writing process.

■ HOW BEATS WORK TOGETHER

Beats in sequence add up to a scene. When you are editing a scene, it is important to stay aware of how this sequence is composed and particularly how the individual units of action connect or don't connect. Ideally, most beats link through cause and effect. The sample beat from *Hamlet*, for example, links directly to the next beat, which begins:

> BERNARDO. How now, Horatio! you tremble and look pale:
>   Is not this something more than fantasy?
>   What think you on't?

The activity in focus has now changed. The ghost has gone, so the group can no longer question it. Bernardo and Marcellus have switched their attention, therefore, to Horatio, the most educated of the three, and his opinion of what just happened. This beat would not have occurred, however, if the ghost beat had not preceded it. By linking beats through cause and effect, you can create a chain of beat events in which each beat contributes something essential to the larger main event of the scene.

In some cases, the relationship between beats is not causal. If the beat stimulus is purely from the inner life of a character or from forces outside the prior action of the scene, the relationship between two beats may be psychological or coincidental. In the opening of *Hamlet,* for example, the sample beat's relationship to the previous beat is coincidental, for, while the previous beats prepared us for the appearance of a ghost, they did not actually cause this appearance. The ghost enters of its own volition regardless of what the soldiers have been saying to one another.

■ ANALYZING THE BEATS OF YOUR SCENE

To do a full beat analysis, you need to know the broad strokes of your scene: who drives most of the action, what scenic objective is being pursued, what central conflict stands in the way, what's at stake, and what main event occurs. Though these broad strokes may change as you look at the scene from a beat perspective, they will provide a context within which to do the following detailed technical analysis:

1. *Mark the beats.* How many beats should be in your scene and how long should each one be? There is no formula to answer such questions, since every scene is something new. A short scene may consist of only one beat. A long scene may have several. The beats may be as short as one line or continue for pages. Most scenes have at least three beats so that the end can be different from the beginning because of what happened in the middle.

Remember that each beat is about one thing and that the process of identifying beats is subjective. As an exercise, draw lines to divide up the beats of your scene visually and create a simple map of its beat structure. As you do this, you may begin immediately to make discoveries about your scene. If you find yourself unsure of where one beat ends and another begins, for example, you may have uncovered areas that need editing and refocusing. Or, you may realize that you don't know what a particular beat is really about.

> As you break down the scene, err on the side of making the beats too large rather than too small. If you chop up the scene too much, you may find yourself getting lost in details.

2. *Give each beat a label.* Think about what happens in each beat and briefly identify what it's about. You can do this by focusing on the beat topic (such as "the ghost appears") or the beat action (such as "to find out what the ghost wants"). Either approach can work as long as the beat has a clear single focus. Make sure that you know what this focus is and stick to it if you need to reshape the dialogue or physical action later.

3. *Define the beat transitions.* Think about how the beats in the scene connect or don't connect. For each beat, look at the stimulus and determine whether the transition between this beat and the prior action is *causal* (this beat is the result of that beat), *psychological* (this beat is the result of something that a character imagined, felt, or remembered) or *coincidental* (this beat starts something new and is not a result of what's happened so far in this scene.)

4. *Evaluate the beat transitions.* Scenes may take an unexpected turn now and then because of beats that arise out of the blue—for example, an unexpected emotional outburst, a chance occurrence, or an accident—and such surprises can be dramatically effective. True to the law of diminishing returns, however, too many surprises defeat their own purpose. For a scene to have a strong throughline, most of the beats need to be linked through cause and effect. If most of your beat transitions are not causal, you may have too many starts and stops, and a throughline that lacks continuity and coherence.

5. *Look for unnecessary beats.* Each beat is a unique and essential part of the scene's main event. Review your beat labels. Does any beat feel unnecessary because it only repeats another beat without adding anything new? Or because it is a tangent that exists for its own sake and doesn't really contribute to the main event? Or because it is just not that important? If your scene has too many beats, flag those that can be either combined or eliminated during revision.

6. *Look for missing beats.* As the characters interact and the main event unfolds, we in the audience may not always understand everything that is happening. For example, certain characters may be hiding information or concealing their true intentions. However, we need to know enough to participate in the story emotionally and intellectually. Look at the sequence of beats in your scene. Does the action flow in a way that will allow us to follow the transitions from beat to beat? Are there any significant gaps in this flow that may cause confusion or distance us too much from the dramatic action? If your scene has any missing beats, briefly note what needs to be added during revision.

7. *Evaluate the French scenes (if more than one).* A "French scene" is a unit of action that begins and ends with the entrance or exit of a character. Each time someone important arrives or leaves, the dynamics change and a new French scene begins. Each is a separate configuration of characters in which something happens. If the scene you are analyzing is comprised of more than one French scene, mark where each begins and ends. Then look at the cluster of beats within each French scene and how they add up. What is the event of this scene section? How does this serve the whole scene? If you find French scenes where nothing happens, you may have underdeveloped or missing beats in the cluster. Or, you may have unnecessary entrances or exits interrupting the action.

Long ago in France, before the convenience of copy machines, scripts for actors had to be hand copied. As a way to reduce the burden of this task, actors in rehearsal often received only the section of a scene in which they appeared. This led to the term "French scene" and implies that there is something worth rehearsing in each scene section.

8. *Clean up the beat changes.* A new beat may be triggered by such stimuli as the entrance or exit of an important character, by a change of topic, or by a change of behavior or emotion. Know where each beat begins and ends. Don't muddy the beat changes. If two beats have a casual relationship, for example, know which speech or physical action in the first beat triggers the

second beat, and reduce or eliminate any unnecessary wordage between that stimulus and its response. Watch out also for beats that bleed into each other because one of the beats ended or started too soon.

9. *Evaluate beat length.* The amount of time you devote to each beat suggests its importance in this particular scene. Review the length of each beat in relation to the beat label. Is the size appropriate for the content? If you are not devoting enough time to an important topic or activity, you may need to develop the beat further. If you are spending too much time on a topic or activity that is not so important here and now, you may need to streamline the beat. Flag any beats that need to be beefed up or trimmed down during editing.

10. *Evaluate the rhythm.* Beats in sequence create the rhythm of the scene. Short beats speed up the pace and are common in comedy. Long beats slow things down and may be more appropriate for serious subjects and moods. For best results, aim for a variety of beats and, during editing, stay aware of the rhythm you are creating. Make sure that it matches the content and mood of the scene.

11. *Review common scene problems from a beat perspective.* As you conclude your technical analysis of the scene, think again about the main event and how it develops from beat to beat. If, after revision, you detect any dramaturgical problems at the scenic level, you may need to go back and look at the beats again. For example:

- *If the scene rambles or loses focus*, there may still be unnecessary beats in the chain of action. If you can remove a beat without affecting the beats before or after, the beat in question is probably not necessary. Remove it.
- *If the scene feels disjointed or doesn't add up*, one or more important beats may still be missing.
- *If the scene feels choppy or hard to follow*, especially at an emotional level, some beats may still be underdeveloped. Flesh them out more.
- *If the scene feels static or overwritten*, some beats may still be overdeveloped. Trim them down to what matters most.

WRAP-UP

When you are developing the first draft of a scene, it's usually best not to plan out all of the beats in advance but rather to find most of them instinctively as you write the scene with its broad strokes in mind. Once you have a rough draft of the scene, you can go back and rework the beats you found.

During editing, some scenes will require more attention than others. The level of technical analysis that you bring to each scene will depend on its importance and how well it works. Doing occasional beat analyses can help you stay aware of beat principles, pinpoint dramaturgical problems, and evaluate your writing process, particularly your ability to think in beats as you flesh out the scenes of your story.

Related tools in *Character, Scene, and Story.* For more about beats as a series of character strategies to achieve a scenic objective, go to the "Causing a Scene" section and try "Levels of Desire." To explore how beats add up to French scenes, try "The Scenes within the Scene" in the same section. To examine the opening beats of your story, go to the "Building Your Story" section and try "In the Beginning."

TALKING AND LISTENING

THE QUICK VERSION
Strengthen the dialogue of a scene

BEST TIME FOR THIS
After completing a draft of a scene

DIALOGUE: MUCH MORE THAN EVERYDAY SPEECH
Dialogue has the form and feel of conversation, but is actually a heightened version of everyday language—even when you are writing a story in realistic style. Effective dialogue boils thoughts and feelings down to their most important parts and expresses them in ways that are unique to the characters. At its best, dialogue reveals who characters are rather than explains who they are, and helps move the story forward rather than bring it to a stop.

In some cases, dialogue uses imagery to describe poetically what a character has experienced or how a character feels. Most of the time, however, dialogue is active: it is driven by desire and shaped by conflict and risk. Open to the beginning dialogue of any script, and you are likely to discover that this sense of objective and problem begins with the first line or, if not then, almost always the second line. For example:

> *Play: The Seagull*, by Anton Chekhov
> *First line* (MEDVEDENKO): Why do you always wear black?
> *Objective:* To find out more about the woman he loves.
> *Problem:* He is puzzled by her chronic melancholy.

> *Screenplay: Chinatown*, by Robert Towne
> *First line* (CURLY'S VOICE): Oh, no.
> *Second line* (GITTES): All right, enough is enough—you can't eat the
>   Venetian blinds, Curly. I just had 'em installed on Wednesday.
> *Objective:* To calm down his client Curly.
> *Problem:* Curly is so emotionally upset that he's wrecking Gittes's office.

> *Play: In the Blood*, by Suzan-Lori Parks
> *First line* (HESTER): Zit uh good word or a bad word?
> *Objective:* To find out the meaning of a word scrawled on a wall.
> *Problem:* She doesn't know how to read.

To write dialogue is not simply to reproduce how people talk. It is to use speech to show who characters are, what they want, and what problems and risks they face. Whether the conflict seems large (you don't understand someone you love) or small (your client is biting the Venetian blinds), something is at stake here and now for the character who speaks. The words that come out of the character's mouth embody a need to address this risk. They reflect and reveal a character in action.

In the final analysis, it is the action that matters most. No matter how brilliantly and beautifully the dialogue is written, the story is not about what the characters say, but rather what they do. If there is a discrepancy between a character's words and actions, the actions speak loudest. All of this reflects the idea that we go to the theater to "see" plays and films, not "hear" them.

Your most effective dialogue will come from your characters themselves as you write the scene. In other words, great dialogue is not planned. It is allowed to flow while you put yourself in the moment with characters whom you know well. At some point, however, you need to stop and take an analytical look at what you've put down on the page. Much of the revision process involves making choices about where to clarify, where to add, and—more often than not—where to cut.

ABOUT THE EXERCISE
This exercise presents general guidelines to help you revise the dialogue of a scene you've written. Remember that they are guidelines and not rules. The terms *speech* and *line* are used interchangeably here and refer to whatever one character says at one time. It may be as short as a word or phrase and can sometimes run on for pages, depending on the complexity and importance of the message.

If you have trouble writing dialogue in a scene, it may be a sign that you don't know your characters well enough yet or that you don't really understand the dramatic event taking place between them.

■ STRENGTHENING THE DIALOGUE OF A SCENE
Keep these questions in mind as you review a scene:

1. *Does each character have a unique voice?* What characters say grows out of who they are, what they have experienced in life, and what they want now. Ten characters with the same need can find ten different ways to express it. Some characters are educated, some aren't. Some speak formally, some use slang. Some are crude, some refined, some terse, some verbose. Most use language that reflects their lifestyle, occupation, location, heritage, and special interests. Make sure your characters each have a dis-

tinct voice. If lines of dialogue are easily interchangeable, you have not yet found the voices of your characters.

If each character does not have a unique way of talking, go to the section "Developing Your Character" and try "Finding the Character's Voice."

2. *Is most of the dialogue active?* Except for special moments where imagery may be used to evoke extraordinary feelings or ideas, dramatic characters are almost always trying to influence whomever else is here now—to make the other character feel good or bad, to convince the other character of something vital, or to find out a critical piece of information.

Beware of speeches where characters are preoccupied with self-reflections, elaborate explanations, or brilliant analyses rather than affecting each other in a specific way. Know what your characters want from each other during the scene and let these objectives guide what they say and don't say.

3. *Is the meaning clear?* We may not always know what the characters are really up to, but we should at least understand what they are saying. If we get confused by the basic meaning of a line or by a reference, our attention wanders from the action while we figure it out, and we may have a hard time catching up with the story that has continued on without us. Great dialogue communicates the information we need to know in order to understand the characters, action, and ideas of the story here and now.

Try to reread your dialogue as if for the first time and hear what would be communicated to an audience if these characters said these things at this point in the story. Clean up any speeches that might be confusing because their content is not stated clearly enough, or because they are too complicated or too detailed, or because they rely on too many references to the past or offstage world.

Big confusion can sometimes be traced to little words, particularly pronouns used incorrectly. When you're deep into a story, it's easy to forget what you knew in elementary school—for example, that the word "she" in a line refers to the female most recently named. If another female has been named since then, we will have the wrong "she" in mind as we hear the dialogue. A good way to test the clarity of your script is to ask someone you trust to read it and sum up what happened.

4. *Does the dialogue make room for subtext?* Great dialogue travels the surface of the character's thoughts and feelings, presents the most important details, and lets us infer the rest from the clues given. This approach is the opposite of "writing on the nose," where everything is spelled out in the lines. Ironically, the more you explain, the less we care. For the audience, part of being engaged is listening to the dialogue and figuring out what's

not being said. If there is no subtext to be discovered, we tend not to believe the lines we have heard.

If Max says to Benny, "I trust you," we are likely to think he doesn't, because we assume instinctively that there must be something else going on. If Max says, "I want you to have my house key," we read between the lines and infer a sense of trust beneath the line. Look for dialogue in your scene where characters make "on the nose" statements, draw conclusions, or put forth generalizations. Some of these statements may be needed, but most will serve you better if they are moved to subtext and suggested by the details presented in the dialogue.

5. *Does the dialogue tap the dynamics of listening as well as talking?* One speech can trigger an array of different responses, depending on who's listening and how they feel. In each case, the listener hears what's said, interprets it a certain way, and responds accordingly. During this process, we can learn a lot about the speaker, the listener, and their relationship. Suppose Joe says, "You look like you could use a vacation." If the other character is Pete, a grumpy neighbor, he might interpret Joe's line as a criticism and reply, "If I need your advice, I'll ask for it." If the other character is Joan, an office rival, she might interpret Joe's line as a threat and reply, "You think it's that easy to get rid of me?" Or if the other character is Maggie, Joe's wife, she might interpret the same line as loving support and reply, "You're right, honey. Let's go to Hawaii."

In your scene, listen to what's being said through each character's ears. Are the responses unique and appropriate? Have you missed opportunities to reveal character through more telling or surprising interpretations of the lines uttered?

6. *Are the characters focused on what's new rather than rehashing what they already know?* When characters sit around and relive their memories at length or remind each other of things that should be obvious to them both, the dialogue tends to feel expositional and phony. More often than not, it's the writer's clumsy way to set things up for the audience. Watch for dialogue that begins with exposition flags such as "I remember . . . ," "Do you remember when . . . ," and "As I said before . . ." Keep the focus of the scene on the here and now. Let the characters refer to the past and offstage world only when it is necessary to make something happen in the present, and keep these references as brief as possible. It is more dynamic to infer the past than to explain it.

7. *Is all of that information really necessary?* Great dialogue is transparent. It envelops the audience rather than impresses them. In the end, every speech matters because it not only reveals something important about the character, but also advances the dramatic action. Read through your dialogue to weed out speeches that don't perform both functions. It is not unusual to find characters making speeches that impress the writer but have little to do with the story. These are what screenwriter William Gold-

man refers to as "darlings" that get in the way of the dramatic action and should be "killed."

If speeches can be cut without changing what happens in the rest of the scene, it's a sign that those speeches should go. They have shifted the scene into neutral gear. These idle moments may be small, only a line or two, or large, a beat or more of action. Either way, they form loops of wordage that exist only as tangents to the dramatic action rather than integral parts of it. In some cases, it's the topic that's unnecessary. In other cases, it's not the topic, but the amount of detail devoted to it. In a dramatic story, time is valuable. Make every minute count by boiling the dialogue down to what is essential for these particular characters in this particular scene.

WRAP-UP

Most of writing is rewriting, and you will probably revisit your scene many times. A good way to review the dialogue during this process is to read each character's lines separately and focus on what that one character is doing in a scene. If you have a character who has only been asking questions, for example, the dialogue may be getting stale and predictable. Remember that characters can probe without asking questions and that too much of anything will ultimately work against the scene. For best results, try to vary the approach and speech rhythms as much as possible while staying faithful to your characters.

"The Bones of the Lines" later in this guide can help you through a technical scene edit. Try it as a final step to refine the language of your characters and tweak the action of a scene.

Related tools in *Character, Scene, and Story.* To continue exploring dialogue, go to the "Causing a Scene" section and try "Phrase Book" or "Anatomy of Speech."

UNSPEAKABLE TRUTHS

THE QUICK VERSION
Use subtext to reveal character and drive story action

BEST TIME FOR THIS
During scene planning, writing, or revision

READING BETWEEN THE LINES
What the characters don't say to each other is often a critical part of what happens between them. Whether through experience, imagination, or leap of faith, characters sometimes develop beliefs and feelings so profound, so painful, or so secret that they cannot be uttered in dialogue and must remain instead in the subtext of the scene. These unspeakable truths are a rich source of dramatic action because they are powerful motivators of what the characters do here and now.

A skillful dramatic writer can show us what's really going on by creating a context which suggests—but never explains—the unspeakable truths. We observe the behavior of the characters within this context, listen to what they say, and read between the lines to infer meaning. The unspeakable truths may be positive or negative, and may sometimes contradict what the characters say. Some characters want to communicate their unspeakable truth. Others want to hide it.

In *Ballad of the Sad Café*, a play adapted by Edward Albee from a novella by Carson McCullers, we enter the world of the poor rural South where we meet two eccentric characters: Marvin Macy and Miss Amelia. Unknown to Miss Amelia, Marvin Macy has suddenly fallen in love with her, even though they have never dated or even had much of a friendly exchange. When he pays her a visit one summer night, his goal is to win her hand in marriage, and his unspeakable truth (I love you) is a message he wants to make clear. The ever-practical Miss Amelia also has an unspeakable truth (I want your ten acres of timberland) which, for now, she wants to conceal.

Though these truths are never uttered aloud, the dynamics of the scene show us that Marvin Macy really is in love and that Miss Amelia has something else in mind when she accepts his proposal of marriage. As a result, the subtext of each character becomes knowable to a certain degree without having to be explained. We learn about Marvin Macy's (I love you) subtext through devices such as these:

- *Character objective.* One of the easiest ways to make subtext known is to give the character an objective that stems from the unspeakable truth and will drive action which embodies that truth. Marvin Macy wants to convince Miss Amelia to marry him. This simple choice of objective goes a long way toward making his (I love you) subtext known.

- *Behavioral clues.* Unspeakable truths are often revealed through the tactics characters choose to achieve their objectives. Though Marvin Macy never utters the words "I love you," there is no mistaking that this is what he wants to communicate to Miss Amelia as he attempts to portray himself as a reformed person, showcase his thriftiness, and assure her that he is a landowner who can provide for her.

- *Emotional clues.* You can suggest a lot of information by showing us how the character feels about what's going on. Marvin Macy is nervous. He stammers and is unsure of himself. This emotional adjustment to his task suggests high stakes for him and helps us see how much he loves her.

- *Physical clues.* The physical life of the scene offers many opportunities to show, not tell, unspeakable truths. Marvin Macy has worn his best jacket even on the hottest of nights. He has brought precious gifts—chitterlings and swamp flowers—as well as a silver ring which he finally works up the courage to present. Such details help us know and believe his (I love you) subtext.

In the same scene, Miss Amelia is more of a mystery, because, unlike Marvin Macy, she wants to conceal her unspeakable truth (I want your land). However, a number of clues suggest a hidden agenda in her agreement to marry him. Even though we don't yet know what that agenda is, we sense its presence because of what we have observed in the scene: her objective (she wants to find out why he has come here) in relationship to her emotional adjustment (cold and suspicious), and her behavior—she spends more time talking about land and inspecting the silver of the ring than she does discussing the prospect of marriage. A hidden agenda like this can be suggested by any of the following:

- *Statements that appear illogical.* If something said now doesn't make sense because of something said or done earlier, we sense a subtext contrary to the text. For example, why would Miss Amelia accept Marvin Macy's marriage proposal when she has not shown even the remotest sign of loving him? Her agreement to marry appears illogical and implies that there is more going on than meets the eye.

- *Actions that contradict words.* You can suggest a hidden agenda by creating contrast between what the character says and what the character does. If the two don't match, we believe the actions more than the words because actions speak louder. Miss Amelia says yes to Marvin Macy's proposal, for example, but won't let him kiss her afterward.

- *Inappropriate emotions.* We may suspect ulterior motives when characters manifest emotions that do not seem to fit the situation at hand. Miss Amelia is unfriendly toward Marvin through most of his marriage proposal, and almost hostile after she accepts it. These surprising emotions call into question her motive for marriage.

Whether the character wants to communicate the unspeakable truth, as Marvin Macy does, or conceal it, as Miss Amelia does, the words that are not spoken often ring louder than those that are. What is the unspeakable truth for each character in your scene? How can you reveal this subtext without explaining it? How much of this subtext do you want us to know at this point in the story?

To have dramatic value, the subtext must be knowable to some degree. If the subtext is so buried that it can't be detected, we have no way to realize that something more is going on.

ABOUT THE EXERCISE

Use this exercise to explore the subtext for a scene that you want to write or edit. This subtext may be an unspeakable truth that a character wants to communicate or an unspeakable truth that a character wants to conceal. Either way, it should be a subtext that you want us in the audience to know or at least sense to some degree.

You can repeat this exercise for each character in the scene, but focus on one character at a time. As you do this, look for new story ideas while staying true to the character and his or her relationship to whoever else is here.

■ FINDING THE UNSPEAKABLE TRUTH OF THE SCENE

Think about the scene you are developing and begin to view it from one character's perspective. Imagine that, under the specific circumstances of this scene here and now, the character has an unspeakable truth—a certain knowledge, understanding, suspicion, desire, interest, emotion, or other development—that is too profound, too painful, or too secret to put into words. Yet it is a truth that will significantly influence the character in the scene. As an exercise:

1. *Identify the unspeakable truth* as simply as possible—for example (I love you) or (I want your land).

2. *Tell why this truth is unspeakable.* For example, Marvin Macy's love is too profound for mere words, and Miss Amelia's true intentions, if revealed now, would defeat her plan to acquire Marvin Macy's property.

■ EXPLORING THE UNSPEAKABLE TRUTH

Determine whether your character's subtext is a truth to be communicated or a truth to be concealed. Then go to the matching step below:

1. *If the unspeakable truth is to be communicated* to another character in the scene and/or to us in the audience, try these steps:

- Marvin's (I love you) subtext leads to his scenic objective: to win Miss Amelia's hand in marriage. Think about your character's unspeakable truth and the different desires it might arouse. Identify an objective that could grow out of—and suggest—this unspeakable truth, so that the character's very pursuit of this goal is a clue to the subtext.
- Marvin's (I love you) subtext is also reflected by his courtship strategies, such as assuring Miss Amelia of his reformed nature. Think about your character's unspeakable truth and the different behaviors it might foster. Identify two or three actions that could point to your character's subtext.
- Marvin's nervousness contributes to our discovery of his (I love you) subtext. Think about your character's unspeakable truth and the emotions it might trigger. Identify at least one emotion that could serve as a clue to your character's subtext.
- The gifts in Marvin's hands and the engagement ring in his pocket also contribute to our awareness of his (I love you) subtext. Think about the physical life of your scene. Identify one or two physical objects or elements that could serve as a clue to your character's subtext.

2. *If the unspeakable truth is not to be revealed* to another character in the scene but suggested to us in the audience as a hidden agenda, try these steps:

- Miss Amelia's (I want your land) subtext is not revealed until later in the story. Yet we sense a hidden agenda now, because, after her cool behavior toward Marvin in the scene, her offhanded acceptance of his marriage proposal doesn't add up. Think about your character's hidden agenda and how it might lead him or her to say something that doesn't seem to make sense at the moment. Give an example of a seemingly illogical statement that your character could make and that could suggest a hidden agenda without revealing what it is.
- Though Miss Amelia accepts Marvin's marriage proposal, she won't let him touch her. Think about how your character's unspeakable truth might lead to a contradiction between word and deed. Give an example of how the hidden agenda might be implied by having your character say one thing but do its opposite.
- After accepting Marvin's proposal, Miss Amelia gets angry at his attempt to kiss her. Think about how your character's unspeakable truth might lead to a surprising emotional response in the scene.

Give an example of an unexpected emotion that could suggest a hidden agenda without revealing it.

WRAP-UP

If a heartfelt exchange between characters feels false or unbelievable to the audience, or if the dialogue of a scene seems melodramatic or corny, the problem may be that an unspeakable truth has been spoken. Putting such truths into words betrays their significance and creates dialogue that rings hollow because it has no subtext for the actors or audience to discover.

As you work on your story, think about the unspeakable truth in each scene. Whether your character wants to communicate it or conceal it, look for interesting ways to show, not tell, the subtext. By focusing on the unspeakable truth of each scene, you can avoid "on the nose" writing and keep us actively involved as we piece together the clues and dig deeper to find out what is really going on.

Related tools in *Character, Scene, and Story*. To explore subtext in more depth, go to the "Causing a Scene" section and try "Better Left Unsaid."

UNIVERSAL TRUTHS AND LIES

THE QUICK VERSION
Elevate the dialogue of a scene by raising some lines to a universal level

BEST TIME FOR THIS
During scene revision

TWO LEVELS OF DIALOGUE
Dialogue engages us in two different ways. First, it tells us the unique details of a world that we have never encountered before. Each character is someone we've never met and speaks in a distinct voice that reflects who that particular character is and how he or she fits into the specific story being presented. These are the details that give us the plot. The focus of these details are the plot points—the dramatic events—that allow us to follow the story step by step.

In scene 2 of *Glengarry Glen Ross* by David Mamet, for example, real estate salesman Moss tries to draw his depressed coworker Aaronow into a plan to exact revenge on their ruthless bosses Murray and Mitch and get rich quick in the process. "Someone should rob the office," he says. The target of the robbery is the company's real estate leads, which could then be sold secretly to a competitor named Jerry Graff. Aaronow asks: "How many leads have we got?" Moss replies: "The Glengarry? . . . the premium leads . . . ? I'd say five thousand. Five. Five thousand leads."

Everything the characters discuss here is plot-specific. They are hatching a particular plan that involves a particular real estate company and its rival. The robbery they are planning is a key event of the story, with much of the second act centering on who did or didn't steal the leads. The dialogue surrounding this robbery applies only to the unique world of this play.

Ideally, every line of dialogue moves the story forward as it reveals more about the characters, so, in a sense, every line of dialogue is plot-specific. However, some dialogue has a second function as well. It reaches above and beyond the world of the story to include the world at large: the world that we, the audience, also inhabit. This is the other way that dialogue engages us: it presents universal statements—generalizations, adages, laws, principles, beliefs, or advice—that are meant to apply not only to the characters but also to us sitting in our theater seats. These are the universal truths and lies of the characters. Regardless of what the characters think, we will see these statements as "truths" if we agree with them and "lies" if we don't.

Great dialogue is sprinkled with universal truths and lies. We listen to these lines differently. They make us sit up in our seats because they challenge us to think about our own life experience and either agree or disagree. Some of these universal truths and lies are small. They offer little insights into everyday life. Some try to be profound statements about the human condition. For example, the world of *Glengarry Glen Ross* is a heartless one driven by ruthless greed. Here are some of the universal truths and lies sprinkled throughout the text:

- *About money*, Aaronow says, "People used to say that there are numbers of such magnitude that multiplying them by two made no difference."
- *About luck*, Levene says, "Bad *luck*. That's all it is. I pray in your *life* you will never find it runs in streaks. That's what it does, that's all it's doing. Streaks."
- *About sales*, Moss says, "What did I learn as a kid on Western? Don't sell a guy one car. Sell him five cars over fifteen years."
- *About taking chances in life*, Roma says, "When you *die,* you're going to regret the things you don't do."
- *About hell*, Roma says, "Bad people go to hell? I don't *think* so. If you think that, act that way. A hell exists on earth? Yes. I won't live in it."
- *About life*, Roma says, "What I'm saying, what is our life? (*Pause.*) It's looking forward or it's looking back. And that's our life. That's *it*. Where is the *moment? (Pause.)* And what is it that we're afraid of? Loss. What else?"
- *About work*, Levene says, "A man's his job . . ."
- *About the world today*, Roma says, "I swear . . . it's not a world of men. . . it's a world of clock-watchers, bureaucrats, officeholders . . . what it is, it's a fucked-up world . . . there's no adventure *to* it. (*Pause.*) Dying breed. Yes it is. (*Pause.*) We are the members of a dying breed. That's . . . that's . . . that's why we have to stick together."
- *About truth*, Roma says, "Always tell the truth. It's the easiest thing to remember."

Each of these dialogue excerpts presents a universal statement. We may accept them as either truths or lies, but either way, we must look beyond the characters and see ourselves as well. This type of dialogue is quite different from that about the plotting and planning of the robbery. In a great story, most dialogue is plot-specific, but it is interwoven with great truths or great lies that elevate our emotional experience of the story. We walk out of the theater with much to think about.

For the dramatic writer, the key to using universal statements is to interweave them so seamlessly and appropriately into the dramatic action that we take them in without ever leaving the story. Balance is important. Too many universal statements will make the dialogue feel like a lecture. Too few will make the dialogue seem trivial.

ABOUT THE EXERCISE

Try this exercise to help you revise dialogue that you have already written. The goal is to strengthen the impact of the dialogue by blending universal statements into the plot specifics. To begin, choose a scene with dialogue that you want to revise and write down the names of the two most important characters in it.

■ WHAT YOUR CHARACTERS HAVE TO SAY ABOUT THE WORLD

1. *Identify topics.* Read the scene you have chosen to revise and think about what happens. As the event of the scene unfolds, different topics enter the dialogue. Some may relate to small, everyday matters—such as a streak of bad luck—and some may encompass larger issues of importance—such as the meaning of life. List the general topics, large or small, trivial or profound, that your characters discuss or mention in the dialogue of the scene now.

2. *Highlight universal topics (if any).* Review what your characters have to say now about the topics you listed. Most or all of this dialogue is probably plot-specific ("Someone should rob the office"), but you may already have some universal statements among these lines ("A man's his job"). Highlight any universal statements—large or small—that you find in the dialogue now.

3. *Select topics to explore in more depth.* Think about the two most important characters in the scene and how they each see the world. As an exercise, step out of the scene for a moment and imagine that each character will make a universal statement about some of the topics you just listed. Circle the most interesting topics on your list.

4. *Develop universal statements.* Remember that a universal truth or lie may be large or small, and may express a generalization ("It's a world of clock-watchers, bureaucrats, officeholders"), opinion ("Bad people go to hell? I don't *think* so"), question ("What is our life? . . . Where is the *moment?*"), adage or law ("Don't sell a guy one car. Sell him five cars over fifteen years"), warning ("When you *die,* you're going to regret the things you don't do"), or advice ("Always tell the truth. It's the easiest thing to remember"). Such statements are broad in scope.

Think about your unique characters: who they are, how they express themselves, and what they each might have to say about the topics you circled in your list. For each topic, write two universal statements—one from each character. Think of these lines as completely separate from each other rather than dialogue exchanges. Let each line stand on its own and reflect what the character believes independently of the other. Express each line briefly and in the character's unique voice. Look for similarities and differences between the characters. When you complete this step, you will have two sets of universal statements—and you may have learned something new about your characters in the process.

5. *Integrate universal statements.* Review the universal statements you wrote. Which of these can be integrated into the scene so that they heighten the dialogue without interrupting the dramatic action? How seamlessly can you accomplish this?

Try to blend some of these statements into the plot specifics of the scene. As you do this, keep in mind who is saying this to whom, how these characters each feel, what they are each thinking about, what they each want, and why the speaker is saying this here and now.

WRAP-UP

Continue looking for opportunities to add impact to your dialogue by weaving in universal statements that speak to the audience on a higher level. As a follow-up exercise, pick up a favorite play or screenplay. Read a scene with the two levels of dialogue in mind—plot-specific and universal—and see what you can learn.

Related tools in *Character, Scene, and Story*.
To learn more about your character's credo, go to the "Developing Your Character" section and try "Beyond Belief."

THE BONES OF THE LINES

THE QUICK VERSION
Refine the dialogue of a scene through technical analysis

BEST TIME FOR THIS
During the final stages of editing

SPEAKING, TECHNICALLY SPEAKING
Dialogue includes what your characters say, what they don't say, and what they hear as they listen. These activities can be so emotionally charged and can unfold in so many unique ways that no rules of diction will always hold up. Nevertheless, certain basic principles of dialogue are usually at work in most dramatic scenes. These principles govern to some degree how lines operate and connect, what patterns they form, and what impact they have on the mood and action of the scene.

From a technical viewpoint, for example, dialogue helps set the pace for what's happening. Short speeches move the story at a faster pace and force the characters to keep interacting. Long speeches slow the action down and isolate the characters in their words. For most writers, short speeches work better than long ones. Short speeches are especially important for comedy and for times of tension. Long speeches work best for special moments where extraordinary or serious ideas are being revealed or where poetry is elevating the language above ordinary speech. For best results, vary the pace and rhythms of language throughout the scene.

ABOUT THE EXERCISE
This exercise asks you to step out of a scene you have completed and look at it from a technical viewpoint so that you can see the "bones" of the lines: the word choices, sentence constructions, line lengths, and speech patterns that fuel the talking and listening of your characters. This more detached viewpoint can help you look at the dialogue analytically and refine its performance. The terms *speech* and *line* are used interchangeably and refer to whatever one character says at one time. It may be as short as a word or phrase and can sometimes run on for more than a page, depending on the complexity and importance of the message.

■ **SUGGESTIONS FOR EDITING DIALOGUE**
The following technical guidelines can help you through the later stages of editing. Review these suggestions within the context of your unique writing

style and script, and remember that they reflect principles worth considering, not rules which must always be obeyed. That said, many dramatic writers have found these tips helpful in crafting great dialogue:

1. *Express one idea per speech*. Each time your characters open their mouths, let one—and only one—thought come out. This approach forces the characters to keep interacting, and helps make the content clear and crisp. It can feel awkward when two or more ideas have been worked into the same speech. Review the lines of your scene to see if any seem too complicated. You may need to trim content or use more exchanges to explore it.

2. *Save the best for last.* Just as drama builds to a climax, a line of dialogue builds to the most important word or words in it. By putting the operative part at the end, you force the other character—and us—to listen to the full line in order to grasp what's being said. This approach also lets the listener respond immediately to what matters most.

Suppose Jack says, "If it weren't for the money, I would never have agreed to be here doing something like this." And Jill says, "What money?" The word that explains Jack's motivation and prompts Jill's response is "money." When he is one third through his line, she wants to react, but must wait artificially through the rest of the line before she can do so. This delay can be avoided by switching the construction of Jack's line to read "I would never have agreed to be here doing something like this if it weren't for the money."

As you edit your scene, know what matters most in each speech and triggers a response. Try to keep these cues at or near the ends of the lines. This approach will build a strong stimulus-response pattern through the scene and help keep it from feeling wordy and slow.

3. *Balance everyday and elevated language.* Depending on your story, genre, and voice as a writer, your dialogue may be totally realistic or totally poetic. Most of the time, however, a blend of the two works best. Too much ordinary language can make the story feel flat. Too much extraordinary language can make it difficult to follow or believe. Even if you are writing a realistic scene, look for opportunities to use metaphors and similes to bring poetry to the lines, let your characters soar during special moments, and say more with fewer words. A "metaphor" is a word picture that compares one thing to another and may be either stated ("You are a mule") or inferred ("Stop braying at me"). A simile does the same thing, but uses the words *like* or *as* ("You sound like a mule").

4. *Stay true to the world of the story.* Your characters exist in a certain place, time, and culture. Know what terms, idioms, and references fit this world. If the story is realistic and takes place in 2001, for example, a character might use a little "down time" to put on some "rap music," visit a "chat room," and meet a vet from "Nam." If the story is realistic and takes place in 1951, however, the use of such expressions would be jarring and weaken

the authenticity of the story's world. Check your dialogue for any anachronisms or inaccurate historical references. Do research if anything is in question.

5. *Stay true to the emotional landscape of the scene.* A dramatic story is primarily an emotional experience. We don't learn the story. We live it. The dialogue serves this experience by giving us access to the emotional lives of the characters. We often learn more by how characters express themselves than by what they actually say. Look at your dialogue from an emotional angle to see if the word choices, sentence constructions, and speech rhythms match how your characters feel. If they are angry or nervous, for example, are they speaking in a way that—for them—is angry or nervous? Try to avoid writing stage directions to the actor about how the lines should be delivered. A good test of your dialogue is to see how it reads with all of the stage directions removed.

6. *Use the "rule of three" for important details.* Dialogue is heard, not read, so we can't go back and review it if we missed or forgot what someone said. When a critical fact is being communicated, you can stress its importance by thinking in threes. Suppose that Mr. Godot, an offstage character being discussed now, will be key to action later in the story. Since we never see Mr. Godot in this scene, we may not remember him later if he has only been mentioned once. Why does it work to state something three times? Stating a fact once may not be enough to make it stand out; saying it twice feels like a mistake; and saying it four or more times feels redundant. Of the facts presented in your scene, which will matter most later in the story? Would any of these benefit now from the rule of three?

7. *Unleash verb power.* Good diction relies more on verbs of doing than verbs of being. Verbs of doing—such as *tiptoe, squeeze,* and *kiss*—suggest movement and change. Verbs of being—such as *is, are,* and *were*—describe passive states. Too many verbs of being will make the dialogue feel weak and static. Look for opportunities in your lines to transform being into action—for example, change "She isn't here now" to "She flew out the door a few minutes ago."

8. *Avoid repetition unless it's for dramatic effect.* Selective repetition of words or lines can be a powerful way to stress information, stir emotions, or heighten mood in a dramatic story. Most of the time, however, repetition feels like a mistake. Try to say things well the first time so you don't need to say them again. When a topic must be revisited for the sake of the story, it's usually best not to repeat the same exact words. Look for different ways to express the same information—for example, use synonyms and different language constructions.

9. *Trim the fat.* The last step of the revision process is to see what else can be cut to heighten—not diminish—the dramatic power of the scene. Look first for any unnecessary lines that remain and then for unnecessary words within lines. Be especially wary of the following types of dialogue:

- *Lines that don't advance the action*, such as "What?" "What do you mean?" "What are you saying?" and "Tell me that again." Look for listener interjections that only break up a long speech—for example, "And then what?" "Really?" "No kidding!" and "What happened after that?" If the speech is overwritten, you may be tempted to compensate for its length by having the listener interrupt to make comments here and there. Instead, get rid of the commentary and shorten the speech.
- *Lines that only set up or announce other lines*, such as "Tell me all about it," "Listen carefully, I'm going to explain something to you now," and "You want to hear something funny?" Don't labor to set it up. Just do it.
- *Lines that needlessly echo the previous line.* If the character asks, "When did Jill decide to leave Jack and start running around with that liquor dealer from Chicago?" the response doesn't need to be "Leave Jack and start running around with that liquor dealer from Chicago? I thought she and Jack just got engaged." The reply can simply be "I thought she and Jack just got engaged."
- *Words that slow down the stimulus-response pattern.* A character may sometimes say something that seems out of the blue and is a delayed response to an earlier stimulus. Most of the time, however, characters respond immediately to what has sparked their interest or need. A lot of excess wordage can be found by knowing what each line really answers. Look again at what triggers each speech and remove any remaining deadwood between the stimulus and its response. Make sure the operative words are usually at or near the ends of the lines.
- *Words that only take up space,* such as "Well," "Anyway," and "As I was saying" at the beginning of a line, or unnecessary details or excessive description during the line. A lot of revising consists of piecemeal trimming: getting rid of a word here and a phrase there until only the essential words remain. As you do this, remember that characters don't have to speak in complete sentences and seldom address each other in paragraphs. Sometimes a sentence fragment, phrase, or even a single word will better fit the emotional life that the actor will bring later to the line.

WRAP-UP

When you are first developing a dramatic scene, the last thing you need to think about is how long the speeches are or where the operative words fall within them. Your story will be best served if your focus during writing is on your characters and the dramatic events they create and experience as they act to satisfy their needs.

Before you send out your script, however, your dialogue may benefit from some technical analysis and editing. By looking at the bones of the lines and seeing where you can refine, rearrange, trim, and cut language, you can create a more powerful blueprint for the actors who will bring your story to life.

Related tools in *Character, Scene, and Story*. For another technical look at dialogue, go to the "Causing a Scene" section and try "Anatomy of Speech." To focus on language that is unique to your character's world, try "Phrase Book" in the same section.

Building Your Story

Story is what happens when a character tries to accomplish something that is not only extremely important but also extremely difficult. The struggle to achieve this goal triggers a chain of events that challenges, reveals, and often changes the character. Use the exercises in this section to help you explore the roots of the dramatic journey, develop an effective throughline, and get a clear big-picture view of the story so that you can better understand what it's really about.

WHOSE STORY IS IT?

THE QUICK VERSION
Choose a character focus for your story: single, dual, or group protagonist

BEST TIME FOR THIS
During story planning or any time you are not sure whose story you are writing

FIGURING OUT WHO MATTERS MOST
Choosing a character focus for a dramatic story is one of the most fundamental and important decisions a writer makes. Sometimes the choice is easy—an inherent part of the story concept—and other times it is a challenge that requires a lot of thinking and rethinking. In some cases, the writer gets distracted and begins to develop the script without really deciding whose story it is. In other cases, a choice is made but gets muddied as the details of story ideas begin to flow. For example, the writer sets out to write one character's story and ends up writing another's.

In the universe of dramatic possibilities, a story may center on one main character, two main characters, or more—even a whole group—depending on the nature and scope of the story concept. Each approach has its own unique set of dimensions and issues. In the end, what matters most is that the writer has made a clear choice about which approach to develop and whom to spotlight within it.

ABOUT THE EXERCISE
Use this exercise to help you define a character focus for the story you are working on now. You also may wish to use this exercise during the writing and editing process if you feel that the character focus has become unclear.

■ DIFFERENT WAYS TO CENTER A STORY
Will your story focus on the dramatic journey of one, two, or more characters?

1. *Single protagonist.* From *Hamlet* by William Shakespeare, to *Wit* by Margaret Edson, to *Doubt* by John Patrick Shanley, the vast majority of dramatic stories have focused on the quest of one main character—whether it's a prince of Denmark who has seen a ghost, an English scholar dying of cancer, or a nun running a Catholic school in the Bronx.

For the dramatic writer, a single main character provides the easiest way to unify the action of the story, communicate its theme, and create an experience that feels dramatically complete. Traditionally called the "protagonist," the main character is the one who commands the spotlight as the story unfolds and usually drives most of the dramatic action. In the end, he or she emerges as the character most revealed—and affected—by story events.

The more characters you add to the center spotlight, the more difficult it will be to find and maintain a clear focus for your story. This may explain why most dramatic stories center on one—and only one—main character.

2. **Dual protagonist.** Many dramatic writers have looked beyond the boundaries of the single-protagonist structure and successfully centered their stories on two main characters who have something of importance in common.

Whether they are Estragon and Vladimir waiting for Godot, Thelma and Louise fleeing the law, or Max Bialystock and Leo Bloom producing a Broadway flop, two individuals can share the role of protagonist by having the same goal and equal time to pursue it. It is their common quest that unifies them as "one" and provides a central focus for the chain of events that make up the story.

Or, instead of sharing the role of main character, two equally dominant characters can compete for it, as in *Topdog/Underdog* by Suzan-Lori Parks or *True West* by Sam Shepard, which each feature a pair of competitive brothers trying to best each other. In this type of duo, the characters have related but irreconcilable goals that unite them as adversaries. Each is the hero of his own story and the antagonist of the other's.

Other dramatic stories with some type of duo at their center include *Romeo and Juliet* by William Shakespeare, *Rosencrantz and Guildenstern Are Dead* by Tom Stoppard, Oscar and Felix in *The Odd Couple* by Neil Simon, Sam and Willie in *Master Harold and the Boys* by Athol Fugard, and Gil and Ray in *Thief River* by Lee Blessing.

3. **Group protagonist—or, no protagonist.** Sometimes it "takes a village" to tell a story. This has been demonstrated many times in plays like *The Cherry Orchard* by Anton Chekhov and films like *Nashville* by Robert Altman, where no single character or throughline dominates. Such stories focus instead on a set of individuals who either have a common purpose or comprise a larger collective identity. For example, a story may center on a group of individuals with the same goal, such as the taxi drivers fighting management in the play *Waiting for Lefty* by Clifford Odets or the airline crew and

passengers resisting terrorist hijackers in the docudrama film *United 93* by Paul Greengrass.

Or, a story may center on the collective identity that is suggested when a group of different story lines are combined with a common focus. This collective identity often functions as a metaphor for something greater than the sum of the story lines we have seen, just as the collective identity of *August: Osage County* by Tracy Letts might be defined as the dysfunctional American family, and the collective identity of *Crash* by Paul Haggis might be viewed as racially divided American society.

Other dramatic stories with a multiple focus and no single main character include *Ghosts* by Henrik Ibsen, *The Women* by Clare Boothe Luce, *The Hot L Baltimore* by Lanford Wilson, *Angels in America* by Tony Kushner, and *Dealer's Choice* by Patrick Marber.

■ DECIDING WHOM TO SPOTLIGHT

Think about what happens in your story, who is involved, what they want, and how they function in relationship to one another. Use the following checklists to help you select a specific single, dual, or group protagonist from the characters you are developing.

1. *Single protagonist.* If your story will revolve around one main character, you need to know who among the population of your story is best suited for this role. He or she will need to be someone who can stir up and maintain your interest as well as ours, dominate the dramatic action, and cause the story to happen. This character is most likely to succeed dramatically if he or she

- is the character most affected—in a positive or negative way—by the inciting event of the story;
- embarks on a quest that begins with the inciting event, drives the story forward, and does not reach its success or failure point until the story ends;
- has a strong will and is so motivated to complete the quest that it seems virtually impossible to compromise or give up;
- pursues the goal actively by tackling problems and initiating strategies rather than passively responding to the actions of others;
- has the most to do and say in the story, and consequently commands and receives the most attention;
- has the strongest emotional investment in the story;
- provides the dominant point of view for dramatic action;
- faces bigger problems than anyone else and has to make the most difficult decision in the story;
- is sympathetic—someone we like—or at least empathetic— someone we understand and care about even if we do not like what the character does; and
- embodies the subject and theme of the story.

If your story will center on one main character, who is it? What does this character want overall? What is his or her central conflict? What is at stake?

2. *Dual or group protagonist who function dramatically as one.* This approach will pose the same demands as a single-character journey, except that you will be juggling more than one individual in the central role. The challenge is to keep the focus on these characters equally balanced. A pair or group acting as a single character is most likely to succeed dramatically if these individuals

- are pursuing the same story goal;
- have an equally important motivation to achieve the goal;
- face the same problems or equally challenging ones;
- remain in synch as they move forward through the story;
- are equally active in their pursuit of the goal;
- equally shape the story's point of view;
- carry the same dramatic weight so that neither character dominates;
- face either the same crisis or an equally demanding one; and
- have to make an equally difficult crisis decision.

If your story will center on two or more characters who function dramatically as one, who are the characters and what is their common goal? What is the biggest obstacle they both face? What is at stake?

3. *Dual or group protagonist who function dramatically as more than one.* This approach will pose the same demands as a single-character journey, but repeatedly, since each story line must be composed as a dramatic journey of its own. The key challenge is to bring focus to the script where there is no single dominant character or throughline to anchor it. You will need to figure out what the different journeys have in common, how they intersect, and why their presence in the same script is not arbitrary. A story with no main character is more likely to succeed dramatically if the individual dramatic journeys

- are essential because each tells part of the whole story, reflects a common theme, or suggests part of a central collective identity;
- are unique because each represents a quest different from the rest;
- each center on a character with a difficult but important objective and a reason to achieve it;
- are limited enough in number that we have time in each story line to find out who the characters are, understand their situations, and track their progress;
- unfold at a complementary pace;
- raise enough interesting questions to keep all of the story lines moving forward as the focus shifts from one to the next;
- intersect without disrupting our interest or creating a competition for our attention;
- have ties that become evident as different journeys intersect and

either affect or inform one another in increasingly significant ways; and

- carry similar dramatic weight so that no single character begins to dominate the script to the extent that he or she might be mistaken for a weak protagonist in an underdeveloped central plot.

If your story will center on two or more characters with individual story lines, who are the principal characters? What traits, actions, circumstances or other elements will provide a common focus among them? If they suggest a central collective identity, how would you describe it?

WRAP-UP

For any dramatic story, you need to know who has the center spotlight and why he, she, or they are more important than anyone else. If two or more characters share this spotlight, you need to understand what brings them together in the same story. If they each have a separate goal, you also need to juggle the demands of a multistory structure where different journeys must unfold without distracting from one another. In effect, you face the challenge of not only writing a great story, but also writing a great story again—and again and again—all in the same script.

Related tools in *Character, Scene, and Story.* To address other fundamental questions about the world of your characters, go to the "Building Your Story" section and try "Facts of Life" or "In the Beginning."

HOW WILL THE TALE BE TOLD?

THE QUICK VERSION
Determine the point of view from which your story will be presented

BEST TIME FOR THIS
During early story development

SETTING THE STAGE FOR YOUR STORY
Regardless of whom or what you are writing about, you face a number of basic decisions about how to develop your story. For example, you need to determine its genre, such as drama or comedy, and style, such as realism or expressionism. You also need to know whether the script will be short or full-length and, if full-length, how many acts it will require. As you think about your story at this fundamental level, one of your key tasks is to define its point of view.

"Point of view" in this case does not refer to opinion, but rather to the vantage point from which we will see story events. This vantage point may offer a view that is broad or narrow, personal or impersonal, reliable or unreliable. Like Bryony Lavery's *Frozen,* for example, a dramatic story may be presented from an omniscient viewpoint which lets us see and hear anything happening in both the external and internal worlds of the characters. Or, like *The Glass Menagerie* by Tennessee Williams, the story be may presented from the more limited and subjective point of view of a narrator. Or, like *Rabbit Hole* by David Lindsay-Abaire, the story may be presented from an objective point of view which shows us only external events with no literal access to the inner workings of any character.

Point of view is a unifying principle that affects how we will experience your characters and story events. It will contribute to how well we understand each character, which events we see and how much we learn about them, and how close or distant we feel emotionally to the dramatic journey in progress.

ABOUT THE EXERCISE
Every story is unique. Use this exercise to explore storytelling possibilities for the script you are working on now, and then develop a point-of-view "contract." This basic set of rules will govern many of your writing choices and later determine what we in the audience can know and not know as we watch your story unfold.

During the writing and editing process, you may wish to revisit this exercise periodically either to ensure that you are playing by the rules you established, or to revise these rules if they no longer seem to be serving the story.

■ **DIFFERENT WAYS TO VIEW THE EXTERNAL WORLD OF THE STORY**

From what vantage point will we see character interactions and story events?

1. *Unlimited external view.* From this standpoint, you can take us freely through time and space to see and hear anything happening anywhere in the world of the story. As a result, we can find things out before characters do and know more about the whole story than any single character does. In *Hamlet,* for example, we get an omniscient view of the kingdom of Denmark. This enables us to learn about the ghost of the dead king before Hamlet does and to observe many activities that Hamlet doesn't, such as Claudius plotting to kill him.

2. *Limited external view.* In many cases, a story is about what we do *not* know. The withholding of vital information for a certain time and the revealing of it later become key elements of the storytelling process. Here are some of the most common ways to limit our knowledge of your story's external world:

- *Main-character perspective.* We accompany a main character through time and space and discover the story only as he or she does. Our view is limited, therefore, to what this character experiences. In David Mamet's *Edmond,* for example, we follow the title character through many places—from a fortuneteller's parlor to a prison cell—over an extended period of time. However, we never see or hear anything that Edmond doesn't. The Alfred Hitchcock film *Rear Window* written by Cornell Woolrich and John Michael Hayes adopts a similar vantage point: the main character is a photographer confined to his apartment with a broken leg and a third-floor view of his neighbors' apartments. We can see only what he sees. The implied rule is that the main character must be present in every scene.

- *Dual or multiple-character perspectives.* In some cases, it is a certain set of characters whom we follow through time and space in order to experience the story. They may be two protagonists, a protagonist and antagonist, or some other combination of two or more important characters. Our knowledge of story events is limited to what they—and only they—collectively know. In Edward Albee's *Who's Afraid of Virginia Woolf?*, for example, we see things from the perspective of George and Martha as they entertain their late-night guests. The implied rule is that George or Martha must be present in every scene. As a result, we never see or hear the guests, Nick and Honey, by themselves.

- *Narrator perspective.* We learn the story through a narrator who may be the main character (*How I Learned to Drive* by Paula Vogel, or *Wit* by Margaret Edson) or a minor character who steps out of the action to report from the sidelines (*A View from the Bridge* by Arthur Miller, or *Our Town* by Thornton Wilder). Either way, the view is not omniscient, since it is limited to what this particular narrator could conceivably know. Nor is the view objective, since it is colored by the narrator's emotions, attitudes, memories, abilities, and needs. As a result, the narrator may be a reliable or unreliable source of information.

    In some stories we see the narrator, and in other stories we only hear the narrator as a voice that introduces scenic action or is heard over it. The narration may be addressed directly to us, to the world at large, to a particular onstage or offstage character, or to someone outside the story, even someone famous. The implied rule is that— right or wrong—we can learn only what the narrator shares with us.

We traditionally watch the events of a play or film through the "fourth wall," an imaginary boundary that separates us from the characters and makes us invisible to them. When narrators speak to us, they "break" the fourth wall through a device known as "direct address."

- *Special space limitation.* This technique enables us to travel freely through time, but not space. Our knowledge of external events is limited to what happens in a certain setting, as in A. R. Gurney's *The Dining Room*, which, though it spans generations of New England life, never takes us out of the dining room of a house, and in Jean-Paul Sartre's *No Exit*, where three strangers find themselves eternally trapped with one another in a windowless drawing room in hell. The implied rule is that we can observe the characters only when they are in the designated setting.
- *Special time limitation.* Our knowledge of the story also may be limited by an overriding time factor, as in Marsha Norman's *'night, Mother*, which unfolds in ninety minutes of real time before a woman's suicide, or in Bernard Slade's *Same Time, Next Year*, where each scene occurs one year after the previous scene so that we can watch a love affair unfold as a series of annual weekend trysts. The implied rule

is that all of the dramatic action must occur within the designated time period.

- *Any combination or variation of these techniques.* If you wish to limit the external view of your story, you can combine any of these techniques—or others—in whatever ways best fit your script. Possibilities are limited only by the imagination. The classic Kurosawa film *Rashomon*, for example, experiments with character perspective by showing us four versions of the same rape and murder—each from a different viewpoint: that of the murderer, the rape victim, the murder victim, and a witness. While designed to explore the elusive nature of truth, *Rashomon* also highlights the power of character perspective as a dramatic technique.

The film *Sunset Boulevard* written by Charles Brackett and Billy Wilder gives narrator perspective an unusual twist by letting a dead man tell us his story after we see his corpse floating in a swimming pool. This approach creates immediate suspense by raising questions about why he is dead.

The film *Groundhog Day* written by Danny Rubin and Harold Ramis uses a unique time frame to limit our external view of the story: the dramatic action takes place on a particular Groundhog Day—not just once, but over and over again as a weatherman keeps reliving the same February 2 with slightly different consequences.

Betrayal by Harold Pinter creates another unusual time limitation: the story is revealed backward, starting with the end of an affair between a married woman and her husband's best friend, and ending with the start of the affair. This approach forces us to know the future of most scenes as we watch them and lets us view the initial moment of betrayal with the ironic knowledge of how it will later ruin several lives.

The film *Memento* by Christopher Nolan uses two timelines to control our view of a story about an insurance investigator who can no longer build new memories. One timeline moves in forward direction as he struggles to figure out his past. The other timeline moves in reverse direction to reveal more and more about what really happened.

■ **DIFFERENT WAYS TO VIEW THE INNER LIFE OF THE CHARACTERS — IF AT ALL**

In drama, the most common ways to access inner life are interior monologue and interior dramatization. In an interior monologue, a character thinks out loud so that we can hear what's going on in the character's mind, as in Hamlet's "to be or not to be" speech. This technique is also known as "soliloquy" and, in abbreviated version, as an "aside." The implied rule is that no other characters can hear these words.

In an interior dramatization, a character's thought, dream, hallucination, memory of the past, or vision of the future is presented to us in some way—for example, as an image, voice, sound effect, beat of dramatic action, or even a whole scene. This enables us to see and/or hear literally what's happening in the character's mind, as in Arthur Miller's play *Death of a Salesman*, where we move in and out of Willy Loman's inner world to witness imaginary events and flashbacks of the past, or in the Roman Polanski film *Repulsion*, where we see the world of an apartment through the distorted vision of a woman who is going mad. The implied rule is that no other characters can see or hear these inner phenomena.

Will you let us literally enter the hearts and minds of your characters? If so, how?

1. *Unlimited inner-life view.* You can take us into the hearts and minds of any of your characters at any time so that we can discover what they are really feeling and thinking, as in Tony Kushner's *Angels in America*, where at one moment we may be in the inner world of a pill-popping housewife worried about the ozone layer, and in another moment we may be in the inner world of a young man facing death in the early days of the AIDS epidemic.

2. *Limited inner-life view.* You give us a transparent view of one character—typically the main character—but not others, as in the Martin Scorsese film *Taxi Driver* written by Paul Schrader, where we hear the thoughts of the main character as he writes in his journal about the world he sees around him. In this type of approach, the implied rule is that only one character can do interior monologues or trigger interior dramatizations. As a result, we can enter this character's heart and mind, but must remain psychologically distant from the rest of the story's population. In other words, we must experience them as the main character does. We cannot read their minds, so we must interpret their words and actions.

3. *No inner-life view.* You may wish to keep your characters opaque and restrict us from entering any one's inner world, not even the main character's. The implied rule is that there will be no interior monologues, flashbacks, dream sequences, or other interior dramatizations in the story. We in the audience will have to discover the characters as if we were observing them in real life, just as we do in *The Piano Lesson* by August Wilson and *Blackbird* by David Harrower. We may be able to reach meaningful conclusions about what we see and hear, but—since characters may be misinformed, delusional, or deceitful—we have no way to know for sure how right or wrong we are: it's a matter of opinion and often a subject of debate.

■ DEVELOPING A POINT-OF-VIEW CONTRACT

You can develop your story from any dramatic point of view and set whatever rules you wish for employing it. As you define this point of view, you are establishing the rules of the game for your storytelling approach and implying a "contract" with the audience.

You can develop this contract either before you begin writing your script or after you have a developed a few scenes and have a working sense of how to approach this unique story. Following are a few summary questions to help you explore possibilities:

1. *Will we view the external world from an unlimited or limited vantage point?* If unlimited, skip ahead to question 3. If limited, go to question 2.

2. *If our view of the external world will be limited, how will it be so?* Remember that our knowledge may be limited by any combination or variation of these techniques (answer whichever questions apply).

- *Character perspective.* Whose perspective will determine what we see and what we don't see? If the perspective of more than one character will serve this function, which two or more characters will it be?
- *Narrator perspective.* Will the narrator be a main character or a minor character? To whom will the narrator speak—for example, to the self, us in the audience, someone specific from the story or outside it, or humanity in general? Why will the narrator tell this story? How reliable will the narrator be, and why?
- *Special space or time limit.* What will be the overriding space or time factor? Why will this limitation be important? How will it help tell the story?
- *Other techniques.* To make this unique story work, is it appropriate to adapt or combine any of the above techniques? If so, how?

3. *Will we be able to enter the inner world of at least one of your characters, or will they all remain opaque?* If all characters will be opaque, skip ahead to question 5. If at least one of them will be transparent, go to question 4.

4. *If we will be able to view inner life, will our access be unlimited or limited?* Whether access will be unlimited—any character can become transparent—or limited—only one character can become transparent—you need to address such questions as the following:

- *Whose inner life will be accessed?* Which characters will become transparent so that we can see and/or hear what's happening in their minds?
- *How will this access occur?* Will you use interior monologue, interior dramatization, or both? If you use interior monologue, to whom will the character(s) be speaking? If you use interior dramatization, what specific form(s) will they take—for example, visual images? Voiceovers? Sound effects? Beats or whole scenes of dramatic action?

5. *Will you use any special storytelling techniques to control the dramatic point of view? If so, what?* Take a creative leap and see if you can discover

any other storytelling techniques that might be appropriate for the story you are developing now.

WRAP-UP

As a dramatic writer, you need to make certain basic storytelling decisions at two levels: the external world of observable events and the internal world of emotion and thought. Your point-of-view contract reflects the decisions you have made about how to limit—or not limit—our vantage point at each of these levels.

We in the audience will never see this contract or read its terms and conditions. However, we will sense and trust its presence in our experience of story events, and if the contract is broken, we may also sense—perhaps without quite knowing why—that something has gone askew. For best results, set clear, simple rules for yourself, and once they have been established, honor them.

Related tools in *Character, Scene, and Story.* To review other fundamental questions about the world of your characters, go to the "Building Your Story" section and try "Facts of Life" or "In the Beginning."

AS THE WORLD TURNS

THE QUICK VERSION
Flesh out your character's world and how it operates

BEST TIME FOR THIS
During early story development

KNOWING THE WORLD OF YOUR STORY
A good story creates a world that we enter through the characters. We live in this world for a while and experience what it's like to be there. This realm may be naturalistic, as in *A Streetcar Named Desire* by Williams or *Long Day's Journey into Night* by O'Neill. Or it may surrealistic, as in *Endgame* or *Waiting for Godot* or almost anything else by Beckett.

The world of the story also may be a blend of the real and surreal to give us an environment that is primarily naturalistic but not quite. For example, it might have one or two non-naturalistic features, such as the worlds of Shakespeare's *Hamlet* or Noel Coward's *Blythe Spirit*, where ghosts return from the dead, or the world of Eugène Ionesco's *Rhinoceros*, where ordinary people turn into rhinos, or the world of Kushner's *Angels in America*, where angels descend from above and wrestle with mortals.

No matter what kind of world you create, it is important to know the rules of the game, that is, what the world is and how it operates. To some degree, every world has its own power structure, its own culture and language, it's own values and expectations, its own customs and logic. All of these elements affect how characters see things, behave, and express themselves.

In *Glengarry Glen Ross*, for example, Mamet takes us into the cutthroat world of real estate where client leads are gold, lying and cheating is utterly acceptable, and a man's worth is measured by how many sales he has posted on the board. In *Road to Nirvana*, Arthur Kopit takes us into another ruthless world: Hollywood. Loyalty here is more important than integrity, celebrity is golden, and anything can be justified by the size of the movie deal it will generate. In *The Beauty Queen of Leenane*, Martin McDonagh takes us into a very different world: that of a rural Irish family that is isolated in an oppressive countryside, has a matriarchal power structure, prizes family ties, and reveres the serving of oatmeal which is not lumpy.

You can find the world of your story through your characters. As you flesh them out and make decisions about their home life, social life, and work life, you begin to define the context for story events.

Use this exercise to learn more about the world of your story: what it encompasses and how it operates. As you do this, keep building on what you already know and try to avoid repetition.

■ **DEFINING THE WORLD OF YOUR STORY**

Through the centuries, dramatic writers have invited us into many different types of worlds—for example, those of royal families (*Lion in Winter*), taxi-cab unions (*Waiting for Lefty*), college faculty (*Oleanna*), therapists (*Beyond Therapy*), three-card monte dealers (*Topdog/Underdog*), southern family life (*Crimes of the Heart*), concentration camps (*Bent*), psychopathic killers (*Frozen*), Catholic school (*Doubt*), international arms negotiations (*A Walk in the Woods*), boarding houses (*Vieux Carré*) and jazz clubs (*Side Man*). Think about the world of your story: the arena in which all or most of your characters operate.

1. *Define the overall world of your story.* There may be a number of ways to do this. Prioritize the options and decide what one world your story most encompasses. This is the primary context in which most—not just one—of your characters act, and it tends to affect them in certain ways.

2. *Identify the general style of this world*—for example, naturalistic, semi-naturalistic, or surrealistic.

■ **EXPLORING THE WORLD OF YOUR STORY**

1. *Setting and time.* Where and when is the world of your story situated? Identify the general setting and time frame. Look for responses that can encompass all of the places and time shifts in your story.

2. *Physical environment.* What is the physical environment like and how does it affect character perceptions and behavior? The physical realm may be primarily interior or exterior. It might include weather, time of year, property conditions, proximity to natural resources, urban or rural surroundings, freedom of movement, barriers to movement, objects, interior decorating—anything physical. In a few sentences, describe what's most important and unique about this realm and its impact on most characters here.

3. *Spiritual realm.* The spiritual can encompass what lies beyond the physical: beliefs in God, higher powers, afterlife, religious systems, the occult, reincarnation, or extrasensory perception, or the utter lack of such beliefs and systems. Look not for what one character holds to be true, but rather what overriding spirituality, if any, affects most of the characters here directly or indirectly, whether they individually believe in that spirituality or not. In a few sentences, describe the spiritual realm and its impact on most characters here.

4. *Rules of the game.* Begin to think about the special facts of life or "rules of the game" that help define the world of your story and govern how it operates. These are the laws or principles that are always true in the

story and cannot be otherwise because you, the creator of this world, say so. They are rules that no character can break and every character must live by. These rules of the game reflect important truths about the world of your story.

- *If your world is naturalistic,* focus on the truths or rules that most affect how characters behave during the story. In *Glengarry Glen Ross,* one rule of the game is a legality: a customer has forty-eight hours to renege on a sale. This leads to a scene in which a salesman tries to avoid a customer who has come to cancel a high-pressure land deal within that legal time frame.
- *If your world is seminaturalistic or surrealistic,* focus on the facts of life that are different from those of the naturalistic world. In *Endgame,* one rule of the game is that there is no life left outside. In *Bedroom Farce* by Alan Ayckbourn, two couples live in the same physical setting without seeing or hearing each other.

Be specific and identify any special facts of life, or rules of the game, for the unique world of your story.

5. **Law and order.** Think about the laws and principles that are supposed to be honored in the world of your story, but may be violated by those who are behaving badly. These are "should" or "should not" rules that are generally upheld as legal, moral, or right, and dictate what is expected of your characters.

In the servant world of *Caroline or Change* by Tony Kushner, family members should remember to remove all change from the pockets of their clothing before giving it to the maid for laundry. It's a governing principle enacted by the mother of the family, but often neglected by the son. Find three specific "should" or "should not" rules that all or most of your characters are expected to obey.

6. **Power structure.** Who controls the immediate world of your story? In *Search and Destroy* by Howard Korder, the driving power is the IRS, represented by an onstage tax auditor who threatens to send the main character to jail. In *Waiting for Lefty* by Clifford Odets, it's the offstage taxi company management. In *Long Day's Journey into Night* by Eugene O'Neill, it's the onstage father James Tyrone. Onstage or offstage, what person or group has the greatest direct power over all or most of your characters? This may be but is not necessarily your main character.

7. **Power dynamics.** How would you describe the person or group who most controls the world of your story? In *Search and Destroy,* the IRS is merciless. In *Waiting for Lefty,* the company is greedy and uncaring. In *Long Day's Journey into Night,* the father has a weakened but grasping hold over his family. In a word or phrase, describe the driving power you named.

8. **Pecking order.** In every power structure, there is a certain chain of command. Think about the hierarchy of power in the world of your story. List your onstage characters and then rank them from most to least powerful,

with 1 being most powerful. If you have more than five characters, list and rank only the top five.

9. *Economics.* Think about the economics of your story's world for most of the characters. This may be a world where money is plentiful and used freely for pleasure, or a world where money is difficult to get and limits what characters can do and how they live. In a few sentences, describe the economics of this world and how it affects most characters.

10. *Sociology.* How do most characters in the world of your story relate? Think about the general social dynamics of this world. It may be a world where most characters usually interact with warmth and intimacy or a world where most characters feel alienated and estranged from one another. These social dynamics may be planned and organized with clear rules, or they may be freewheeling, haphazard, or even chaotic in nature. In a few sentences, describe the social dynamics of this world and how they affect most characters.

11. *Communications.* From cave drawings to smoke signals to office memos, from carrier pigeons to cell phones to secret notes, people have found many different ways to communicate when they can't or don't want to talk face to face. Think about life in the unique world of your story. Identify at least three ways that people communicate here other than by talking face to face.

12. *Customs and rituals.* Think about the unique culture of your story's world and the customs and rituals it fosters. Families, clubs, businesses, sports teams, communities, and other worlds have unique ways of doing things that reflect the needs and logic of the world and which become customary over time. These may be large rituals, such as burning everything you own every seven years, or small rituals, such as taking off your shoes before entering the room. They may be everyday customs, such as kneeling in a group as a family and saying the rosary aloud together, or customs for special occasions, such as meeting in a motel room on the same day every year for an extramarital affair.

In any case, these customs have become commonplace and seem logical and appropriate to the general world of the story. For most characters, these customs help ensure the smooth running of this world. Name three specific examples of customs that are common in, and unique to, the world of your story. These may be everyday customs or customs for special occasions.

13. *Center.* In the musical *Cabaret,* the emcee sings that "money makes the world go round." In *Romeo and Juliet,* it's love that makes the world go round. In *Lion in Winter,* it's power. Think about what lies at the core of your world: the force around which the activities of most characters whirl. This is a key to what your story is about. It reflects what your most important characters most want to attain (if your world has a positive core) or most

want to escape (if your world has a negative core.) In a word or phrase, what makes your world go round?

14. **Highest values.** Whether it's love or money or something else, what makes your world go round is either the thing it wants most or fears most. Without repeating your last answer, think about the values that most characters here would see as desirable and would want to attain and protect. Name three things that are most valued in the world of your story. You can interpret this any way you wish. List them and rank them, with 1 being most valued.

15. **Lowest values.** Name three things that are abhorrent and repellent in the world of your story. These might be the opposites of the values you just named or they might be other things. List them and rank them, with 1 being most abhorrent.

16. **Lingo.** Every world has, to some degree, its own language. Certain terms are used commonly and reflect the shared experiences of those who live or work here. These expressions may suggest personal terms of endearment or the jargon of professions or hobbies, or shared histories, or geographical or time period influences. Think about language unique to the world of your story. List at least three terms that are special to this world and define each one in a simple phrase.

17. **Success.** Think collectively about your characters and their relationships and histories. Give one specific example of something that most characters would agree is a success in the world of your story.

18. **Failure.** Give one example of something that most characters here would agree is a failure, sin, or crime in this world.

19. **Beauty.** Different worlds have different standards of beauty. Give one example of something or someone that most characters here would agree is beautiful.

20. **Ugliness.** Give one example of something or someone that most characters here would agree is ugly.

21. **Advantages.** Every world has certain resources that people can tap when they need help—for example, friends, institutions, tools, nature, rules of conduct, social clubs, religious organizations, rich uncles, police officers, nest eggs, family heirlooms, hidden treasures. What are three resources available to most characters in the world of your story? These are positive elements—people, places, or things—that are specific to this world and are potentially helpful.

22. **Obstacles.** Every world also has certain disadvantages that can make life difficult, and limitations that can get in the way. What are three obstacles that affect most of the characters in the world of your story directly or indirectly? These are negative elements—people, places, or things—that are specific to this world and can potentially block characters from getting what they want.

WRAP-UP

You need to know the world of the story as thoroughly as you know each of the characters whom we will meet here. It is essential to understand what this world is, how it operates, what makes it unique, what it values, and what is expected of those who populate it. Once this groundwork has been established, make sure that the story unfolds in a way that is logical and appropriate to the world you have defined.

Related tools in *Character, Scene, and Story.* To dig deeper into the world of your story and how it works, go to the "Building Your Story" section and try "Facts of Life." To explore the language of this world, go to the "Causing a Scene" section and try "Phrase Book."

INCITING EVENT

THE QUICK VERSION
Identify and analyze the event that triggers the main character's dramatic journey

BEST TIME FOR THIS
During early story development

THE EVENT THAT STARTS THE STORY ENGINE
The inciting event is a key element of your story. It is what causes the story to happen. The inciting event does this by changing the dynamics of the main character's world. For example, something is added: guests arrive in the middle of the night (*Who's Afraid of Virginia Woolf?*). Or something is altered: you move your family to a new country (*In America*). Or something is taken away: your son disappears (*Missing*).

Whether positive or negative, large or small, this change in dynamics may be caused by the main character or by someone or something else. It may be the result of intention, accident, coincidence, luck, or the forces of nature. It may take the form of a decision, discovery, opportunity, loss, external development, or other event.

For example, your father's ghost appears and tells you he has been murdered by your new stepfather (*Hamlet*). Or you learn that you have a terminal illness (*Wit*). Or you, your house, and your dog are suddenly whisked away by a tornado and left in a strange land far from home (*The Wizard of Oz*). Even if the inciting event is only a quiet spark, such as the glance of an attractive stranger across the way (*Romeo and Juliet*), it is a powerful force that sets the character moving in a new direction.

Among the turning points of the story, the inciting event is unique in that it triggers the goal that drives the main character's dramatic journey. This goal reflects a desire to do something about the change that has occurred— for example, to avenge the murder of your father (*Hamlet*), to understand what matters most in life (*Wit*), to find a way home (*The Wizard of Oz*), or to unite with your love (*Romeo and Juliet*).

The inciting event works best when it occurs during the story—not the backstory. It is often the first important thing that happens. Sometimes this turning point is delayed so that we can develop a better understanding of the life that will be changed. However, the event is not usually delayed for long, because until it happens the engine of the story has not really started.

For the inciting event to function dramatically, two things must occur.

First, the main character has to know it happened. If he or she is not present when the event takes place, therefore, the character must learn about it as soon as possible. Second, the character must be incited into action. If the inciting event is a problem, the character may want to solve it or avoid it. If it's an opportunity, the character may want to take advantage of it. If it's a mystery, the character may want to uncover its meaning.

In screenplays more often than plays, the inciting event may be delayed so that subplots can be introduced. In films like **Butch Cassidy and the Sundance Kid** *and* **Fargo,** *for example, the inciting event may not occur until the end of the first act or even the beginning of the second act.*

Regardless of how it changes the dynamics of the world, the event triggers in the main character a desire that cannot be dismissed or delayed. This is the kind of desire that burns: one so important and so urgent that the character will do everything possible to satisfy it and, even in the face of the worst conflict, will not consider compromise or surrender along the way. When the character finally achieves the goal or when it becomes clear that the character can never accomplish the goal, the dramatic journey— and the story—are over.

Sometimes the goal that drives the story is conscious—the character knows what must be done or at least believes so—and does not change. For example, you set out to find a valuable treasure that has been hidden (*Raiders of the Lost Ark*). In more complex stories, the inciting event may trigger a subconscious goal as well. This hidden desire is often contrary or even contradictory to the conscious one. For example, you may be consciously striving for political success but subconsciously trying to defeat yourself and create personal failure (*Macbeth*). In such cases, it is the subconscious goal that drives the story and doesn't change.

Drama is the art of showdown, and the inciting event is the first indicator of what this showdown will be. For example, we have a sense that in the end there will be a face-off between you and your father's killer (*Hamlet*), between you and the forces of death (*Wit*), or between you and the strange world around you (*The Wizard of Oz*). This foreshadowing raises a big question that begins to engage us and does not get answered until the story ends.

ABOUT THE EXERCISE

Use this exercise to find and flesh out the event that triggers your main character's dramatic journey. Look for new possibilities as you explore this key event and how it can influence the rest of your story.

■ THE INCITING EVENT OF YOUR STORY

Think about the unique world of your story, who populates it, and what goes on there. The dynamics of this world could be changed by many different types of events—large and small, positive and negative. Consider the possibilities that could affect your main character and launch a dramatic journey.

1. *What if* the dynamics of your character's world were changed by a discovery that he or she makes—for example, someone who owes him money refuses to pay the debt (*The Bear*). Briefly identify a discovery.

2. *What if* the dynamics of your character's world were changed by a conscious decision that the character makes—for example, to walk out of an abusive marriage (*Alice Doesn't Live Here Any More*). Briefly identify a personal decision that makes sense for your character.

3. *What if* it were a conscious decision of someone close to your character—for example, the man she loves asks her to marry him (*Rebecca*). Briefly identify a personal decision or action of someone close.

4. *What if* it were a decision of someone whom your character knows from work or from the community—for example, a neighbor burns down his cotton gin (*Baby Doll*). Briefly identify the decision or action and who initiates it.

5. *What if* it were the action of an organization with strong but impersonal ties to your character—for example, the police arrest him (*The Wrong Man*). Identify the decision or action and the organization that initiates it.

6. *What if* it were an external event caused by an individual or small group with no prior connection to your character—for example, escaped convicts invade his home (*The Desperate Hours*). Briefly identify the event and who initiates it.

7. *What if* it were an external event caused by a large group or organization with no prior connection to your character—for example, Nazi forces blow up the radio studio where he works (*The Pianist*). Briefly identify the external event.

8. *What if* it were an accident or coincidence—for example, a car crash leaves her paralyzed and widowed (*Resurrection*). Briefly identify what happens.

9. *What if* it were an act of God or force of nature—for example, your character's wife dies and leaves him alone (*About Schmidt*). Briefly identify what happens.

10. *What if* it were something completely different? As a final brainstorm, look back through the possibilities you've imagined for an inciting event and, in any one category, add an opposite possibility. For example, if you came up with a discovery that is negative—your character finds out that someone who owes him money can't pay the debt (*The Bear*)—consider one now that is positive—he finds out that he has inherited a castle (*Frankenstein*).

A CLOSER LOOK AT HOW THE DRAMATIC JOURNEY BEGINS

As you complete the next steps, continue to think about the unique world of your story, who populates it, and what goes on there:

1. Choose one inciting event to explore further. Develop a few more details about what happens, where and when it happens, and who's there.

2. How close to the beginning of the story does the inciting event occur? If it happens in the backstory, how could you move it forward into the story itself? If it occurs late in the story, do you have a compelling reason for delaying the inciting event? If not, how could you move it closer to the opening?

3. When does your main character learn about the inciting event? If the character is not present when it happens, how might you condense the time between the event and your character's awareness of it?

4. What is the immediate emotional impact of the inciting event on your character?

5. The inciting event launches the dramatic journey. What conscious goal does this event trigger in your main character?

6. In some stories, the inciting event sparks not only a conscious goal, but also a more powerful subconscious need. If this is true for your character, what is the subconscious need and how does it compare to the conscious goal?

7. Think again about your character's goal. Is it truly a new desire that the character did not have prior to the inciting event? If this desire is not new, how can you change the story or backstory so that it is?

8. What is at stake for your character as a result of the inciting event? How might you make the stakes higher? How might you make the situation more urgent?

9. In the short term, does the inciting event move the character's life in a positive or negative direction?

10. In the long term, does the inciting event move the character's life in a positive or negative direction? How does this compare to the short-term impact?

11. Identify two or three of the biggest obstacles that your character will have to overcome in order to achieve the new goal that has been incited.

12. What is the showdown that this inciting event foreshadows? Identify at least two forces that are introduced now and will collide later.

WRAP-UP

Whether the inciting event is caused by the main character or results from forces beyond his or her control, it changes the dynamics of the character's life in an important and irreversible way. Be sure you know what this event is, how it affects your character consciously and subconsciously, and what story goal it triggers. Many dramaturgical problems can be traced back to an inciting event that did not arouse a strong enough or clear enough goal in the main character.

Related tools in *Character, Scene, and Story*.
To learn more about the inciting event of
your story and the quest it triggers, go to
the "Building Your Story" section and try
"Character on a Mission."

THE ART OF GRABBING

THE QUICK VERSION
Analyze the opening of your story

BEST TIME FOR THIS
After you have completed at least ten pages of your script

DRAWING THE AUDIENCE INTO YOUR STORY
One of Billy Wilder's tips to dramatic writers is to "grab 'em by the throat and never let go." This "grabbing" needs to occur as soon as possible and preferably within the first ten minutes—that's usually ten pages—of your script.

Most audiences will watch just about anything for ten minutes. After all, they have come to the theater to have a worthwhile experience; they have invested time and money in this endeavor; and they are usually eager to prove to themselves and each other that they made the right decision. They *want* your story to succeed.

However, all of this can change rapidly after ten minutes. The audience can move from rapt interest to distraction, confusion, boredom, impatience, irritation, and sometimes even hostility. If you lose the audience, it is extremely difficult to win them back. It is essential to use your first ten minutes wisely. If you win the audience over during this critical time—if you have truly grabbed them—they are more likely to participate in the journey and forgive any problem spots along the way.

The story's opening needs to accomplish certain things, therefore, if the rest of the story is to succeed. During the first ten minutes, you need to establish what the story is about and who it's about. The audience typically wants some understanding of this as soon as possible so that they know—at a gut level—where to put their focus.

For example, they want to know that this will be Tony and Maria's journey to love, or Homebody's journey to truth, or Mary Tyrone's journey to refuge. The audience doesn't want the ending spelled out, but they do want a general sense of destination: where they will be heading in the story and who will be leading them there. In other words, they want a "ticket" at the beginning that identifies the journey ahead.

Such knowledge allows them to settle into the world of the story, pay most attention to what's most important, get emotionally invested in a main character, and begin to follow a throughline. Until this knowledge is acquired, the audience is working hard to get a handle on things. If they have to work too hard for too long, they may begin to feel it's not worth the effort.

A key goal is to make the audience care about what's going on. You have to somehow capture their attention and hopefully their hearts—you have to grab them—during the first ten minutes so that they will begin to focus not only on what's happening right now, but also on what could happen later. From a technical point of view, the function of story is to make the audience worry. They are most likely to do so if they like or at least empathize with the character in front of them.

By the time they are ten minutes into the story, the audience is consciously or subconsciously asking questions they want answered. Good stories tend to center around one big question that is raised early on and not answered until the end, and then lots of little questions that get raised and answered along the way. Questions keep the audience in two places at once: the present of the story (what's happening now) and the future (what might happen later). When the audience is in two places at once, they are leaning forward in their seats and fully engaged.

During the first ten minutes, you also need to show what the rules of the game are, especially if you are presenting a world which is in any way different from the everyday world outside the theater. Chekhov's advice is to establish these rules within the first few pages. If this is a world where ghosts will appear, for example, something ghostly or at least eerie should happen near the top of the story. The audience also wants a sense of genre as soon as possible. If it's a comedy, they want to know up front that they have permission to laugh. If it's a thriller, they want early warning signs of scary stuff ahead.

ABOUT THE EXERCISE

The following ten questions can help you strengthen the grabbing power of your story and are based on the idea that suspense comes from knowledge: in order to be grabbed, the audience needs to know what's going on. Exercise examples are from David Mamet's play *Edmond*.

■ THE FIRST TEN MINUTES OF YOUR SCRIPT

Read over the first ten pages of your script and answer these questions:

1. *Whose story is it, and how well have you established this?* When the story begins, we, the audience, are like strangers at a party who don't know anybody. We're all alone and want to latch on to someone as soon as possible so that we can start meeting the others through this new acquaintance.

You need to determine how quickly and how clearly you will let us know whose story it is. The sooner you do this, the better. We want to know where to put our focus, whom to invest ourselves in, and whose journey we will be following.

In *Edmond*, for example, the main character is Edmond. We know this from the title even before the story begins. If the play had a different title, we would still know it is Edmond's journey after the first few moments of scene 1, when he is having his fortune told: the focus is entirely on him and his future. If we had any doubts about this, we would know for sure moments later when scene 2 begins and it is not the fortune-teller but Edmond we see next at home.

2. *In one sentence, what happens during the first ten minutes?* During this time, the audience will be entering the world you have created, meeting your characters, and experiencing the first story events. They also will be consciously and subconsciously deciding whether or not to get involved in this dramatic journey. What happens during this time is critical. Hopefully, it introduces an interesting character in an interesting situation with strong emotional qualities.

By compressing your opening into one sentence, you may get a clearer vision of what's there and whether or not you need to heighten its impact. You may discover that you need to make more happen. Or you may discover that you need to make less happen. Either way, aim for character and story choices that will make the audience eager for more.

In one sentence, for example, here's what happens in *Edmond* during the first ten minutes, which includes three short scenes: a grim fortune spurs Edmond to walk out of a miserable marriage of many years and enter a threatening world of violence, racism, and back-room sex. The mysterious power of the fortune-telling, the emerging desire to change a life, and the radical shift in environment promise lots of dramatic and interesting, though certainly not easy, things ahead.

3. *What is the strongest image in the first ten minutes?* Theater is a highly visual experience. The living pictures that we see on stage or on screen often reveal more about the characters than their words do. Think about the visual images that come and go as your characters interact with each other and with their physical environment and the objects in it. Ideally, you have written a script that demands interesting and compelling images because of what's happening and what's being said. Look at the images you have built into the first ten minutes and see if they are strong enough to add grabbing power to your story.

In the opening of *Edmond*, for example, one of the most interesting and compelling images is that of the fortune-teller reading Edmond's palm. In some ways, it's a familiar sight—we have seen palm readers before—and, at the same time, it is unfamiliar. This is not an everyday occurrence for most of us, and its presence suggests a voyage into the unknown. It's the type of image that draws us in by automatically raising questions: what's the fortune-teller saying to this man? Is this for real or only a hoax? Will her predictions come true?

4. *What is the strongest action in the first ten minutes?* Characters are re-

vealed by what they do more than by what they say. So we, the audience, watch them and make inferences based on what we see and feel. This process engages us in the characters and helps us get to know them on an emotional level. What your main character does during the story's opening may be a critical factor in your ability to make the audience care.

A character's most important actions are usually those in which he or she is trying to affect another character in a meaningful way—whether positive or negative. They are actions driven by desire, obstacle, and high stakes, and they often center around important turning points in the character's life. Sometimes physical action rises to this level as well, especially in film.

In the opening of *Edmond*, one of the most interesting and compelling dramatic actions is that of Edmond ending his marriage after his wife complains about the maid breaking an antique lamp. His action is fueled by strong desire (to convince his wife that he doesn't love her), by an obstacle (he's been unable to express this to her for years), and by high stakes (his yearning for a new life).

One of the peaks of action here is Edmond's brutal confession to his wife: "You don't interest me spiritually or sexually." It's a sign of how deeply his soul has been stirred by the fortune-teller and a measure of how strong his motivation is. Characters at turning points like this have a way of grabbing our attention whether we like it or not.

5. *What is the inciting event, and has it happened yet?* Every story is a quest triggered by some type of turning-point experience that upsets the balance of the character's life in either a good or bad way. Ideally, this inciting event occurs onstage or onscreen after the story begins, but not too long after. In most plays and screenplays, the inciting event happens during the first ten minutes—or at least begins by then—because, until the inciting event occurs, the real engine of the story has not yet begun. In some screenplays, the inciting event is delayed to make room for a subplot.

In *Edmond*, the inciting event is the fortune-teller's warning that he is not where he belongs. This occurs on the second page and it's the first dramatic event of the story: it's what causes the story to take place.

6. *What new goal does the inciting event arouse in the main character, and how well have you established this?* The inciting event matters only when the main character knows about it and makes a conscious decision to do something about it: to restore the balance that has been upset.

A key word here is "conscious." The character knows what he or she must accomplish, or at least thinks so. In complex stories, there may also be a stronger subconscious goal that the character and the audience do not discover until much later. In either case, the story goal defines and drives the quest, and is only achieved, if ever, at the very end of the story. To grab the audience, let them in on what the main character is after, and why that's important. This knowledge will get us wondering whether or not the character will succeed, and will guide us to what's most important as the journey unfolds.

In *Edmond*, for example, the fortune-teller's warning arouses in Edmond the need to find where he belongs. This is implied by Edmond in the second scene when he tells his wife, "I'm going," and then later, "I'm not coming back," and then later, "I don't want to live this kind of life." All of this, coming right after the fortune-telling, shows us how much it has affected Edmond and defines his quest in the story. He doesn't find the kind of life he wants to live until the story's end—twenty-one scenes later.

7. *What are the rules of the game, and how well have you established them?* Drama is heightened reality, so even a naturalistic story may operate under laws, customs, and values that are unique to the world of the characters. Know the rules of the game for your story and show them or imply them as soon as possible. This is especially important if your story will depart from everyday reality, as in the case of magic realism. While establishing the rules, be sure it's clear what genre, or type of story, we are in.

Edmond, for example, is naturalistic drama. However, it takes us from the ordinary surface of New York life to a dark underworld where the top values are power, sex, and money, and the most common means to acquire them are treachery, theft, prostitution, violence, rape, and murder.

The nature of this world is established in scene 3 when Edmond meets a stranger at a bar who spews racial hatred, educates him about where to find a prostitute, and seals the deal with the buying of drinks. Within the first ten minutes of the story, we know what type of world Edmond is entering. We also understand that he can never return to what he left behind. The rules of the game have been drawn. We also have been prepared for a drama that will be told in short scenes of escalating tension.

8. *What big question has been raised?* Ideally, while watching a good story, the audience always has a big question lingering somewhere in the back of their minds. This big question is raised during the opening pages of the story and not answered until the final pages. It's a version of "How will it all turn out?" Know what big question you want the audience to ask and try to raise it within the first ten minutes.

In *Edmond*, the big question is "Will Edmond ever find his true place in the world?" This question begins to get raised right away with the inciting event—the fortune-teller's warning that he is not where he belongs—and is reinforced by the action of Edmond walking out of his marriage and the comforts of a middle-class home to seek a new life. The big question doesn't get answered until the end, after Edmond has been put in prison for murder and assaulted by a fellow prisoner. He finds his true place—and redemption—in the prison cell he shares with his attacker.

9. *What will make the audience wonder what happens next?* Ideally, while watching a good story, the audience is always wondering "what happens next?" These smaller questions tend to lead us into the next scene

or sequence, where they are usually answered and then replaced by new questions leading us forward again. Know what smaller question you want the audience to ask after the first ten minutes. This is the gateway to the rest of the story.

By the time we are ten minutes into *Edmond*, the stranger at the bar has stirred up some dangerous ideas and sent Edmond to the Allegro to meet a B-girl. The "what happens next" question is "What will happen to Edmond at the Allegro?" This question is raised by the trouble brewing: Edmond is a desperate man who has been drinking and is about to get more entangled in a dangerous underworld for which he is ill prepared. The question gets answered in the next scene: he does meet a B-girl, but gets ripped off and kicked out of the Allegro without getting sex.

10. *What is the strongest hook in your opening pages now?* Think about the characters, imagery, action, dialogue, backstory, and other elements at work in your first ten pages. Ideally, there is a hook that will grab the audience and make them want to go along for the ride. You may have already found this hook in your answers to the other questions. Determine what the hook is, what emotional response you want from the audience—for example, laughter, pity, anxiety, or anger—and whether you need to do more to make the audience care.

In *Edmond*, what grabs the audience by the throat is Edmond's desperate need to reinvent himself after seeing the awful truth about his life. Mixed in with this is the threat of danger that looms in the underworld. After the first three scenes, we are on a tightrope of emotion, hoping for the best and prepared for the worst. We are worried about where Edmond's quest will lead.

RETHINKING HOW YOUR STORY BEGINS

Focus on your response to the last question—what's the hook?—and explore some new possibilities:

1. In your mind's eye, watch what happens during the first ten pages of the story when you are introducing your characters. Focus on one important image in this sequence and how you might boost its grabbing power by changing it in some way—for example, by adding something, removing something, or exaggerating what's there now. Suppose the image is a man and a fortune-teller seated across the table from each other. The image could be heightened by moving the man's hand, palm up, into the fortune-teller's hand. This simple change creates a more visually dynamic interaction between them and more clearly defines without words what's going on. Briefly describe a new version of your image.

2. Bring the revised image to life with a line or two of dialogue that, like a photo caption, adds meaning to the visual content—for example, the fortune-teller is saying to the man, "You are not where you belong."

3. Look at the opening sequence again and take another, even bigger, creative leap. Find a completely new image that could be added to

this sequence. Imagine that this new image is more interesting and more powerful than anything you see there. Imagine that it has three elements: it centers around your main character, it has a strong emotional quality, and it is somehow startling or unusual. In other words, there is something about this new image that would make us look twice, raise a question, and make us want to know more. Describe the new image.

4. Bring the new image to new life with a line or two of dialogue that adds meaning to the visual content.

5. Will either or both of these images work in your opening? If so, how and where?

WRAP-UP

Use the opening of your story wisely. It's your best time to grab the audience by the throat and make them want to take the dramatic journey with you. Here is a summary of how to add grabbing power to the first ten minutes of your story:

- Introduce an interesting character with whom we can empathize, and make it clear that this is the main character of the story.
- Introduce an interesting dramatic situation with strong emotional qualities.
- Build in at least one interesting and compelling dramatic image, preferably one that centers around the main character.
- Make the main character active and use the actions to reveal something important and interesting about him or her.
- Introduce the story's inciting incident and let the main character be aware of it.
- Define the quest by establishing what story objective has been aroused consciously in the main character as a result of the inciting event.
- Establish the rules of the game so that we are prepared for the world we will be exploring.
- Raise an important big question that will not be fully answered until the end of the story.
- Raise an interesting smaller question that will make us want to see the next scene or sequence.
- Know what your strongest hook is and what emotional response you want from the audience at this point in the story.

Related tools in *Character, Scene, and Story.* For more help with the opening pages of your script, go to the "Building Your Story" section and try "In the Beginning."

STEP BY STEP

THE QUICK VERSION
Use a step outline to track and manage the events of your story

BEST TIME FOR THIS
Any time you want to identify story events and see how they connect

DRAMA AS LIFE IN TRANSITION
Webster defines transition as "a passing from one condition to another." In drama, this passing is the step-by-step movement from how a character is at the beginning of a story to how the character is at the end. We often enter the character's life just before—or sometimes just as—an important turning-point experience occurs. This event arouses a desire that turns the character's life in a new direction, either positive or negative. By the time the story ends, the character has changed. Something dramatic has happened. A transition has occurred.

Imagine a traveler who is in San Francisco and headed by train to New York. To reach the final destination, the traveler must make a journey and pass through a number of different cities along the way. Dramatic characters also make journeys. Instead of going from one city to another, they travel between other types of places—for example, from cowardice to bravery, or from honesty to corruption, or from failure to success. To make the journey, they must move through a number of different experiences along the way. These experiences are the steps of the story.

As you develop scenes, try to keep an eye on your main character's big transition, step by step, from beginning to end. A common problem in new scripts is a weak throughline. The main character's journey is not clear or seems illogical for that particular character. Or the journey unfolds too quickly or too slowly. Or it has too many steps or not enough. In some scripts, there simply is no transition. The whole story is told over and over in each scene, with the same dynamic repeated in slightly different ways. To create a big transition that works, you need these elements:

An established starting point. We won't know that a transition is taking place unless we first have a clear understanding of the starting point. If this is not well defined, we have no way to know when we have left it for somewhere else. If the character will move from honesty to corruption, for example, we will not understand the change unless the character's honesty has first been clearly demonstrated. Or, to use the travel analogy, we will not know that we left San Francisco unless we realize that's where we were to begin with.

An established end point. We also need to know where we have ended up. If this end point is not clearly shown, we have no way to compare it to the starting point and see that something important has changed. This is not to say that the story must avoid ambiguity—great stories often leave questions unanswered—but we need to sense that things have changed in a certain way. In the journey from honesty to corruption, for example, we must experience the corruption. Or, in the travel analogy, we must see the landmark that finally welcomes us to New York.

Steady movement. While life is full of sudden changes, it is difficult for a dramatic journey to hold our interest unless it unfolds steadily in a series of steps. If we stay in the same place too long, we grow tired of being there. (Is this still San Francisco?) If we move too quickly from one place to another, we have trouble following the journey. (How did we get to Chicago already?) By creating a steady, step-by-step transition, you enable us to follow and become part of the journey. These steps vary in size and importance, but their overall effect is one of ever-forward movement.

Steps that are unique. Each scene of the character's journey is different from the rest. Once we leave San Francisco, we arrive in Las Vegas and not San Francisco again. Once we leave Las Vegas, we arrive in Salt Lake City and not another Las Vegas. If each next step is truly different, we keep entering new territory and moving ahead to the final destination.

Steps that are connected. The steps of the story are woven together through cause and effect. Because that happened then, this will happen now. These dynamics make each event essential in the chain of events and create a logic that we can follow at gut level. In the journey by train from San Francisco to New York, for example, we would get confused if there were a stopover in Paris. While surprise can be effective dramatically, an illogical surprise can take us out of the story or make us feel we have gotten off track.

Steps that fit the character. There is no magic formula to determine what steps or how many steps a character must take in order to complete a dramatic journey. Just as there are a variety of possible routes and stopping points between San Francisco and New York, there are many different ways to move from honesty to corruption, or from love to hate, or from injustice to justice. Figuring out the steps of the story is one of the hardest tasks you face. It requires that you know not only who your character is, but also—at each new step—how the character's experience and knowledge has now changed as a result of the previous step.

Change that matters. If the transition of the story is too small, we will have a hard time staying interested in what goes on. We go to the theater to experience journeys that are meaningful and profound. For example, a journey from one thing to its opposite—from cowardice to bravery, from ugliness to beauty, or from infidelity to fidelity—can certainly be a journey worth watching. When in doubt, err on the side of being too bold.

Some stories go even further by taking us around the world so that the end point is the starting point again. In other words, we leave San Francisco and return there in the end. This type of journey can work dramatically if the San Francisco we ultimately reach is not the San Francisco we left. For example, if an honest man faces increasingly powerful temptations, succumbs to them, corrects his errors, and resists corruption in the end, his final honesty has more meaning because it has been tested in the real world and strengthened.

ABOUT THE EXERCISE

Use this exercise to create a step outline: a planning and revision tool that sums up the key events of your main character's dramatic journey. By compressing this journey to a manageable size, you can see it all at once, explore how events connect or don't connect, and determine whether you have the right events in the right order for the story you want to tell. A step outline is also a useful tool for eliminating events that do nothing more than duplicate other events or are tangents that lead nowhere and fail to support the central throughline.

To develop a step outline is to explore the dramatic continuum of the story, its inseparable past, present, and future. While focusing on what's happening here and now, each step reflects certain consequences of what has happened earlier and implies certain possibilities of what might happen later. This continuum is what creates the throughline and enables the big transition to occur.

You can use step outlines different ways. Some writers don't begin writing scenes until they have mapped out the whole story. Others wait until they have finished a first draft and extract the outline to see where to revise. Still others develop the step outline as they write so they have an ongoing way to track what they have so far.

Regardless of when and why you use the step outline, aim for one page per act and one or two sentences per event. Too much detail defeats the purpose. In *Search and Destroy* by Howard Korder, for example, the main character is Martin. Here are the first three steps of his dramatic journey as they might appear in a step outline:

1. A Florida state accountant informs Martin that he owes the state a lot in back taxes and will go to jail if he doesn't pay by a certain date.
2. Stressed out, Martin goes to his wife Lauren for comfort, but she asks him to leave: the relationship is over.
3. With nowhere else to turn, he goes to a party with brother-in-law Robert, who tells him about a New Age guru named Doctor Waxling.

As the dramatic journey continues, Martin will end up pursuing Waxling as part of a strategy to raise the money needed to stay out of jail. Martin's loneliness and isolation will push him to commit desperate and finally criminal acts. These first three events of the story prepare the way. The first event incites the whole story and leads directly to the second event which then leads to the third event, and so on.

■ DEVELOPING A STEP OUTLINE OF YOUR STORY

Identify the steps of your story and summarize each in a sentence or two. Remember that each step is a dramatic event: something important begins, ends, or changes and has an impact—positive or negative—on the world of the characters. In some cases, a "step" may be the equivalent of a "scene." In other cases, more than one step may occur within the same scene. For best results:

1. *Highlight the key steps.* The events of the story are not equally important. Some matter more than others. Identify the most important steps that occur as your character's big transition unfolds:

- *Inciting event.* What event arouses the main character's superobjective—the goal that drives the rest of the story—and thus launches the character's quest? (For more details about this type of dramatic event, review "Inciting Event" earlier in this guide.)
- *End-of-act reversal(s).* Each act ends with a significant turning point, often a reversal that radically changes the world of the story. For example, peace changes to war. Or war changes to peace. If your script has two acts, what is the turning point at the end of act 1? If your script has three acts, what are the turning points at the end of acts 1 and 2? (For more details about this type of dramatic event, review "Turning Points" next in this guide.)
- *Crisis.* The final act typically includes a crisis that leads to the climactic action and resolution of the dramatic journey. What step will pose the greatest crisis for your character? (For more details about this type of dramatic event, review "Crisis Decision" later in this guide.)

As you develop your step outline, remember to keep event descriptions brief. By keeping each act to about one page, you will have an at-a-glance view of the story and how it unfolds.

2. *Identify the connecting steps.* The key events of the story are connected by a certain number of intermediate steps that shape how the dramatic journey unfolds. Work in sections—sequence by sequence, act by act—to see how the story builds. For example, what intermediate steps connect the inciting event to the end-of-act reversal? If you are working with a three-act structure, what steps connect the reversal at the end of act 1 to the reversal

at the end of act 2? What steps connect the second reversal to the crisis of the story?

■ EVALUATING THE STEPS OF YOUR STORY

Use questions like these to review the steps of the story as you write and edit your script:

1. Are these the right steps for this unique character in this unique situation?

2. Does each step make sense based on what the character has experienced up to now, what the character knows now, and how the character feels now?

3. Is each step truly unique? Can any be eliminated because it duplicates what another step already accomplishes?

4. Does each step connect to least one other step in the story? Can any be eliminated because it is only a tangent with no significant impact elsewhere?

5. Do any new steps need to be added in order to motivate a later action or show more clearly why a later step occurs?

6. Is this the best order for these steps? What would happen if a critical event happened earlier or later in the chain of events?

7. What big transition does your main character undergo as a result of all these steps? Identify the poles of the journey: the starting point and end point.

8. How well do early steps establish the starting point?

9. How well do final steps establish the end point?

10. In summary, how well does the overall sequence of steps connect the starting point to the end point?

WRAP-UP

As you develop your story, try to stay aware of the big transition that your character is undergoing. Track the steps of this journey and be sure they make sense for this character in this situation. Many forks in the road will present themselves as you work, and it is easy to take a wrong turn every now and then—for example, to write a scene that doesn't really serve the whole. A step outline can help you avoid such pitfalls by keeping the throughline in view.

> **Related tools in *Character, Scene, and Story*.** To continue thinking about the events of your story and how they connect, go to the "Building Your Story" section and try "The Dramatic Continuum" or "Two Characters in Search of a Story."

TURNING POINTS

THE QUICK VERSION
Flesh out two basic types of turning-point experiences

BEST TIME FOR THIS
Any time during story development

MANEUVERING THE TURNS OF THE DRAMATIC JOURNEY
A character's dramatic journey typically includes a number of turning points: experiences, large or small, positive or negative, that move the character's life in different directions. These are often times when decisions must be made.

It is typically a turning point that launches the character's quest, that brings each act to its conclusion, and that triggers the climax of the story. To function as a true turning point, the experience must change the character's course of action from this point forward so that a new, untried path must be taken. The first step on this new path may be a small, subtle shift or a large and obvious change.

Some turning points are things that happen to the character. They are caused by someone or something else, but have a significant impact on the character's future. The agent of change might be an individual, group, organization, or government. Or it might be the force of nature or chance. The character here is passive. This type of turning point usually works best early in the story, when we are more likely to accept character passivity and believe events that occur only by chance. In many cases, the inciting event of the story is something that happens to the character. For example, the city where you live is invaded by Nazis (*The Pianist*).

Some turning points are things that your character does. Whether the action is wise or unwise, and whether its consequences are expected or unforeseen, the character initiates a change. For example, you decide to become a ballet dancer in spite of your father's disapproval (*Billy Elliot*). The character in this case is active: a doer who causes a new sequence of events. This type of turning point can work well anywhere in the story and becomes increasingly important in the latter half, when we most need active characters to keep us engaged.

Turning points vary in size and scope. Major turning points are sometimes known as "reversals": experiences so powerful that they force the dramatic journey into a radically different—often opposite—direction. A reversal can be something that happens to the character or something that the character does. Either way, its effects are large and far-reaching. The turning point at the end of each act is often a reversal. At the end of act 1, the reversal forces the story into the new territory of act 2. In the final act, the reversal forces the story to its climax and conclusion.

ABOUT THE EXERCISE

Use this exercise to explore the causes and effects of two basic types of turning points: something that happens to the character and something that the character does. As you do this, look for opportunities to flesh out what you already know about your story, and try to make new discoveries in the process. Exercise examples are from my play *How I Became an Interesting Person*.

■ **SOMETHING THAT HAPPENS TO YOUR CHARACTER**

Think about the different turning points that your character experiences in the story. Choose one where something important happens to your character. It's a change caused by someone or something else. In *How I Became an Interesting Person*, for example, someone leaves a matchbook on Wayne's desk with an ad that reads, "Ever feel like you're just too boring?" If you can't find this type of event in your story, look for one in the backstory. Briefly sum up the turning point: the important thing that happens to your character. Then use the following steps to explore this event in more depth:

Causes of this turning point

1. *Agent of change.* You already know that this is someone or something other than your character. Identify the primary direct cause of the turning point—for example, the matchbook was the anonymous work of Wayne's boss Judy.

2. *Reason.* The turning point may be the intended result of someone wanting to affect your character. Or it may be a matter of accident or chance. In the case of the matchbook, Wayne's boss fully intended to send him a message about his personality. Think about what happens to your character. Did the agent of change intend to affect your character in some way?

- *If the impact was intentional*, identify the specific motivation behind it. For example, Wayne's boss wanted him to realize how boring everyone in the office thought he was.
- *If the impact was not intentional,* consider the reason for what happened. If the agent of change is another person or group, what motivated the action? If the agent of change is a thing or blind force, what set it into motion?

3. *Contributing factor.* Other forces from the past or from the bigger picture of the present may have played a less direct role in what happens to your character. These background influences may be other people, organi-

zations, or perhaps even society itself. Or they may be events that occurred in the past or are taking place elsewhere now. For example, office politics played a background role in the decision to taunt Wayne: it was a way of establishing the pecking order. Think about the contributing factors that could possibly share the credit or blame for what happens to your character. Identify an important contributing factor.

Effects of this turning point

1. *Immediate emotional impact*. If this is indeed a true turning-point experience, it will produce an important change of some kind, positive or negative, and set your character on a new, untried path of action. Think about the significant short-term impact of this experience on your character, starting with its emotional effect. After discovering the matchbook on his desk, for example, Wayne experiences a gamut of feelings—from anger to hurt to panic. In your story, what is the short-term emotional impact of the turning point on your character?

2. *Immediate intellectual impact*. Think about how the experience affects your character intellectually. It will somehow influence what's going on in the character's mind. Perhaps it will rekindle old memories or stir up new ideas. These thoughts may later prove to be true or false, profound or trivial, helpful or harmful. After discovering the matchbook on his desk, for example, Wayne realizes that he is, in fact, a boring person. In your story, what is going through your character's mind immediately after the turning-point experience? Briefly identify an important memory, idea, perception, or conclusion, and state it in your character's unique voice like a line of inner monologue.

3. *Analysis*. Wayne's feelings of distress and realization of boringness will eventually prove to be a helpful first step in his escape from an isolated life. Though painful, it's good that he sees the truth now. If you were to step back from your character's turning point and look at it within the context of the whole story, how would you evaluate your character's thoughts and feelings now?

4. *New desire*. Thoughts and feelings often lead to desires which, in turn, lead to behavior, and that puts us into the realm of drama. Some desires are short-term: they drive only the next scene or sequence of the story. Some are long-term: they drive the rest of the story. Wayne's matchbook experience, for example, is the inciting event of the play so the desire it sparks is a big one: the need to find a connection in the world. This is Wayne's primary objective in the play. Short- or long-term, what new desire is stirred up in your character by the turning point?

5. *Personal impact*. Some of the traits that define us individually are genetic. We inherit them from our parents whether we like it or not. Some traits are acquired: the product of our life experiences. Such traits may be physical, psychological, or social. A turning-point experience probably has a

significant effect on your character in one or more of these areas. It may re-inforce a trait that's already there, change a trait that's already there, or lead to the development of a new trait or habit. For example, Wayne's match-book leads him to change several defining traits by the time the story is over. He evolves from an isolated narcissist who cannot handle the truth into a socially involved and loving person who can face the world honestly. In your story, how does the turning point affect your character? Describe at least one important way that the experience affects your character's identity.

6. *Resulting event.* Dramatic events are connected through cause and effect. A turning point, by definition, will lead to a new chain of events that would not have otherwise happened. In most cases, the experience triggers the next event, but sometimes the effect is not seen until later. For example, Wayne's discovery of the matchbook prompts the next step of the story: Wayne goes out and buys the self-help book being advertised. This, in turn, prompts him to follow several different sets of advice from a guru named Doctor Betty X.

Think about your story and identify one important event that is directly caused by the turning point you are exploring. This is a discovery, revelation, success, failure, or other event that can be directly linked back to this turning point and occurs only because of it.

7. *New possibility.* Think about your unique character's dramatic journey. Then try to see the turning point and its possible effects with new eyes. As an exercise, look for something completely new and define another event that the turning point could possibly lead to either next in the story or later down the road. This is an event that could conceivably make sense for your particular character in your particular story, but is not actually in your script now. Take a creative leap and briefly describe this new possibility.

8. *Key short-term change.* Think about how you would sum up the imme-diate effects of this turning-point experience in your story. In the short term, for example, the matchbook ad prompts Wayne to begin a self-help program that he would not otherwise have even considered. In your story, what is the most important short-term change that the turning point pro-duces or might produce?

> *A turning point is a river of no return. Once this river has been crossed, the characters cannot go back to the other side. They must continue forward into the unknown territory that now lies ahead.*

9. *Key long-term change.* Now consider the long-range consequences of this turning point. These effects may be less direct than the one you just identified, but still have an important link back to this event and the knowl-

edge and experience your character gained from it. In the long term, for example, the matchbook ad leads Wayne to find love and truth where he least expected it: in his landlady Mrs. Walker. In your story, what is the most important long-term change that results from this turning point?

■ SOMETHING THAT YOUR CHARACTER DOES

Some turning points are caused directly by the character. For example, Wayne decides to romance his much older landlady Mrs. Walker. This decision leads to a major shift in his behavior in the second act, when he begins to pursue Mrs. Walker rather than flee from her. Think about your story and choose one character action that significantly changes the direction of the character's life for better or for worse. Then use the following steps to explore this action in more depth:

Causes of this turning point

1. *Reason.* Think about your character's motivation. Identify the most direct and immediate reason for this action here and now. Include what your character expects to happen as a result of it. For example, Wayne decides to romance Mrs. Walker because he has fallen in love with her. He is worried, however, that he will say or do the wrong thing and drive her away.

2. *Highest stake at risk.* What's at stake for your character is what will be gained if the action is successful or lost if it's not. If this is a critical turning point, the stakes are probably high, but are they high enough? Consider what the character has experienced so far in life, and what the character now knows and believes. See if you can raise the stakes in a way that would add importance and urgency to the story. For example, what's at stake for Wayne is love. This high stake could be even higher if he sees Mrs. Walker as his last chance for love: it's now or never. Briefly identify the highest version of what's at stake for your character.

3. *Contributing factor.* Think about the contributing factors from the past or from the bigger picture of the present that could possibly share some of the credit or blame for your character's turning-point action. Identify one important contributing factor or background influence. For example, Wayne has felt lonely and isolated since his last girlfriend unexpectedly jilted him.

Effects of this turning point

1. *Immediate emotional impact.* Think about the immediate consequences of what your character does, starting with the emotional impact. Briefly describe how your character feels as a result of this turning-point action. For example, Wayne feels exhilarated and anxious about his decision to woo Mrs. Walker.

2. *Immediate intellectual impact.* Think about the short-term intellectual impact of this action on your character. Briefly identify one new belief, idea, perception, discovery, or conclusion that results from the experience and state it in your character's unique voice like a line of inner monologue. When Wayne now compares the other parts of his life to a life with Mrs. Walker, for example, he realizes that "nothing—*nothing*—seems quite as interesting as it did before."

3. *Analysis.* How would you evaluate this thinking within the context of the whole story? For example, is it true or false, profound or trivial, helpful or harmful? Wayne's fundamental shift in interest from his own little world to Mrs. Walker's world is a healthy change that will lead eventually to his redemption.

4. *New desire.* Think about how this action reflects a change in what your character wants—either in the next scene or perhaps for the rest of the story. Short-term or long-term, briefly identify the new objective that results. In making the decision to woo Mrs. Walker, Wayne now wants to find out who she really is.

5. *Personal impact.* Identify one key way that the experience affects your character physically, psychologically, or socially. Wayne's interest in Mrs. Walker begins to make him more interesting and attractive to other people in his life.

6. *Resulting event.* Name one important event that this turning point causes—either next in the story or later on. This is a discovery, revelation, success, failure, or other experience that can be directly linked back to this turning point and occurs only because of it. Wayne will invite Mrs. Walker up to his room for dinner and end up spending the night with her.

7. *New possibility.* As an exercise, look for something completely new and identify another possible consequence of this turning-point action— something that could result either next in the story or later on. Try to find an event that could conceivably make sense for your particular character in your particular story, but is not actually there now. Take a creative leap and describe the new possibility. Wayne's affection for Mrs. Walker will prompt her to reveal her deepest secret: her son Bobby killed her husband Colonel Walker to put him out of his misery and is now serving a life sentence at San Quentin Prison.

8. *Key short-term change.* In summary, what is the most important short-term change that occurs as a result of your character's turning-point action? Wayne becomes one who fights for what he wants instead of one who flees from what he doesn't want.

9. *Key long-term change.* In summary, what is the most important long-term change that occurs—directly or indirectly—as a result of your character's turning-point action? Wayne ends up in a meaningful relationship with Mrs. Walker.

WRAP-UP

Whether a turning point is something that happens to your character or something your character does, it has causes and effects worth exploring. Know how turning points arise and, for better or for worse, how they change the world of the story.

Related tools in *Character, Scene, and Story*. To explore a turning point in more depth, go to the "Causing a Scene" section and try "Why This? Why Now?" Or go to the "Building Your Story" section and try "What Just Happened?"

WHAT HAPPENS NEXT?

THE QUICK VERSION
Explore ways to build suspense in your story

BEST TIME FOR THIS
After you are well into story development

THE ART OF SUSPENSE
One of the functions of dramatic storytelling is to keep the audience in two places at once: the present and the future. This means that, as the audience participates in the "here and now" events of the story, they are also anticipating the possible outcomes of what they see. They are wondering what happens next. When this phenomenon occurs, the audience is in suspense.

Suspense is a critical element of not just thrillers but all dramatic stories. "Suspense" here refers to a state of being undecided or uncertain, and even in comedy is characterized by anxiety. If the audience is worried about what happens next, they are involved in the story. If they are not in a state of anticipation—a state of looking forward—you may have lost them, because they either don't care about the future of your characters or have already figured it out.

As Alfred Hitchcock pointed out in his interview with François Truffaut, suspense is different from surprise. When we are surprised, we had no idea what would happen. Something popped out of the blue and took us off guard. Surprise may produce an emotional reaction—perhaps a laugh or even a gasp—but lasts for only a moment. When we are in suspense, we have clues about how a situation may unfold, but cannot be sure of what the actual outcome will be. More than one outcome is possible, and we worry about which will occur. Suspense, unlike surprise, can last for a long time—even for the whole story, if handled properly.

To get involved and to anticipate outcomes, we need to know—or at least think we know—what the character is trying to accomplish here and now. This means that suspense is as much a product of knowledge as lack of knowledge. We believe we know what the character wants, but we don't know whether or not this objective will be achieved. Knowledge and lack of knowledge: both must be present for suspense.

Some of the questions that create suspense are small. They lead us, beat by beat, through the scene. Some of the questions are bigger. They lead us, scene by scene, through the story. Such questions tend to get answered soon after they are raised, so we keep gaining enough new knowledge to feel in on what's happening instead of shut out from it. One scene often answers a question raised by the previous scene.

In Tony Kushner's *Angels in America*, we are introduced to two men in an office. One is Roy Cohn, a powerful, ruthless lawyer juggling a barrage of demanding phone calls at his desk. The other is Joe Pitt, a Mormon who waits across the desk and manages to request that the shouting, cursing Cohn please not take the name of the Lord in vain. This scenario stirs up the question "Why are these two very different men together?"

The question is answered near the end of the scene: Roy has brought Joe here to offer him a big job in Washington with the Justice Department. This answer then raises a new question: "Will Joe accept the job and move to Washington?" This question, however, is not answered during the scene. Joe must think it over and talk with his wife first. Though a complete event has occurred—Joe gets a job offer—the scene ends in uncertainty. This leads us to wonder what will happen next, creates the need for another scene, and weaves a pattern of suspense where questions are answered as they are raised, and raised as they are answered.

Drama also creates suspense by stirring up a grand question that draws us in at the beginning and doesn't get answered until the end. This keeps us ever involved and looking forward with uncertainty. The grand question is what holds us in suspense during those small, quiet moments of the story. It is what keeps us from leaving at intermission or dozing off in our seats if we didn't like this scene or that. It is the big question always somewhere in the back of our minds waiting to be answered.

How will Hamlet avenge his father's mysterious death? What drives George and Martha to play dangerous games with people they've just met? How will George and Lennie ever make their dream of a rabbit farm come true? Grand questions like these keep us glued to our seats for hours if we empathize with the characters, know what they want, and worry about their destinies. We have both knowledge and lack of knowledge. We await the outcome. We watch in suspense.

ABOUT THE EXERCISE

This exercise asks you to think of your story as a series of questions and answers. You may need to find new material to complete some of the steps. Stay true to what you know about your story and take creative leaps from there. Examples are from *A Streetcar Named Desire* by Tennessee Williams.

■ SUSPENSE AT THE STORY LEVEL

Think about the questions your story raises and how they do or don't get answered:

1. *Grand question.* Imagine your main character's dramatic journey as a question—not three questions, not two questions, but one question: a

grand question. This is the biggest question that your story raises. Ideally, it is stirred up near the beginning of the story and never fully answered until the end. For example, the grand question might be "Will Blanche find a safe refuge in a cruel world?" Identify the grand question of your story.

2. **Prompts.** Suspense results from both knowledge and lack of knowledge. In order to ask a question, we must first acquire certain information. These are the facts that form part of a picture, but not all of it, and help us figure out what to ask. Such facts must be established as quickly as possible so that the suspense of the story can begin to build early on. Will Blanche find a safe refuge in a cruel world? To stir up this question, author Williams establishes the following facts about Blanche:

- She has entered a harsh environment: a French Quarter where heat bakes everything in sight, prostitutes wait on corners, and the forlorn songs of flower women echo through the streets.
- She has arrived at a new home where she doesn't fit: her married sister's home is a small, shabby apartment with little room for a third.
- She is a desperate person who's not what she seems. When alone, Blanche rummages through the apartment to find liquor and down a strong belt. With Stella later, however, Blanche pretends she's not much of a drinker.
- She no longer has a home of her own. This is revealed when Blanche tells Stella that Belle Reve, their family estate, has been lost.

All of these facts are established in the opening two scenes of the play and lead us to form a question about this desperate, homeless woman finding herself in a harsh environment where her only shelter is an apartment with no room for her. What's she going to do? Will Blanche find a safe refuge in this cruel world? This is the grand question that the play has raised and will proceed to answer.

Think about your story and the grand question it raises. What knowledge do we need in order to begin asking this question? Identify at least three facts that are introduced early in the story to prompt the grand question and begin building suspense. State each fact simply and objectively.

3. **Final answer.** What is the final answer to the grand question of your story? This is the information that is not provided until the end. It is what we discover as a result of watching all of the story events unfold. Will Blanche find a safe refuge in a cruel world? The final answer is "Yes, but it's a mental asylum."

Think about the final answer to your grand question. If it is a complex question, the answer may be complex, too, as in *Streetcar*, where Blanche gets what she wants, but it's not what she expected. Identify the final answer to your grand question. Try to include a "but" qualification that deepens or colors its meaning.

4. **Supporting evidence.** Think about the final answer to your grand ques-

tion and the events that must occur before it can be answered logically and truthfully. In *Streetcar,* the final answer—"Yes, but it's a mental asylum"—can be true only if Blanche has no other options. During the story, therefore, the following events will occur:

- Blanche will lose the only place she has left to stay: the home of Stanley and Stella. Blanche accomplishes this by alienating and then enraging Stanley. He wants her out of his home so badly he buys her a bus ticket himself.
- She will lose Mitch, her last hope for marriage and a home of her own. She accomplishes this by lying to Mitch about her age and tawdry past, and then getting Stanley angry enough to rat on her to Mitch.
- She will lose herself: the shreds of what's left of her ability to take care of herself. This happens when she is attacked by Stanley in the climactic scene and ends up with nothing left to rely on but the kindness of strangers.

Once developments like these have occurred, the final answer to the grand question of *Streetcar* becomes logical and truthful. Think about your main character's actions and what happens as a result of them. Name three of the most important events that must occur in the story to make the answer to your grand question logical and truthful. State each event simply and objectively.

■ SUSPENSE AT THE SCENIC LEVEL

Choose any one scene from your story for suspense analysis. You've already explored material from your early story, so, to avoid duplication, you might want to choose a later scene. The following examples are from scene 9 of *Streetcar*.

1. *Scenic question.* The grand question of your story breaks down into smaller but still important questions that move us from scene to scene and, within each scene, from beat to beat. In *Streetcar,* when Stanley informs Mitch that Blanche is not a genteel aristocrat but a prostitute fleeing a scandal, the question is raised "Will Blanche be able to keep Mitch now that he knows the truth?" This is the question that scene 9 will answer.

Ideally, your scene also addresses an important question that is triggered near the start of the scene or that has been raised previously—for example, a question that was left undecided or uncertain in the last scene. The current scene then goes about the task of answering this question. Think about what happens in your scene. Identify the most important question that it tackles and indicate when this question is raised: during the scene or before it.

2. *Scenic answer.* While the grand question isn't answered until the end of the story, the scenic- and beat-level questions get answered along the way while the audience is still involved in them. In *Streetcar,* it doesn't

take Mitch long to act on the tawdry news about Blanche. Once the question is raised—"Will Blanche be able to keep Mitch now that he knows the truth?"—we are into the scene which answers it. A drunk Mitch comes to the apartment to confront her as a whore, hold a lightbulb to her face to see her true age, and break off the relationship in disgust. When the scene is over, the answer to the question is clear: "No, Blanche has lost Mitch forever." Think again about your scene and the main question it tackles. Write the answer that is shown to us by the scene.

3. **Supporting evidence.** When a scene tackles a question that has been raised earlier, certain events must occur during the scene to make the answer logical and truthful. Suppose the answer to the scenic question is: "No, Blanche has lost Mitch forever." To make the answer logical and truthful, the scene must show us certain events, such as:

- The truth must be aired. Mitch has to confront Blanche with the sordid details that he now knows about her.
- Mitch must destroy everything between them by treating Blanche like a whore and letting her know that they are finished.
- Blanche must do everything she can to win Mitch back and she must clearly fail.

These scenic developments show us that the answer to the question is true. The relationship between Blanche and Mitch is over, and there is no way it will ever be repaired. Think about the question and answer you just identified for the scene you are analyzing. Identify at least three things that must happen during the scene to make that answer logical and truthful.

4. **New question.** While a good scene tackles an important question and then answers it, suspense continues because during that answer a new question is raised. When the scene ends, something else is undecided or undetermined. As we witness the failure of the relationship between Mitch and Blanche, for example, we are left with a new question: "What will Blanche do with no hope for love?" This leads us to the next scene, where Blanche retreats into a mad world of fantasy with old fancy clothes from her trunk and ends up being raped by her sister's husband. What new question does your scene raise before it ends? Write the new question to show what is uncertain or undecided at the end of the scene.

WRAP-UP

You've begun to explore how you can use questions and answers to keep the audience engaged. Continue to think about the grand question that your story raises and the final answer it provides. Has the grand question been raised soon enough and clearly enough? Is it an interesting and meaningful question that will hold the audience in suspense for a whole story? Has the final answer been revealed as late as possible? Can it include something unexpected? Whether the answer is positive or negative, does it feel satisfactory for the type of story you are developing?

As you write the beats of the scenes, and the scenes of the story, keep the audience in suspense by giving them the information they need to ask smaller questions along the way. Don't make them wait too long for the answers. Does each scene address a question raised by an earlier scene? Does the scene end with something uncertain so that we want to see what happens next? Can the unanswered question at the end be more interesting? How and when does this question get answered?

Related tools in *Character, Scene, and Story.* To flesh out the causes and effects of a dramatic event, go to the "Building Your Story" section and try "What Just Happened?" To continue exploring how scenes connect, try "The Dramatic Continuum" or "An End in Sight" in the same section.

POINTING AND PLANTING

THE QUICK VERSION
Use foreshadowing to strengthen your story's throughline

BEST TIME FOR THIS
Any time during story development

FIGURING OUT HOW AND WHY EVENTS
FIT TOGETHER IN A SEQUENCE
In a horror movie, when a thunderstorm suddenly begins to rage, we know that trouble lies ahead. If we are engaged in the story, we will now wait to see how and when that trouble occurs. While thunder and lightning have become clichés to foreshadow conflict, they illustrate part of a preparation process essential to the development of any type of dramatic story. This process has two basic steps: setup and payoff.

In some cases, such as the ominous thunderstorm, we understand the significance of the setup as it occurs. It's what shifts our attention forward and makes us worry about what will happen next. In other cases, we do not understand the significance of the setup until later. For example, a botanist sets out to find a rare flower that blooms only in moonlight in a faraway corner of the world. His search is successful but results in an animal attack that he survives without serious injury. Back home a month later, he begins to experience blackouts. A fortuneteller reveals that he bears the mark of a werewolf. This pronouncement is a payoff that makes us think back to the animal attack we saw earlier. We now realize that the attacker was a werewolf and understand how the fortuneteller's words could be true.

A setup that foreshadows conflict and shifts our attention forward, like the thunderstorm, is sometimes called a "pointer." A setup that later authenticates conflict and shifts our attention backward, like the exotic animal attack, is a "plant." Just as a pointer suggests that something might happen later, a plant tells us in retrospect that what's happening now is a believable development in the world of this story. In both cases, the setup is what makes the payoff work. More often than not, the payoff then becomes a setup for another payoff later.

Whether or not you view your story as suspenseful, you are probably creating a series of setups and payoffs as you develop the throughline. Such patterns are an instinctive part of figuring out how and why story events fit together in a sequence. You may benefit from becoming more aware of these preparation tactics and how they can add storytelling power to your script.

This technical exercise can help you use foreshadowing to strengthen your story's throughline and heighten suspense. The exercise might be most useful during revision as you focus on how story events connect and inform one another.

■ DIFFERENT TYPES OF POINTERS

When used near the beginning of a story, foreshadowing can hook us into the dramatic journey by enabling us to sense the type of showdown that looms at the end of the line. The most fundamental way to foreshadow conflict is to introduce equally strong forces and set them into motion on a collision course where neither can avoid the other. This typically translates into willful characters with opposing and uncompromising needs.

In Sam Shepard's *True West*, for example, we meet two very different brothers: Austin, a hack Hollywood scriptwriter with a family and middle-class lifestyle, and Lee, a loner and drifter who makes his living by burglarizing suburban homes. The ever-feuding brothers now find themselves face to face for the first time in five years. Austin has come here to housesit for Mom while she is on vacation, and Lee has shown up unexpectedly. As they clash over the rules of Mom's house and the keys to Austin's car, we begin to witness the competition that keeps these brothers at odds. We also sense a major and possibly violent showdown between them by the time the story ends.

Foreshadowing can be useful not only at the beginning of a story, but also throughout as a way to build suspense. Besides putting two equally matched characters on a collision course, you can use pointers like these to stimulate suspense:

1. **Provoking trait, quality, or condition.** In David Auburn's *Proof,* while Catherine is having a heart-to-heart talk with her father, a famous mathematician who went mad, she suddenly realizes that her father died a week ago and that she really has been talking to herself. As a result of this discovery, we will now wait to find out how much of her father's madness she has inherited.

2. **Provoking action.** In Beth Henley's *Crimes of the Heart*, Babe shoots and nearly kills her husband Zachary. When the police her ask why, she explains that she "didn't like his looks." As a result of her action and unusual rationale, we begin to wonder why Babe really shot her husband and what legal fate awaits her.

3. **Statement of willful intent.** In August Wilson's *The Piano Lesson*, Boy Willie announces his intention to sell the family piano, which his sister wants to keep. He warns that if she resists his plan, he will cut the piano in two and sell his half of it. His words create suspense as we wait to see whether he will actually carry out the threat.

4. **Announcement, warning, or prediction that something will occur.** In Ed-

ward Albee's *Who's Afraid of Virginia Woolf?* though it is now the middle of the night after just getting home from a party, Martha informs her husband George that guests are coming. As we watch Martha spar with George over this news, we wait for the doorbell to ring and worry about what will happen when the guests arrive. In William Shakespeare's *Macbeth*, the three witches make psychic predictions throughout the play that foreshadow future events, such as the brewing mix of victory and evil that will put Macbeth on the throne as the "King hereafter." Because these prophecies are fueled by supernatural powers, we wait to see how and when they will be fulfilled.

5. *Revelation or discovery about the past.* In Edward Albee's *The Goat, or, Who is Sylvia? (Notes Toward a Definition of Tragedy)*, Martin, a famous architect, decides to tell his best friend a secret of many months: Martin has been having a love affair with a goat. The startling revelation leads us to wonder how Martin's marriage, career, and life will be affected.

6. *Unanswered question.* In John Pielmeier's *Agnes of God*, an innocent young nun gives birth to a child found dead in her arms. She claims to have had a virgin birth, but cannot remember it or the infant's death. Martha, a court-appointed psychiatrist, wants to find out what really happened. The mystery generates suspense as we wait to find out who impregnated Agnes, and how and why the child died.

7. *A "loaded" object or other physical element.* In Henrik Ibsen's *A Doll's House*, Nora is being blackmailed over a forgery that she committed years ago and that her banker husband Torvald knows nothing about. Now a blackmail letter incriminating Nora sits visibly in a locked glass letterbox that only her husband can open. We wait to see when he will notice the letter and how he will react to its news.

Each of these pointers leads eventually to a payoff in which a question is answered or an expectation is fulfilled—often in a way we didn't expect. The delay between the setup and payoff varies from story to story, but is generally long enough to give us time to think about the significance of the pointer and to anticipate—and often worry about—the different outcomes that could result further down the road.

■ **DIFFERENT TYPES OF PLANTS**
Placed strategically throughout the script, plants are often key to making the events of the dramatic journey—particularly extreme, unusual, or surprising events—believable and understandable. Plants do this by establishing important character and story facts as true before they are needed to motivate or explain story action. Plants can also add to the emotional impact of such events by enabling us to witness them with broader vision and deeper insight.

Unlike the pointer, which is meant to draw attention to itself, the plant works best when at first its special significance for the future goes unnoticed. The more seamlessly the plant is inserted into the script, the more satisfying the payoff it can produce later. A clumsy plant defeats its own purpose by making its presence feel contrived and its purpose, predictable.

With skillful preparation, a dramatic writer can make anything believable, whether it's a woman who could force her invalid mother's hand onto a burning hot stovetop in Martin McDonagh's play *The Beauty Queen of Leenane,* or a man who could fall in love with a life-size inflatable doll in Nancy Oliver's screenplay *Lars and the Real Girl.* Most of the dramatic elements that can become pointers can also become plants. Instead of arousing anticipation, however, their purpose is to stimulate reflection and acceptance. Plants can be fashioned from such elements as these:

1. *A trait, quality, or condition that will become important later.* In the film adaptation of L. Frank Baum's *The Wizard of Oz*, we see the Wicked Witch acting skittish around water. This behavior may not seem significant, but it's a clue to her greatest vulnerability and ultimate fate: if the Wicked Witch gets wet, she melts into a puddle. In Eugene O'Neill's play *Long Day's Journey into Night*, we learn that mother Mary Tyrone had a restless sleep last night and poor appetite this morning. Such discoveries are preparing us for the news later that Mary has lapsed back into morphine addiction.

2. *A belief or attitude that will motivate later action.* In Tracy Letts's play *Bug,* Peter believes that, during his stint as a soldier in the Persian Gulf War, the army subjected him to secret experiments that have left him infested with bugs. This belief lays the groundwork for a claustrophobic nightmare in which he and his lover Agnes find themselves surrounded by bugs and military predators.

3. *A statement with hidden significance.* In the opening of Clifford Odets's play *The Golden Boy,* Joe talks about a boxer who died in an automobile accident and later describes his own love of fast cars as "poison in my blood." Throughout the story, he is warned about the dangers of fast cars and speeding. As a result of such plants, we accept Joe's death in an automobile accident as a grim inevitability.

4. *A rule or ritual that will be violated later.* In John Patrick Shanley's *Doubt,* when Father Flynn arrives for a meeting with Sister Aloysius, he must wait outside her office door until Sister James arrives because it is taboo for a priest and nun to be alone. This plant adds fire to the confrontation between Flynn and Aloysius at the end of the play when he storms into her office without a third party present.

5. *A physical element that will gain importance later.* In David Lindsay-Abaire's *Rabbit Hole,* a mother sorting and folding her child's freshly laundered clothing does not seem to have much significance. Yet this clothing will add an emotional wallop to the discovery later that her child died eight months ago and that she finally has reached the point in the healing process where she can take his things to Goodwill.

> *Planting can help you avoid* **deus ex machina** *endings in which the solution to a problem is an improbable coincidence that has little to do with preceding story events. By introducing facts and objects before they matter, you will have the elements in place to fashion a credible ending that grows out of what has happened in the story.*

6. *An event that is not what it seems.* In M. Night Shyamalan's film *The Sixth Sense*, Malcolm arrives late for an anniversary dinner with his wife at a nice restaurant. She ignores him, gets up in tears, and leaves. Her departure seems like an understandable reaction to having been stood up for an important date. However, it is actually one of several plants throughout the story that prepare Malcolm and the audience for the surprising discovery that he is dead.

7. *An event that will be mirrored later on a larger scale.* In John Steinbeck's *Of Mice and Men,* Lennie doesn't know his own strength and accidentally kills a mouse that he was only trying to pet. Unknown to the characters at the time, this event presages Lennie's accidental killing of Curley's wife. Because of the plant, we understand that the childlike Lennie was only trying to pet her soft pretty hair.

Each of these plants eventually helps explain an unusual, extreme, or surprising development later in the story, or adds emotional impact to it. As with the pointer, there is a delay between the setup and payoff. In this case, the delay gives us time to accept a certain character or story fact as true so that we have an established context for understanding the payoff and accepting it as a credible event in the world of this story.

■ FORESHADOWING AN IMPORTANT CONFLICT OR EVENT

You can repeat these steps as often as needed to strengthen your story's throughline:

1. *Identify a conflict or event that would benefit from foreshadowing.* This conflict might be an important event that you want us to wonder or worry about before it happens (Boy Willie threatens to cut the piano in half). Or, it might be an event that is so extreme (Lennie kills Curley's wife), so unusual (the Wicked Witch melts), or so surprising (Malcolm is a ghost who doesn't realize he's dead) that we might find it difficult to understand or accept as credible. Or, it might be an event with an emotional impact that you wish to heighten (Flynn confronts Aloysius in her office without a third party present).

2. *Choose a general foreshadowing technique.* Think of the event as a payoff. In doing so, you can no longer look at the event in isolation. Rather,

you must see it in relationship to at least one earlier event or element in the story. This setup may already be in your script in a form that requires further development. Or, there may be no relevant setup in the script yet. Either way, you need to decide what you want the setup to accomplish. Will it be a pointer that stimulates our anticipation of the payoff? Or, will it be a plant that prepares us to accept the payoff when it occurs later?

3. *Choose a specific foreshadowing device.* Brainstorm a few "what if" scenarios to explore dramatic possibilities and determine how you might integrate foreshadowing into the unique throughline of your story.

If you wish to develop a pointer to make us anticipate the payoff, ask yourself the following questions:

- *What if* the pointer were a provoking trait? Which character would you focus on? What trait would you highlight, and how?
- *What if* the pointer were a provoking action? Who would do what to make us anticipate a payoff of some kind?
- *What if* the pointer were a statement of willful intent? Who would state this objective to whom, and why? What would the objective be?
- *What if* the pointer were a statement about the future? Who would make this statement, and why? Would it stem from observation, logic, intuition, or psychic power? What would the forecast be?
- *What if* the pointer were a fact from the past? What would the fact be? Who would reveal or discover it, and why?
- *What if* the pointer were an unanswered question? Who would be involved? What would make the mystery interesting?
- *What if* the pointer were a "loaded" object or other physical element? What would it be? How would it be revealed or discovered?

If you wish to develop a plant to prepare us inconspicuously for the payoff, consider the following:

- *What if* the plant were a character trait that will gain importance later? What would the trait be? How would you show it to us without indicating its future significance?
- *What if* the plant were a character belief, value, or attitude? What would it be? How would you show it to us without giving away its future importance?
- *What if* the plant were a statement with hidden significance? What would the statement be? What significance would it appear to have at the time?
- *What if* the plant were a rule or ritual that will be violated later? What would the ritual or rule be? How would you establish it?
- *What if* the plant were an object or other physical element that will gain importance later? What would the physical item be? How would it be introduced at first?
- *What if* the plant were an event that is not what it seems? What event would occur? What would appear to be happening at the time?

- *What if* the plant were a smaller conflict that mirrors a larger conflict later? What would the smaller conflict be? How and why would it happen?

4. *Decide where in the script this setup should occur.* Find the place or places in the script where the setup could most naturally occur and revise the scene accordingly. As you do this, keep in mind what expectation you are trying to trigger or what information you are trying to establish. Make sure of the following:

- The importance of the payoff warrants the size and scope of the setup. Don't devote too much attention to preparing a simple payoff, or too little attention to preparing a complex or unusual one.
- The setup is dramatically strong enough to fulfill its function as either a pointer that triggers our expectations, or a plant that prepares us to understand and believe something that will happen later.
- There is enough delay between the setup and the payoff for the setup to take hold.

WRAP-UP

Foreshadowing is central to dramatic storytelling because it highlights the relationship between past, present, and future. Important and complex events may require multiple foreshadowings throughout the preceding script. Simpler events may need only a single pointer or plant to be effective. As you develop your story, continue to look for opportunities to use foreshadowing to build or reinforce the throughline.

Related tools in *Character, Scene, and Story.* To learn more about the events of your story and how they connect, go to the "Building Your Story" section and try "The Dramatic Continuum" or "An End in Sight."

CRISIS DECISION

THE QUICK VERSION
Flesh out the decision that your main character faces at the crisis of the story

BEST TIME FOR THIS
After you have a working sense of the characters and the world of your story

THE MOST REVEALING MOMENT OF A DRAMATIC STORY
A dramatic story takes us into the time when the main character has to make the most difficult decision of his or her life. From the moment the story begins, certain forces are set into motion that will push and pull the character to this ultimate turning point: the crisis decision. It is a "crisis" because each alternative poses a loss as well as a gain and because it forces the character to weigh what really matters most. It's the moment on the old television game show *Let's Make a Deal* where the contestant has to choose between the last set of doors. Will the character choose Door Number 1 or Door Number 2? It all depends on who the character is and how the story has unfolded so far.

The crisis decision is neither easy nor predictable because, from the character's point of view, it is not a choice between good and evil. If it were that simple, it would not pose a crisis, since characters always choose what they perceive as good—even when they are doing something really terrible that they later regret. One who murders, for example, may at that time see the act as a necessary means to justice. He chooses this "good" over the evil of allowing injustice to prevail by not murdering.

The crisis decision is more complicated because it forces the character to choose between the better of two goods or the lesser of two evils. If the choice is between goods that are important and if the selection of one automatically eliminates the other, the character faces a true crisis. Suppose she is in love with both Jules and Jim and must decide which one to marry. If she chooses Jules, she loses Jim. If she chooses Jim, she loses Jules. Each alternative is a gain and a loss, and the final decision will reveal a lot about her and what she most values.

The character also faces a crisis if the decision is between two evils and if the choice to eliminate one enables the other. Suppose that the character is a rural drifter during the Depression era when resources are scarce. Suppose also that his best friend is mentally challenged, has killed someone by accident, and is now being sought by an angry mob. If the character turns his friend over to the local law, the friend will be handed over to the mob for a cruel death by lynching. If the character helps the friend escape, the friend might accidentally kill again. Neither situation is good. The decision about which is more tolerable will show what the decision maker is really made of.

Act 1 usually introduces or at least suggests the alternatives that the character will face during the crisis—for example, she meets Jules and Jim. The rest of the story can then more deeply define these alternatives and make a compelling case for each—for example, this is what she loves about Jules and that is what she loves about Jim. If each case has been well presented through story events, the character will end up at the threshold of the crisis not knowing—at least for a moment—which way to turn. It will be the ultimate moment of truth in an unpredictable story.

The crisis decision is the core moment of the story. It's where all roads lead, step by step. Most importantly, the subject, theme, character, and plot all come together in this ultimate turning point where each option is both a good choice and bad choice for this particular character in this particular situation. If you don't understand your main character's crisis decision, therefore, you don't really know what your story is about.

ABOUT THE EXERCISE
Use this exercise to flesh out your main character's crisis decision. Look for new possibilities as you define and explore each alternative. Try to be as objective as possible during the final analysis of your exercise work.

■ **THREE CHARACTER DECISIONS**
Answer these questions about your main character:

1. *Easy decision.* Your story shows us your main character at a number of different decision points. Identify one decision near the beginning of the story that is significant but relatively easy for your character to make. As an exercise, imagine this decision as a choice between two doors: Door Number 1 and Door Number 2. Describe what's behind each door in a simple phrase such as "to have dinner with Jules" or "to go sailing with Jim." You don't need to address the outcome of the decision: just state the alternatives.

2. *Difficult decision.* As the story unfolds, life will grow increasingly hard for your main character. Decisions will be less and less easy. Identify one difficult decision that your character must make near the middle of your story. As before, think of this difficult decision as a choice between two doors. What's behind Door Number 1? What's behind Door Number 2? Identify each alternative in a simple phrase.

3. *Crisis decision.* As the story continues, the stakes will continue to rise and the obstacles in your character's way will become more and more chal-

lenging until, at last, a showdown of some kind occurs near the end of the story. It's when your character must make not just a difficult decision, but a crisis decision. It's the ultimate moment of truth when your character will, in fact, make the most difficult and important decision of his or her life. As before, think of this decision as a choice between two doors. What's behind Door Number 1? What's behind Door Number 2? Identify each alternative in a simple phrase.

■ FLESHING OUT THE CRISIS DECISION

Think about the options your character faces at the crisis of the story. If the decision is truly at a crisis level, the character will perceive something extremely positive and something extremely negative about each alternative.

1. *Look at what's behind Door Number 1* from your character's perspective:
   - Identify the biggest benefit of this alternative. If you can't see a strong plus for this option, revise the choice so that you can.
   - Name three good reasons your character might choose this option at the crisis. State each reason simply and from your character's perspective.
   - Identify the biggest drawback of this alternative. If you can't see a strong minus for this option, revise the choice so that you can.
   - Name three good reasons your character might not choose this option. State each reason simply and from your character's perspective.

2. *Look at what's behind Door Number 2* from your character's point of view:
   - Identify the biggest benefit of this alternative. If you can't find a strong plus for this option, revise the choice so that you can.
   - Name three good reasons your character might choose this alternative at the crisis. If your response overlaps with your analysis of Door Number 1, try to paraphrase the response to find a new angle of meaning.
   - Identify the biggest drawback of this alternative. If you can't find a strong minus for this option, revise the choice so that you can.
   - Name three reasons that your character might not choose Door Number 2 at the crisis.

3. *Sum up your analysis* by identifying this crisis decision from your character's point of view as either a choice between goods or a choice between evils.

4. *Consider your character's traits, values, beliefs, discoveries, experiences, and actions* in the story up to the time of the crisis decision. Based on what you have developed in the story so far, is your character more likely to choose Door Number 1 or Door Number 2?

5. *Rate the likelihood of your character choosing this door* at the time of the crisis decision, based on what you have developed in the story so far. Use one of three responses: very likely, likely, or possibly.

6. *Now look at the door you didn't choose.* This is the door the exercise is really all about. In your story planning and revising, you may need to beef up the case for this other door throughout your story, especially if you responded that your character's choice is very likely or likely. If there's little or no chance that your character could select this other door as well, there's less opportunity to create the stress needed to reveal your character and maintain suspense.

THE OTHER DOOR

Ideally, both doors are viable options by the time your character reaches the crisis of the story. Here are some questions to consider for the door that you did not choose:

1. *Values.* Should you change anything in the main character's value system to help build a better case for this door?

2. *Traits.* Do you need to add, emphasize, remove, or deemphasize any character strengths or weaknesses—such as physical, psychological, or social traits—to make the character as likely to choose this door?

3. *General circumstances.* Should anything about the character's world be altered to beef up the case for this door? One key change may be all it takes.

4. *Relationships.* Do you need to further develop or change the relationship between the main character and anyone else in the story?

5. *Behavior.* Has the character established a logical path of decisions and actions that could possibly lead to this door and, if not, how might you alter the character's choices and behavior along the way?

6. *Events.* Do you need to add or get rid of story events to make this door more appealing or seem more necessary to the main character?

7. *Knowledge.* Does the character need to know more—or perhaps know less—in order to consider this door more seriously?

8. *Backstory.* Is there anything from the backstory that you can find or bring out to help build the case for this door?

9. *Preparation.* Have you foreshadowed the possibility of choosing this door and thus prepared us to believe it might be the character's final choice?

WRAP-UP

The last set of questions can be used to address any of the alternatives your character faces during the crisis decision. However, if you found yourself clearly favoring one alternative over another, stay focused on the option that needs more attention. Keep looking for ways to revise your story so that the character's final choice will be not only challenging but also unpredictable.

Related tools in *Character, Scene, and Story.* To explore other important choices that your character must face, go to the "Building Your Story" section and try "Decision Points."

PICTURING THE ARC OF ACTION

THE QUICK VERSION
Use a series of images to map the throughline of the story

BEST TIME FOR THIS
After you are well into story development and want a global view of what happens

MAPPING THE DRAMATIC JOURNEY
Your main character's dramatic journey is driven by the need to fulfill a certain desire and unfolds in a series of events that reveal and often change the character along the way. What keeps the story moving forward is the throughline that links these events like a strand connecting the pearls of a necklace. To get a clear view of this throughline is to see what events matter most and understand how they relate.

ABOUT THE EXERCISE
This visual exercise taps the power of image to help you better see and understand your main character's dramatic journey. The goal is to find five telling images of your character at critical times during the story. Exercise examples are from *The Beard of Avon* by Amy Freed.

To begin, create five exercise blanks to record your work. Allow a half page per blank and number them chronologically from 1 to 5. Then do the exercise steps in the order given (you will be asked to look at the events of your story out of sequence). As you proceed, think in images. Focus on visual details, and resist the urge to explain their meaning.

■ IMAGE 1: POINT OF DEPARTURE
The Beard of Avon inspires a number of telling images. One of the first is a squalid barn in the middle of an English nowhere in the 1580s. An eighteen-year-old Will "Shakspere" is lying in a scratchy pile of straw and staring up despondently at the cobwebs in the rafters. His wife Anne stands beside him akimbo and glares down at him with fierce anger. In the shadows behind them, his friend Old Colin is grinning, drooling, and lustily eyeing Anne's protruding derriere. All three are plainly and poorly dressed in the rural garb of the times.

In this opening image, the characters appear to be in three different worlds—sadness, anger, and lust. What seems most important here is Shakspere's unhappiness and restlessness. With that focus in mind, the image might be summed up by the single word "Failure." As an exercise, the image might be titled "Lost Like a Needle in a Haystack."

Imagine your main character near the beginning of the dramatic journey: the point of departure. This is most likely when the story's inciting event occurs. Think about what's happening and create image 1 by completing the steps in "Picture This" below. Record your work in the first exercise blank.

PICTURE THIS
1. Look for an important dramatic moment when the character is doing something interesting with someone else. Freeze-frame this interaction in your mind's eye and study the image. Fill in the exercise blank with a description of the image and remember that you are describing, not explaining. Look for interesting details.
2. Focus on what matters most in the image and sum it up in one word.
3. Write a title for the image that adds further meaning

■ IMAGE 5: FINAL DESTINATION

Skip ahead to the end of your story and see what's happening. If you do not yet have an ending, be spontaneous and, as an exercise, make one up based on what you know about the story so far. Remember that your character is completing the dramatic journey. Things are different now. For better or for worse, something fundamental about the character has changed. At the end of *The Beard of Avon*, for example, "Shakspere" has become "Shake-speare." He is now surrounded by cloaked luminaries bringing him scripts that they have ghostwritten under his name. This image might be summed up by the word "Success" and titled "A Beard for All Seasons." Find image 5 for your story by repeating the steps in "Picture This." Look for as much contrast as possible with your opening image, word summary, and title. Record your work in the fifth exercise blank.

■ IMAGE 3: MIDPOINT

Now go backward until you see your character in the middle of the story. In a two-act play, this would be around the end of act 1. In a three-act play or screenplay, it would be in the middle of act 2. Either way, this is a view of your character halfway through the dramatic journey that ultimately connects image 1 to image 5.

Try to find an important event near this midpoint that is changing the character's world and contributing to the transition from the beginning of the story to the end. About halfway through *The Beard of Avon*, for example, Shakspere is now with a surprised Edward de Vere in a pose of oratorical brilliance. This image might be summed up by the word "Fame" and titled: "The Beard Speaks." Create image 3 for your story by repeating the steps in "Picture This." Look for contrast between this middle image and the other two. Record your work in the third exercise blank.

■ IMAGE 2: EARLY TRANSITION POINT

How does your character move from image 1 to image 3? Focus next on what happens between these two points in the journey. Find an event or revelation that contributes to the changes that have taken place between the start of the story and the midpoint. At an early time in *The Beard of Avon*, Shakspere has joined a traveling troupe of actors and is now on stage as a bit player holding a spear. This image might be summed up by the word "Hope" and titled "The Spear Shaker." Create image 2 for your story by repeating the steps in "Picture This." Continue to look for contrast. How is this image different from the others you have created so far? Record your work in the second exercise blank.

■ IMAGE 4: LATER TRANSITION POINT

How does your main character move from image 3 to image 5? Focus now on what happens between these two points in the character's journey. Find an event that contributes to the changes that take place between the mid-point and the end of the story. At a later time in *The Beard of Avon,* Shakspere is busy writing as Edward de Vere sleeps with Shakspere's wife. This image might be summed up by the word "Betrayal" and titled "Obsessions." Create your image 4 by repeating the steps in "Picture This." Continue to look for contrast. Record your work in the fourth exercise blank.

■ EVALUATING THE THROUGHLINE OF YOUR STORY

You've begun to look at the arc of action in your story through a series of telling images, word summaries, and titles. If you look at these elements now in chronological order, you can begin to see the bold strokes of the character's dramatic journey, just as Shakspere moves from Failure (Lost like a Needle in a Haystack), to Hope (The Spear Shaker), to Fame (The Beard Speaks), to Betrayal (Obsessions), and finally to Success (A Beard for All Seasons). Go back and review your images in chronological story order from 1 to 5. Keep these questions in mind:

1. Does the sequence of events make sense?
2. How does each of the five events connect to at least one other event?
3. Is each event different enough from the other four in the sequence?

WRAP-UP

The throughline is sometimes referred to as the "spine" of the story. A strong throughline holds the story together and keeps it moving forward so that the end is different from the beginning because of what happens in the middle. Keep your story's throughline in mind as you continue to make decisions at the scenic level. Know how each scene fits into and strengthens the story's spine.

Related tools in *Character, Scene, and Story.* In the "Building Your Story" section, try "Living Images" to add visceral power to your script, "Two Characters in Search of a Story" to identify character arcs, or "The Dramatic Continuum" or "An End in Sight" to examine how story events connect.

BEFORE AND AFTER

THE QUICK VERSION
Explore how your character is changed and not changed by the dramatic journey

BEST TIME FOR THIS
After you have a completed draft

THE POWER OF CHANGE
Drama shows us characters in transition. They start out one way and end up another because of what they do during the story and because of how the world responds to these actions. The power of change is often what keeps us leaning forward in our seats as we observe characters that we care about. We witness an important turning point, watch its consequences unfold, anticipate—and often worry about—the outcome, and wait to see what happens.

Marketers understand the power of change and often use "Before and After" scenarios to sell their products—for example, a plain person has a makeover and becomes beautiful, a lonely person joins a dating service and becomes popular, a poor person takes a real estate course and becomes wealthy. Because such changes are designed to sell products, the change presented is usually positive.

In drama, which deals not with products but emotions and ideas, the overall change may be positive or negative. Either way, it is a significant transformation, and it has occurred gradually in steps rather than suddenly all at once. A step-by-step transition keeps the world of the story dynamic and unpredictable, and gives us time to observe, digest, and emotionally participate in what's happening from scene to scene. In effect, we watch little bits of the "Before" scenario being slowly replaced by little bits of the "After" scenario until the transition is complete.

To tap the power of change, you need to clearly establish the "Before" scenario: who your character is and how the character feels, thinks, and behaves when the story begins—for example, he is a 98-pound weakling who gets sand kicked into his face by bullies when he goes to the beach. If we do not see this starting portrait clearly and have time to understand it, we will not know later what is being undone. When your story begins, be sure to carefully introduce and define your unique character in relationship to his or her world.

You also need to clearly establish the "After" scenario: who and how your character is when the story ends—for example, the 98-pound weakling has now become a bodybuilder whom bullies fear. If we do not understand this "After" and if we cannot see how it contrasts with the "Before," we will not know that a transition has occurred or be able to measure its impact or significance.

Think about your main character's "Before" and "After" and how they compare. If the character has experienced a journey that matters, it stands to reason that some elements of these two pictures will be very different. For example, a weakling has become strong. However, if the character is to remain identifiable as the person we first met, it also stands to reason that some elements of the two pictures will be the same. For example, the character may have been socially inept in the "Before" picture and, despite his new physical prowess, is still socially inept. How has your character changed and not changed when the story ends?

ABOUT THE EXERCISE

Try this with your main character or a principal character whose transition in the story you want to explore. Use what you already know about the character to make new discoveries. For best results, focus on the big picture of the story and keep your responses brief so you don't get bogged down in details.

■ THE "BEFORE" AND "AFTER" OF YOUR CHARACTER

Think about how the dramatic journey most affects your character:

1. *Before.* Who and how is your character when the story begins? Briefly describe the character's "Before." This is a high-level, but defining summary of whom we meet at the journey's start. This summary may include any backstory information that is critical here. Limit your description to no more than a few sentences.

2. *After.* Who and how is your character when the story ends? Briefly describe the character's "After." This is a high-level, but defining summary of the character at the end of the journey. Look primarily at how the character has changed. If it's especially important, you may also include how your character has not changed. However, try to keep the focus here on contrast more than similarity.

■ FLESHING OUT YOUR CHARACTER'S TRANSITION

Get ready to evaluate how much your character has changed in each of ten categories as a result of the dramatic journey. In each category, compare the After to the Before. Use a simple 0-1-2-3 rating system, where 0 equals "no change" and 3 equals "huge change," to indicate the degree of transition. Then give a specific example to illustrate the measurement. As you do this, focus on the material most important to the story.

1. **Demographics**, or basic identifying facts about the character, such as name, age, gender, and address. If the story spans many years, or if the

character has a sex change or moves to a new location, you might have a level 3 change in this category. Otherwise, you are more likely to be at or close to 0. Compare the After to the Before. Rate the demographic transition and give an example of how the character has or hasn't changed. For example, if there is 0 change, the key fact might be "He never left New Jersey." If there is a level 3 change, the character may have gone from "living in New Jersey" to "living on Mars."

2. *Physicality*, or health, genetics, appearance, body type, or anything else biological about the character. Compare the After to the Before. How much has your character changed physically by the end of the story? Rate the change in this category and give an example.

3. *Sociology*, or your character's traits in relationship to individuals, groups, and institutions. This category includes the family, friends, community, and society at large. For the purposes of this exercise, it excludes romantic relationships, which will be looked at separately. Compare the After to the Before. Rate the change in this category and give an example.

4. *Romance*, or your character's love life, sex life, and related traits, qualities, and behaviors. Compare the After to the Before. How much has the character changed romantically? Rate the change and give an example.

5. *Career*, or your character's work habits, job status, professional reputation, or anything else related to job or career. How much has the character changed professionally? Rate the change and give an example.

6. *Economics*, or your character's relationship to money, the status of his or her financial assets, or anything else economic in nature. How much has the character changed economically? Rate the change and give an example.

7. *Politics*, or your character's political beliefs, relationship to political movements, and traits or behaviors in power-oriented situations. How much has your character changed politically? Rate the change and give an example.

8. *Morality*, or your character's sense of right and wrong, value system, and ethical standards as well as innocence or corruption. How much has your character changed morally or ethically? Rate the change and give an example.

9. *Psychology*, or your character's inner world, mental health, fears and complexes, strengths and weaknesses. How much has your character changed psychologically? Rate the change and give an example.

10. *Spirituality*, or your character's beliefs in God or other higher powers, the afterlife, and organized religion. How much has your character changed spiritually? Rate the change and give an example.

HOW THE CHARACTER HAS CHANGED AND NOT CHANGED

Use what you have learned so far in this exercise to answer these questions:

1. *Key Change That Occurs.* Think about your character's most defining traits and qualities. These are what make your character unique. Some are positive, some negative. Some are changed by story events, some not changed. When all is said and done, what is the most significant character trait, quality, or condition that is transformed by the dramatic journey? This is one big positive or negative change that unfolds step by step through the story. Briefly identify the Before and After of this change—for example, the character changes from being dishonest to honest, or vice versa.

2. *Key Change That Almost Occurs But Doesn't.* Think again about your character's defining attributes. What is the most significant trait, quality, or condition that is nearly changed—it is seriously tested, threatened, or challenged during the story—but survives intact in the end? For example, the character's fidelity to a romantic partner is almost undone but saved at the last minute.

3. *Key Constant.* Among your character's traits, some are so fundamental, so set in stone, and so much a part of his or her identity, that they simply cannot be changed. Whether strengths or weaknesses, they are at the unshakeable core of who your character is. Despite whatever opportunities or problems arise, what significant trait, quality, or condition of your character is least resistant to change? For example, the character is an unswerving optimist, no matter what.

WRAP-UP

By exploring the Before and After of your character, first broadly and then in detail, you may better understand the dramatic journey and what it needs to accomplish. Your answers in the last part of the exercise suggest the big picture of this journey and its impact on the character. As you continue to work on your story, be sure to keep in mind the most significant change that your character will experience, the most significant trait that will be shaken but not changed, and the most significant trait that will defy all challenges.

Related tools in *Character, Scene, and Story.* To continue fleshing out character arcs, go to the "Building Your Story" section and try "Two Characters in Search of a Story."

TWELVE-WORD SOLUTION

THE QUICK VERSION
Work within limits to explore key story events

BEST TIME FOR THIS
After you have completed a draft or are well into the story

STORY AS ONE THING AFTER ANOTHER
Story is the chain of events that occurs when a character sets out to achieve an important but almost unreachable goal. These events come in different sizes and shapes and may be positive or negative in nature. Each changes the world of the story in an important way. Events may center on a discovery, revelation, decision, or action. Some are successes that move the character closer to the goal. Some are failures that push the character away. In most dramatic stories, most events are caused by the main character in pursuit of the goal. Inevitably, however, some events are caused by outside forces beyond the character's control.

ABOUT THE EXERCISE
While all of the events of the dramatic journey may be important, some are more important than others. This focusing exercise asks you to look at your story from different angles, find some of the events that matter most, and identify each in twelve words or fewer. This word limit is designed to help you simplify and prioritize your story ideas. Use either your main character or a principal character as a focal point for your responses. As you do this, interpret qualitative terms such as "positive" and "negative" any way you wish, and remember that their meaning is relative to your unique character.

■ WHAT IS YOUR TWELVE-WORD SOLUTION?
1. *Positive discovery*. Think about the good things that your character learns during the course of the story. These may be self-realizations or insights about other characters, humanity in general, current events, the world, the universe, or beyond. Whether these discoveries are by design or by chance, and whether they actually prove to be good or bad in the long run, they seem positive to your character at the time. For example, the discovery might be: the test results were wrong and he is actually in excellent health. What is the most positive thing that your character discovers during the story?

2. *Negative discovery.* Focus on the bad things your character learns. As before, these may be self-realizations or insights about other characters, humanity in general, current events, the world, the universe, or beyond. Whether these discoveries are by design or by chance, and whether they actually prove to be good or bad in the long run, they seem negative to your character at the time. For example, the discovery might be: her husband has been having an affair with her sister for years. What is the most negative thing that your character discovers?

3. *Positive revelation.* Think about the different types of good news that your character delivers to others: positive or helpful information related to this character, other characters, or the world of the story. Regardless of what others think, and whether or not this news proves to be good in the long run, your character sees it as positive at the time. For example, the revelation might be: she's madly in love with him and wants to get married now. What is the most important positive thing your character reveals to one or more other characters?

4. *Negative revelation.* Some of your character's revelations may be bad news: negative or harmful information about this character, other characters, or the world of the story. Regardless of what others think, and whether or not this news proves to be bad in the long run, your character sees it as negative at the time. For example, the revelation might be a confession: he has been embezzling money from the company every month for years. What is the most negative thing that your character reveals to one or more other characters?

5. *Decision to begin.* Consider the decisions your character makes to initiate new courses of action or new ways of being. These "decisions to begin" suggest movement *toward* something: a pursuit of good or what is perceived to be good at the time. For example, the decision might be: she will throw her hat into the ring and run for mayor. What is the most important "decision to begin" that your character makes?

6. *Decision to end.* Now consider the decisions that your character makes to stop doing or being something. These "decisions to end" suggest a movement *away* from something: a retreat from what is bad or perceived to be bad at the time. For example, the decision might be: he's the worst and unhappiest salesman in the office and he quits. What is the most important "decision to end" that your character makes?

7. *Earned success.* Keep your character's strengths in mind and think about the accomplishments that he or she achieves through good decisions or right action. For example, she finally convinces her son to enter rehab and get off drugs. What is the most important success that your character achieves during the story?

8. *Given success.* Now think about good things that happen to your character: boons or blessings caused by outside forces, such as other people, fate, accident, higher powers, or perhaps good luck. For example, he finds

bags of cash in the back seat of his cab. What is the most important success that your character enjoys but didn't actually earn?

9. *Caused failure*. Keep your character's weaknesses in mind and think about the times that these shortcomings prevent your character from achieving an important goal. These are failures due to bad decisions or wrong action. For example, she's so unprepared for final exams that she ends up not graduating. What is the most important failure that your character causes?

10. *Given failure*. Now think about the bad things that happen to your character due to outside forces, such as other people, fate, accident, higher powers, or perhaps bad luck. For example, his house is struck by lightning and burns down to the ground. What is the most important failure that your character suffers but didn't directly cause?

WRAP-UP

Working within a word limit, you have now identified some key events of your story: discoveries, revelations, decisions, successes, and failures that matter most. How well have you shown the importance of these events in your script? Have you devoted enough time to them? Are any lesser events stealing focus? How clearly have you shown the impact of each key event on the dramatic journey? You might wish to return to this exercise periodically to see how your twelve-word solutions change as your understanding of your characters and story grows.

> **Related tools in *Character, Scene, and Story*.** To learn more about the story event you understand least, go to the "Building Your Story" section and try "What Just Happened?"

MAIN EVENT

THE QUICK VERSION
Clarify your understanding of the main event of the story

BEST TIME FOR THIS
After you have completed a draft or are well into the story

A BIG, OBSERVABLE ACTION SHAPED
BY POSITIVE AND NEGATIVE FORCES
Regardless of the number of characters, the complications of plot and sub-plot, and the complexity of ideas and emotions, most dramatic stories can be boiled down to one main event through which all else is revealed. Whether it centers on adapting a book about orchids into a screenplay (*Adaptation*), saving a marriage on the verge of destruction (*Who's Afraid of Virginia Woolf?*), or saving a whole family on the verge of destruction (*Long Day's Journey into Night*), this main event unfolds in front of us as a big, observable action shaped by both positive and negative forces.

"Big" here means that what happens overall is of vital importance to the characters and hopefully the audience. It is not an everyday trivial event. Nor is it something sort of interesting that happened. Rather, it is the kind of event we find at the edges of human experience: a major turning point which, scene by scene, strips away the main character's superficialities, reveals who the character really is, and typically changes the character in a fundamental way.

"Observable" means that the action can literally be seen. Internal states are implied by external actions, particularly interpersonal actions: how one character tries to affect another here and now. When writing for the page, you may explain that a man is unhappy because he suspects that his wife has been having an affair. When writing for stage or screen, you need to translate such knowledge into dramatic action that we can watch—for example, a man playing a cat-and-mouse game with his wife in order to trap her in a lie, as in the opening scene of *The Real Thing*.

The term "action" means that the focus is on what the characters do more than what they say. Since some characters may be intentionally misleading or unintentionally misinformed, the words we hear are not always reliable. To learn the truth about what's really going on, we look instinctively through the dialogue to the behavior of the speaker, especially when that behavior contradicts the dialogue. In the film *Gaslight*, originally the play *Angel Street*, for example, a husband says he loves his wife, but actually plots to destroy her. His actions speak louder than his words.

The main event is driven by something "positive." This suggests character objective: a quest to attain something important that the character sees as good—for example, to make a difference in the world before you die (*About Schmidt*). The main event is also shaped by something "negative." This suggests conflict: the forces of antagonism that rise up to thwart the quest and create a central problem—for example how to overcome the failures and trappings of the past (*About Schmidt*).

In stories with a single protagonist, the main character and main event are inseparable: they define each other. In stories with more than one protagonist, the same principles tend to apply—the main event is a big, observable action shaped by positive and negative forces—but there are variations on this theme. In *The Hours*, for example, we are presented with three stories, each with its own main character and main event. These stories reflect and inform one another. In films like *Go!*, *Magnolia*, and *Five Corners*, and plays like *The Hot L Baltimore* and *Waiting for Lefty*, the "main character" is not an individual but a group of individuals whose lives intersect through a main event that affects them in different ways.

ABOUT THE EXERCISE

Use this exercise during the revision process to explore the main event of your story and sharpen its dramatic focus. Exercise examples are from the Roman Polanski film *The Pianist* written by Wladyslaw Szpilman and Ronald Harwood.

■ THE MAIN EVENT OF YOUR STORY

1. The main character of *The Pianist* is Wladyslaw Szpilman. Who is the main character of your story?

2. In *The Pianist*, a Jewish composer and pianist during World War II survives the Nazi occupation of Warsaw. In one sentence, what is the main event of your story?

3. The main event of *The Pianist* is triggered by an explosion: Nazi artillery blows up the radio station in Warsaw where Wladyslaw is playing the piano on the air. What triggers the main event of your story?

4. As a result of the inciting incident, Wladyslaw realizes that his life is in danger and that he needs to protect himself. This arouses an objective—to survive—that drives the main event of the story. What story objective is aroused in your main character as a result of the inciting incident?

5. The central problem in *The Pianist* is the lethal Nazi hatred of Jews combined with the Nazi power that has been gained from occupying Warsaw. In your story, what central problem must be resolved to achieve the story objective?

6. What is at stake for Wladyslaw is life—not just his own life, but also that of the Jewish people. What is most at stake for your character?

7. As the main event of *The Pianist* unfolds, Wladyslaw experiences a number of turning points that each change the direction of his journey. For example:

- The Nazis force his family to leave their apartment and move into a controlled ghetto.
- An ally on the Jewish ghetto police force saves Wladyslaw from deportation to a concentration camp.
- A German woman who was a fan of his music helps him escape to a safe house outside the walls of the ghetto.
- A German officer who has discovered his hiding spot spares his life after hearing him play the piano.
- The Allied troops arrive and defeat the Nazis.

In your story, after the inciting incident, what are some of the major turning-point events that set your character's dramatic journey into new directions? Identify at least three important examples.

8. Wladyslaw does many different things in order to survive. For example:

- He allows his family to sell his piano in order to buy food.
- He asks for help from a German woman who was his fan.
- He hides in a safe house and waits patiently for food that sometimes doesn't come for days or weeks.
- He restrains himself from playing a piano in his hideout for fear that his presence will be detected.
- He plays the piano in his imagination and fingers the air as if it were a keyboard.

Think about what your character does—not what your character says—during the story. Some of these actions are critical to the quest and reveal important information about the character. Identify at least three important examples.

9. In *The Pianist*, Wladyslaw is pushed to the limits of human endurance. He must hide in freezing cold, fight illness alone, struggle to get food out of a tin can, and bury himself away from everything he has ever known—all in order to survive. This journey reveals his emotional strength, patience, creativity, and resourcefulness. And it ends as it began—with Wladyslaw playing the piano. However, this is not the same man we first saw. He has become a survivor with a knowledge of himself and his world that he had no need to possess before.

Think about the main event of your story, what this dramatic journey reveals about your character, and how your character changes as a result of what happens. Give at least two examples of what is revealed about your character during the story, and then give at least one example of how your character has been affected by story events.

10. *The Pianist* dramatizes an important historical event from World War II—the Nazi occupation of Warsaw and the extermination of Jews who lived there—and is based on a true story originally written by Szpilman as a book. This makes the main event "big" in every way. It is far removed in size, scope, and significance from the trivialities of the everyday world and offers many lessons and insights about the best and worst of humanity.

Your story does not have to be historical to have importance. It does not have to be based on true events. Nor does it have to be a serious drama. Even if you are writing a comedy that you make up as you go along, you can find big material in your character and story choices. Look for issues, truths, and themes that matter to you and reflect your life experience. Chances are, these things will matter to us, too, or at least provoke us into seeing them in new ways, even if we are laughing in the process.

Think about how big your story is—or isn't. If it feels like big material, what makes it so? If it doesn't feel big enough yet, how can you increase its importance while staying true to yourself as a writer? Regardless of how you feel about your material now, trust your first instinct. There was something about your story important enough to draw you in and make you commit to writing it. Try to explore what may still be in your subconscious waiting to be discovered under the character and story choices you have made so far. Then answer the question: What makes your story big? Or, if it doesn't seem big, how might you make your story more important?

11. You have now answered ten questions about your story. Hopefully, these responses have helped clarify your understanding of the main event. As a final step, revisit your answer to the second question: "In one sentence, what is the main event of your story?" If you have learned anything new about this event and want to revise your answer, do so now. This can serve as an important guide for you during the revision process.

WRAP-UP

A dramatic story is about one thing: a big, observable action shaped by positive and negative forces. Know what the main event of your story is and keep this focus in mind as you make decisions at the scenic level and work through story details.

> **Related tools in *Character, Scene, and Story*.**
> To continue fleshing out the main event of your story, go to the "Building Your Story" section and try any stage 3 exercise, particularly "Different Sides of the Story."

YOUR STORY AS A DOG

THE QUICK VERSION
Learn more about your story by translating it into other forms

BEST TIME FOR THIS
After the first draft or any time you need a clearer vision of your story

FINDING THE ESSENCE OF THE STORY
During the process of script development, from fleshing out characters to seeing the big picture of the story, you are making decisions that bring to your work a certain kind of life. If your work is successful, this life will find a form and meaning that transcend the words of the script and encompass the whole work—characters, structure, subject, and theme—both on and off the page. To experience this life is to know, at some level, the essence of the story.

Though intangible and immeasurable, the essence of the story is what matters most in the end. In many ways, its power will determine how your work is received and understood by others. What is the essence of the story you are developing now? How would you distill this essence? What are its core truths?

ABOUT THE EXERCISE
This is a fun exercise with a serous goal: to learn something new about the essence of your story. Use the following steps to simplify and prioritize story ideas so that you can shake up your material in unexpected ways and see what falls out.

In each round, you will be asked to translate your story into a different form of writing. No matter what you do with the new form or how much fun you have with it, stay true to the story as you know it now. Do each round as quickly as possible and remember that you may learn the most by making bold choices.

■ YOUR STORY AS A LIBRARY CATALOG LISTING
You can locate books in the library by going to an electronic catalog which lists titles, authors, genres, and synopses among other publication information. These entries are purely functional devices with no bells or whistles, since nobody is trying to sell anything. After identifying the genre—for example, mystery, comedy, suspense, drama, farce, science fiction, or horror—the synopsis of the plot is short and simple, usually just a sentence, and

may be on the dry side. It's designed for efficiency and economy. For example:

- *How I Learned to Drive* by Paula Vogel. Drama. A woman looks back in forgiveness on a seven-year relationship with her uncle.
- *Deathtrap* by Ira Levin. Thriller. A washed-up playwright tries to trick one of his ex-students out of a brilliant play, and turns to murder when his efforts fail.
- *Crimes of the Heart* by Beth Henley. Comedy. Three Mississippi sisters try to escape the past and face the future.

Think about your subject and theme, and main story event. What genre does your story fall into? How would you sum up the story in an efficient and functional way that does not exceed one sentence? What is your story as a library catalog listing?

■ YOUR STORY AS A MESSAGE IN A FORTUNE COOKIE

Think about your whole story—its subject, theme, and main event—and how you might translate this into the type of message found in fortune cookies. Written for a tiny scroll, the message is usually only one sentence long. It has the style and tone of a psychic prediction or a statement of profound wisdom from the mysterious and great beyond. For example, a Chinese fortune cookie might contain any of the following:

- A message of enlightenment, perhaps for George and Lennie in *Of Mice and Men*: "There is a true and sincere friendship between you both."
- A foretelling of the future, perhaps for Joe and Harper in *Angels in America*: "If you travel, you will lose your true love."
- Advice for success, perhaps for the real estate agents in *Glengarry Glen Ross*: "You will never find true wealth if it is only money you seek."
- A warning, perhaps for Macbeth: "You walk under a cloud. Beware the storm."
- An encouragement, perhaps for star-crossed pairs of lovers like Rosalind and Orlando in *As You Like It*: "You will yet live to splendor and plenty."

Your fortune cookie message may deliver good news or bad news. It may be about the present or future. It may be directed to your leading character or characters, or perhaps even to your audience. What's important is that it expresses a high-level truth. What is your story as a message in a Chinese fortune cookie?

■ YOUR STORY AS A LETTER TO AN ADVICE COLUMNIST

Advice column letters often suggest story. They tend to be emotional in nature and have a way of getting to the heart of dramatic situations and the people who populate them. They are dramatic in the sense that the writer often has a strong objective, stakes high enough to motivate the writing of the letter, and conflict that cannot be easily resolved. Listen to the drama in this letter to columnist Amy Love:

> Dear Amy,
>
> My boyfriend "Joe" and I have been together for three years, but things haven't been so hot. One day he's here waiting to be fed and have his clothes washed and other needs tended to. Next day, he's gone and so is all of the liquor in the apartment and most of the money in my checking account. He also steals my cigarettes if he can find them. Then one day he's here again acting real lovey-dovey. Now after almost two weeks he came back with a black eye and bruises all over, but he won't tell me what happened. But he does say he's changed and wants to get married. He acts like he means it this time. What do you think?
>
> Wedding Bells

Think about the big picture of your story. How might you translate it into an advice column letter? And how will the letter be signed? You can imagine the letter being written by your main character, another character, or whomever you wish. What is your story as a letter addressed to Dear Amy, ending with the writer's moniker?

■ YOUR STORY AS ADVICE FROM A COLUMNIST

This is the flip side of the advice column letter: the expert advice that addresses the question and offers some kind of solution. Here is Amy Love's reply to the question of whether or not Wedding Bells should marry her boyfriend:

> Dear Wedding Bells:
>
> What do I think? I think you have a very unusual way of seeing reality. I also think you should stop smoking. Next time he's gone, change the locks, get a new checking account, and find somebody else to marry.
>
> Amy

Think about the question you posed in the first round, and now write the reply in the style and tone of an advice columnist. As before, try to keep your subject, theme, and plot in mind and translate these into a different form that distills their essence.

■ YOUR STORY AS A HEADLINE IN THE NEWSPAPER

Think about who your main character is and what happens overall as a result of his or her quest. Translate this main event into an informative, newsworthy, and attention-grabbing newspaper headline that reflects an interesting angle on your story. It's the kind of news headline you might see on the front page of your morning newspaper—for example, "DNA Testing Leads to Justice after a Decade behind Bars." Think about the main event of your story. Translate it into the style, tone, and length of a hard news head-line.

■ YOUR STORY AS A NEWSPAPER ARTICLE

Now start to imagine the news article for the headline you just wrote. It's a more elaborate reporting of the main event. To be written in the style and tone of hard news, it needs a strong factual lead: an opening paragraph that tells what happened and highlights what's newsworthy. The article then gives supporting facts about the who, what, where, when, and why of the event. For the headline "DNA Testing Leads to Justice after a Decade behind Bars," for example, the article begins:

> After serving more than 10 years in prison for a murder he did not commit, a Los Angeles man on Friday was cleared of all charges and immediately released from the Pacific Bay Correctional Center, thanks to DNA tests which confirmed his innocence.
>
> "I never thought this day would come," said Jacob Moore, 38, as he emerged from the prison Friday afternoon with his attorney Maria Wills.
>
> "I used to have a girlfriend. I used to have my own apartment and a good job. Now all that's gone," Moore said. "I've got nothing but freedom and a chance to start over."
>
> During a brief hearing at the Los Angeles Criminal Courts Building, prosecutors dismissed all charges against Moore, who was serving a life sentence for the murder of a coworker found strangled near Moore's home. The dismissal came after a two-year reinvestigation of a case built on forensic evidence that prosecutors now say was flawed from the start.
>
> The case began when . . .

In a hard news story, the opening paragraph objectively sums it all up. The article then moves from what's most newsworthy to what's most newsworthy after that, to what's most newsworthy after that, and so on. Few details are given this early in the article. Think about the main event of your story. How would you report it as hard news for the front page? Write the opening paragraph or two of the story.

■ YOUR STORY AS A TABLOID HEADLINE

Think again about who your main character is and what happens overall as a result of the quest. What is most unusual or emotionally appealing about your story? How would you translate this into the style and tone of a front-page tabloid headline? Your focus now will be more on the personal and sensational aspects of your material rather than a factual recap. For example, here is a front-page headline from a weekly tabloid: "His Ex Returned from the Grave to Wreck My Dream Wedding." What is your story as a tabloid front-page headline?

■ YOUR STORY AS A TABLOID ARTICLE

This is the article for the headline you just wrote and it sums up your story in the style and tone of a tabloid. As with the hard news article, you need to start with a strong lead, but the approach is more emotional than factual, and imagination and embellishment are not discouraged. Here is the opening of the article "His Ex Returned from the Grave to Wreck My Dream Wedding":

> A wedding ceremony at Reno's White Venus Chapel came to a literally screeching halt on Saturday when the ghost of the groom's deceased ex-wife suddenly appeared at the altar and began wailing loudly.
>
> "This was supposed to be my dream wedding," said almost-bride Cathy Taylor, 25, still in her elegant silver satin wedding gown with a deep V halter neckline, dramatic low back, and miniature pearl bead accents. "I guess I should feel lucky that no one got hurt," Taylor said, as she recounted the horror of seeing her groom, wedding party, and chapel full of guests all screaming and fleeing in panic.
>
> The uninvited ghost was described as . . .

Notice how the opening does still recap what the article is about. However, the angle is more subjective and relies on big adjectives and emotional hot buttons. Think about the main event of your story and what's most sensational about it. Write the opening paragraph or two of your story as a front-page article in a tabloid.

■ YOUR STORY AS THE TITLE OF A TOP-TEN LIST

David Letterman's comedic top-ten lists have now worked their way into the fabric of American culture. In reverse order of importance, from ten to one, they give the top ten ways to do something, or the top ten warning signs of trouble, or the top ten signs or clues that something is true—all for the purpose of satire and getting a few laughs. Here are a few examples of titles from the 2001 *Late Show* Top Ten Archive:

- Top Ten Signs Your Radio Shack Manager Has Gone Nuts
- Top Ten Signs You're Talking to a Bad Phone Psychic
- Top Ten Things You Don't Want to Hear from a Gas Station Attendant

Think about your whole story. What's it about? What theme are you exploring? What happens in the story overall? If you were using this exercise to explore the big picture of *A Streetcar Named Desire*, for example, you might write "Top Ten Ways to End Up in a Mental Asylum." What is your story as a top-ten list title?

■ YOUR STORY AS A TOP TEN LIST

Imagine the actual list for the top-ten list title you just wrote. In reverse order of importance, from ten to one, it will list the "top ten" signs, ways, questions, clues, reasons, or whatever you called for in your title. However silly or serious your choices may be, sum up your subject, theme, and story line as faithfully as possible. If the story were *Streetcar* and the title were "Top Ten Ways to End Up in a Mental Asylum," for example, the list might read like this:

10. Marry a guy who is not sexually attracted to you.
9. Get a teaching job and have sex with your students.
8. Get fired from teaching and become a prostitute.
7. Move into a small, one-room apartment with your sister and her husband.
6. Make enemies with your sister's husband as soon as possible by calling him a Neanderthal.
5. Drink like a sailor but only in secret.
4. Try to land a husband by lying about your background and age, and keeping the lights as dim as possible.
3. Try to break up your sister's marriage so she can be completely available to take care of your every need.
2. Deny everything, especially to yourself, while wearing a boa.
1. Have sex with your sister's husband while she's out having a baby.

What is your story as a top-ten list?

■ YOUR STORY AS A POEM

Think about how you might capture your whole story in a poem that accomplishes a lot with relatively few words. For example, it might create a word picture or appeal to the reader's senses in other ways in order to stir emotions and reveal some kind of truth. Your poem might be written in free verse or stanzas that rhyme. It might take the form of a sonnet, limerick, or haiku. Think about the essence of your story. How would you translate it into a poem?

WRAP-UP

No matter what you are writing about or how serious your topic may be, exercises like this can help you find a clearer vision of your story. By distilling the essence of your material and translating it into a different structure, such as a tabloid headline, you can see what rises to the surface of your thinking. Some of this process may feel silly, but it can often lead to surprising new insights. It's the creative equivalent of suddenly finding yourself in a burning building and wanting to save what matters most. With such little time to act, what will you reach for?

> **Related tools in *Character, Scene, and Story*.** To keep fleshing out the big picture of your story, go to the "Building Your Story" section and try any stage 3 exercise, particularly "Coming Soon to a Theater near You!"

THE INCREDIBLE SHRINKING STORY

THE QUICK VERSION
Write a series of synopses to clarify the big picture of your story

BEST TIME FOR THIS
After you have a completed draft

SYNOPSIS: A FOCUSING TOOL
When the Eugene O'Neill Theater Center accepts your play for the U.S. National Playwrights Conference, one of the first tasks is to write a synopsis of the story in advance for *Playbill*. The purpose of the synopsis is to highlight what the story is about and attract an audience in about a hundred words. For example, here is the synopsis that appeared in *Playbill* for my play *Hotel Desperado*:

> There are old blood stains in the carpet, scratching sounds inside the walls, and stranglers on the second floor. The sign outside says Dorado, but those who live here know better. James Maxwell Dean just checked in without realizing it and now he can't check out. He's shacking up with Gil, a.k.a. Gila Monster, and trying to make the past as distant as the dunes he left behind. But doors here don't always open to what they once shut off. The view is unpredictable. And anything can happen when someone knocks. Welcome to the Hotel Desperado.

Whether or not your work is selected by the O'Neill, it's a good idea to have a synopsis of your story ready when you begin to submit it to producers, agents, and competitions. The process of developing a synopsis is an enlightening one because it forces you to prioritize your story ideas, focus on what's most important about your plot and theme, and highlight your story's potential appeal to an audience.

To generate interest, the *Hotel Desperado* synopsis highlights a few concrete details (blood stains in the carpet, scratching sounds inside the walls, stranglers on the second floor) and includes the names of the main character (James Maxwell Dean) and a secondary character (Gil, a.k.a. Gila Monster). It also suggests a sense of mystery and surrealism: "The sign outside says *Dorado* but those who live here know better . . . the doors don't always open to what they once shut off. The view is unpredictable . . . anything can happen when someone knocks."

Most importantly, the synopsis frames the central conflict of the story— the fact that the main character cannot check out of the hotel and is "trying to make the past as distant as the dunes he left behind." All of this is described in the present tense to make it feel immediate and dramatic.

ABOUT THE EXERCISE

The goal of this exercise is to help you simplify and prioritize your story ideas. For best results, complete each exercise round before you begin the next one. As you do this, keep in mind that writing a synopsis is all about working within limits: the stricter the limit, the stronger the need to prioritize, and the greater the opportunity to see what matters most in your story. When the limit is a word count, the story title is not included, but two words hyphenated still counts as two words.

■ **SEVEN WAYS TO SUM UP YOUR STORY**

Remember to go one step at a time without looking ahead:

First summary. Your first limitation is a time limit. After you finish reading this paragraph, give yourself up to fifteen minutes to develop a synopsis of your story. Try to write as much as you can during this time so that you can highlight what you've got so far and find some interesting details along the way. The task is to zero in on your story's most important and most interesting details while also suggesting the central conflict. Remember that there is no wrong way to do this, and it is only an exercise. See what you can say about your story in fifteen minutes.

Second summary. In this round, the goal is the same, but the limitation is different. Instead of working within a time frame, you will now be working within a word count which asks you to tighten the focus on your material. The limitation is 50. As you develop the synopsis, you may use parts of what you wrote during the first round or you may start again from scratch. Write your 50-word summary now.

Third summary. See what happens when you tighten the restriction further and narrow the word count to 30. You can use 30 of the words you have already written or find another way to describe your story within this new limitation. Sum up your story now.

Fourth summary. Now see what happens with a limitation of only 15 words to sum up your story. You can boil down your previous summary or find a new approach. As before, the word count does not include the title, and two words hyphenated still counts as two. In no more than 15 words, how would you describe your story?

Fifth summary. Narrow your vision further by writing a summary in only seven words. You can select seven of the words you have already written or come up with new words that do the job better. Try to express one complete thought.

Sixth summary. Think about how you have summed up your story so far. What if you had to reduce this description to three words? Would you remove words or find new ones to do the job? Since there are only three of them, these words do not need to express a complete thought in a sentence. If you prefer, they can reflect two or three concepts instead.

Seventh summary. By now, you have probably guessed the inevitable conclusion of this exercise, and that is to sum up your story in one word. This is obviously quite an important word. Will it be one you used before or a new one that does the job better? You are about to identify the subject of your story.

WRAP-UP

This has been a focusing exercise to help you explore what matters most in your story. The different-size synopses—or variations of them—may come in handy when you begin to send your work out and need a description to introduce your story in a cover letter or submission form. Your last three synopses suggest words to stress when describing your story to a potential agent or producer.

Related tools in *Character, Scene, and Story.* To boil your story down to the elements that matter most, go to the "Building Your Story" section and try "List It."

WHAT'S THE BIG IDEA?

THE QUICK VERSION
Define the theme of your story

BEST TIME FOR THIS
Any time you need to clarify what you are really writing about

THEME: THOUGHT WRAPPED IN STORY
A great story is more than a great story. It is an experience that stirs our emotions and provokes us to think—to discover new ideas or reexamine old ones—even long after we have left the theater. A key element of a story's lingering effect is its theme: the main idea that the author attempts to show us through the characters we meet and the events we witness.

Some writers insist that a dramatic story cannot be developed until first its theme has been clearly defined. They begin with a premise they wish to explore, and use it to guide their writing choices from beginning to end. This approach brings a certain degree of efficiency to script development—it provides an intellectual focus that helps keep everything on track—but runs the risk of producing a story with a heavy-handed author's message that fails to reach the audience at a gut level.

Other writers adopt a more intuitive approach. They start with a particular character, incident, or situation that has aroused their interest and emotions. Then they write with these specifics in mind, and look later for the universal ideas within them. This approach can lead to a script with powerful moments as the story evolves organically from the characters and their ever-changing world, but runs the risk of producing a script that gets lost in its own labyrinth of possibilities.

Whether the primary approach to your story is intellectual or intuitive, you need at some point to decide what theme you are illustrating. A complex story typically embodies a number of different themes but, if all these ideas are equally important, the script may end up being about none of them. Ideally, one theme is more important the rest. It is a core insight that unifies the different steps of the journey and elevates it to a higher level. What is the central theme of your story?

ABOUT THE EXERCISE
Defining your story's theme is usually not a matter of drumming up a big idea that you can bring to your story, but rather uncovering a big idea that is already woven into it. The goal of this exercise is to help you uncover the

main theme in the story you are developing now, and to state this theme as simply as possible. By keeping the theme statement short, you can create a guide that focuses on what matters most and is easy to keep in mind as you write or edit.

The approach of the exercise is inductive, moving from the specific to the universal. So you will first need to know whose story you are writing, and have a sense of what happens—or at least what could happen—in the dramatic journey. This exercise may be most useful when you are at a critical decision point in story development and not sure which way to turn next. You also may wish to revisit the exercise at different times to see if your theme has evolved or changed. Such reviews can be especially helpful when you are about to begin a round of revision.

■ SEARCHING FOR CLUES THAT MAY LEAD TO A THEME

In choosing characters and stories to develop, most writers instinctively also choose themes that matter to them. At first, the writer may not be aware of the themes within a particular story, and it is not unusual for a writer to tackle the same themes over and over—just as Arthur Miller in plays like *The Crucible* and *After the Fall* addresses the blurred line between good and evil, and August Wilson in plays like *Fences* and *Joe Turner's Come and Gone* explores the African American experience in different decades of the twentieth century.

The terms "subject" and "theme" are often confused. The "subject" of a story is the main topic—for example, "social equality." The "theme" is a point of view about the subject—for example, "Social equality leads to freedom" (A Doll's House). A subject can be expressed in a word or phrase, but a theme requires at least a complete sentence.

There is no correct or incorrect theme. No one else can tell you what it should be, and there is nowhere to find it except in yourself. What's most important is that you believe the theme to be true and have strong feelings about it. Know also that you are probably not the first person to ever think of this theme and that it's all right if it sounds familiar. What will make your piece original is probably not so much the theme itself but rather how you demonstrate it through the details of your story. For example, here are a few old sayings that could also be viewed as themes for dynamic and original work: "Money is the root of all evil" (*Glengarry Glen Ross*); "The truth shall set you free" (*Who's Afraid of Virginia Woolf?*); and, "Lies beget lies" (*Betrayal*).

Your theme may come to you quickly and easily. Or it may require a lot of time and thought. To find the theme, look for clues embedded in your story choices so far—whether you are in the planning stages, working your way through a first draft, or revising a script that's well on its way. Elements to consider:

1. **Main character.** Look again at the main character of your story. Identify his or her defining traits—strengths and weaknesses—and see if you can find any clues among these traits that might lead to your story's theme. Why did you choose to write about this particular character? If he or she is overly trusting, for example, you may have unconsciously picked a theme that relates to this trait, such as "Blind faith leads to failure" (*King Lear*).

2. **Quest.** Every story is a quest. What is your main character after? This primary goal—and the motivation to achieve it—may uncover a path to your story's theme. If your main character gains power and will do anything not to lose it, for example, you may find a theme such as "Power corrupts" (*Macbeth*).

3. **Main action.** Your main character exhibits different types of behavior and performs a number of different deeds during the dramatic journey. What is the most important thing your character does? This defining action, its motivation, and its outcome may suggest part of the story's theme. If the main action is to commit murder to exact revenge, for example, you may uncover a theme such as "Injustice breeds revenge" (*Medea*).

4. **Central conflict.** Drama is what happens when strong opposing forces collide. What are the two most important forces in conflict in your story? Which force prevails, and why? Your story's theme may be suggested by either this central conflict or its outcome. If the clash is between a labor union and management, for example, you may find a theme such as "Capitalism thrives at the expense of the working class" (*Waiting for Lefty*).

5. **Dominant emotion.** Think about the emotional landscape of your main character's dramatic journey. What feeling dominates this journey? You may discover your theme in the roots of the strongest emotion. What idea is contained there? If the dominant emotion is love, for example, you may uncover a theme such as "Love conquers all" (*Romeo and Juliet*).

6. **Final destination.** The theme is embodied ultimately by the whole story. So think again about what happens in yours. See if you can find any clues in the main event that might help you uncover the theme. The strongest clues can often be found in how the story ends. What is the final destination of the dramatic journey? If your character winds up isolated from loved ones, for example, you may find a theme such as "Dishonesty leads to isolation" (*A Streetcar Named Desire*).

Other ways to uncover your theme

If you have trouble finding a clear theme among your character and story choices so far, try these steps:

1. *Personal priorities.* The theme reflects a subject important to the writer—for example, love, honesty, or religion. What subjects have you written about in the past or considered writing about in the future? What topics most attract you when you are selecting a play or film to see, or a book to read? What subjects in the news make you stop and pay attention? List a few topics that matter most to you. Then see how your list matches the story you are developing now. In a word or phrase, what subject are you really writing about?

2. *Personal beliefs.* The theme reflects your view about the subject you have chosen. What point have you been trying to make with this story? Or, if you're still in the initial stages of script development, what point do you want to make? If your subject is jealousy, for example, you may wish to show that "jealousy destroys both the lover and the loved" (*Othello*). In a sentence that includes the subject you chose, what theme are you writing?

■ YOUR THEME STATEMENT

Once you know your theme, state it in writing as simply as possible. Do not include character names or other plot specifics. Make the statement universal in scope so that it rises beyond the world of your characters to include the world we all inhabit. A few suggestions:

1. Your theme statement is a guide to story development: a reminder of what you're really writing about. This guide will be most useful and easiest to remember if you can boil it down to one sentence.

2. If a story is to avoid being didactic, its theme will not be explained by the characters but rather implied by what they do and experience. Since the theme will not be stated in dialogue, you can word it any way that makes sense to you, as long as it expresses a complete thought that you believe and want to demonstrate as true.

3. For a more useful point of reference, develop a theme statement that stays contained in a single sentence and highlights two of the story's most important elements: character and conclusion. Suppose your story centers on the idea "Money is the root of all evil." You may create a more workable guide to story development by restating the theme as "Greed breeds poverty."

This rewording highlights "greed" as a defining trait of the main character and shows that he or she will end in "poverty"—either literally or figuratively—like the greedy real estate agents in *Glengarry Glen Ross* who wind up morally bankrupt. Unlike the static verb of being "is" in the first version, the verb "breeds" adds action to the statement. In effect, the second version becomes a map of the whole story: a reminder to the writer that the main character's greed must be clearly established and that the chain of story events must show how this defining trait causes the character's downfall.

WRAP-UP

As you use your theme statement to guide writing and editing, find a balance between what you say and don't say in the script. Remember that, if you spell out the theme for us, we may feel like we're being hit over the head with it. Great stories often raise more questions than they answer. Instead of providing pat solutions to complex issues, they provoke us to think. However, if your theme is too buried or too ambiguous, we may miss the point.

Related tools in *Character, Scene, and Story*. To convert ideas into dramatic terms and find a main theme for your story, go to the "Building Your Story" section and try "Found in Translation." To examine the story's theme from a new perspective, try "Coming Soon to a Theater near You!" in the same section.

WHAT'S IN A NAME?

THE QUICK VERSION
Use the naming process to explore the big picture of your story, figure out what matters most, and maybe even find a title

BEST TIME FOR THIS
After you have completed a draft or are well into the story

THE IMPORTANCE OF BEING A TITLE
The title is a powerful symbol of the whole story, and literally or figuratively infers what's most important about it. As a result, the naming process is an excellent way to explore your material, set priorities, and clarify your ideas. How well do you know what you are really writing about?

ABOUT THE EXERCISE
This focusing exercise asks you to consider different categories of titles and come up with new alternatives for your story. These categories have been created solely for the exercise. Some, such as the one-word title, highlight form. Some, such as the main-event title, highlight content. Categories often overlap, so that one title could fit more than one category. The purpose here is not to figure out how to sort titles, but to use the naming process to help you examine your story from different angles—twenty of them—and see what matters most.

■ THE NAMING PROCESS: A KEY TO WHAT MATTERS MOST

1. *What would your title be if it summed up your whole story in only one word?* This is the lean muscular approach to titles, for example:

Proof	*Endgame*	*Memento*
Notorious	*Hairspray*	*Rent*
Loot	*Contact*	*Wit*
Cats	*Arcadia*	*Plenty*

2. *What would your title be if it used so many words that we could barely remember them all?* This is the chatty approach. It breaks the title barrier by using as many words as it wants to give a detailed account of the subject or create an image. Such titles are still around, but were more popular in the sixties and seventies, for example:

Oh Dad, Poor Dad, Mama's Hung You in the Closet and I'm Feeling So Sad
For Colored Girls Who Have Considered Suicide/When the Rainbow Is Enuf
The Effects of Gamma Rays on Man-in-the-Moon Marigolds
Everything You Wanted to Know about Sex But Were Afraid to Ask
The Fearless Vampire Killers or: Pardon Me, But Your Teeth Are in My Neck

3. **What would your title be if it asked a question?** Some titles pose a question that will be addressed by the story, and sometimes this inquiry is directed to a specific character. For example:

Whatever Happened to Baby Jane?   *What Price Glory?*
Where's Poppa?   *Who's Afraid of Virginia Woolf?*
Whose Life Is It Anyway?   *Is Paris Burning?*
Isn't It Romantic?   *When You Comin' Back, Red Ryder?*

4. **What would your title be if it issued an order, warning, or advice?** This is a more demanding title that expects some kind of result, for example:

Take Me Out   *Dial M for Murder*
Play It Again, Sam   *Go!*
Don't Drink the Water   *Come Back to the Five and Dime, Jimmy*
Wait until Dark   *Dean, Jimmy Dean*
Stop the World, I Want to Get Off   *I Love You, You're Perfect, Now Change*
Kiss Me Quick, I'm Double Parked

5. **What would your title be if it named your main character?** This title implies that a main character is so fascinating that nothing need be said except his or her name. The identifier might be a first name only, last name only, full name, title and name, nickname, or description and name, for example:

Hamlet   *Elmer Gantry*   *Major Barbara*
Macbeth   *Henry IV*   *Anna in the Tropics*
Fosse   *Uncle Vanya*   *Killer Joe*
Hedda Gabler   *Tiny Alice*   *Agnes of God*

6. **What would your title be if it described your main character?** This title describes an important trait or condition of a principal character without using his or her actual name, for example:

The Singing Detective   *The Miracle Worker*
The English Patient   *A Man for All Seasons*
Lord of the Rings   *Last of the Red Hot Lovers*
Rebel Without a Cause   *Psycho*
Side Man   *Dirty Blonde*

7. **What would your title be if it were a personal statement from the main character?** This title declares something important from the main character's point of view, for example:

I Never Sang for My Father	*I Married a Werewolf*
I Remember Mama	*I Am a Camera*
I Am My Own Wife	*I Am a Fugitive from a Chain Gang*
I Led Three Lives	*I'm Not Rappaport*

8. **What would your title be if it named the two most important characters in the story?** This "dynamic duo" title identifies the most important relationship in the story, for example:

Antony and Cleopatra	*Bonnie and Clyde*
Thelma and Louise	*Topdog/Underdog*
Romeo and Juliet	*Dr. Jekyll and Mr. Hyde*
Harold and Maude	*Butch Cassidy and the Sundance Kid*

9. **What would your title be if it described more than one character in the story?** This title describes a set of characters, from just a couple to the whole population, without naming anyone, for example:

Angels in America	*The Grifters*
The Producers	*Assassins*
The Boys from Oz	*The Stepford Wives*
Lesbian Vampires of Sodom	*The Cook, the Thief, the Wife, and Her Lover*
The Odd Couple	*Children of a Lesser God*
A Few Good Men	

10. **What would your title be if it highlighted the setting?** This title tells where the action takes place, either literally or figuratively. It implies that the setting has a lot to do with what happens in the story, for example:

Avenue Q	*Our Town*
The Cherry Orchard	*In the Shadow of the Glen*
Animal Farm	*Bus Stop*
Cape Fear	*Chicago*
Little Shop of Horrors	*Hotel Desperado*
Chinatown	*Cabaret*

11. **What would your title be if it highlighted when the story takes place?** Telling when important action takes place, literally or figuratively, this title implies that a certain time or circumstance is key to what happens in the story, for example:

Fifth of July	*Twilight: Los Angeles, 1992*
Night of the Iguana	*The Desperate Hours*
The Children's Hour	*The Year of Living Dangerously*
The Birthday Party	*The Day the Whores Came Out to Play Tennis*
Twelfth Night	
When Pigs Fly	*Last Night at the Ballyhoo*

12. **What would your title be if it focused on something physical?** This title identifies one or more physical objects, elements, or personal qualities that are pivotal to the story action or somehow represent it, for example:

The Rose Tattoo	*Seven Guitars*
Fried Green Tomatoes	*The Diary of Anne Frank*
Quills	*Skylight*
Schindler's List	*The Full Monty*
The Glass Menagerie	*Krapp's Last Tape*
The Chairs	*The Piano*

13. **What would your title be if it highlighted a certain feeling or mood?** This title suggests emotional life that is important to the action, for example:

Frozen	*Body Heat*
Desire under the Elms	*Shakespeare in Love*
Laughing Wild	*Wicked*
Darkness at Noon	*Look Back in Anger*
Ballad of the Sad Café	*Blues for Mister Charlie*
High Anxiety	*Hurlyburly*

14. **What would your title be if it combined two elements not usually thought of as a pair?** This "odd combo" title suggests that two elements have an important relationship that is not apparent at first glance, for example:

Arsenic and Old Lace	*Brimstone and Treacle*
Tea and Sympathy	*Cries and Whispers*
Bread and Roses	*Blood and Sand*
Summer and Smoke	*Laundry and Bourbon*
Love and Drowning	

15. **What would your title be if it highlighted a lesson that your story has to teach?** This title acts instructional and explains what is supposed to be learned by the characters or the audience as a result of the story, for example:

How I Learned to Drive	*How to Succeed in Business without*
How the Other Half Loves	*Really Trying*
How to Marry a Millionaire	*The Piano Lesson*
How the West Was Won	*How to Make a Monster*
How I Became an Interesting Person	

16. **What would your title be if it were a metaphor?** This title describes a leading character, important story element, or even the whole story itself by making a poetic comparison to something else, for example:

American Beauty	*A Thousand Clowns*
Cat on a Hot Tin Roof	*Dark at the Top of the Stairs*
Lost in Translation	*The Silence of the Lambs*

A Streetcar Named Desire	Separate Tables
A Doll's House	Lion in Winter

17. **What would your title be if it summed up the main event of the story?** This title tells what happens literally or figuratively, for example:

Death of a Salesman	Judgment at Nuremberg
Long Day's Journey into Night	Waiting for Godot
Breaking the Code	The Marriage Proposal
Entertaining Mr. Sloan	One Flew Over the Cuckoo's Nest
The Killing of Sister George	Finding Nemo

18. **What would your title be if it identified the subject of the story?** This title goes above and beyond the plot to the highest level and identifies the subject embodied by the story, for example:

Betrayal	The Invention of Love
Love! Valour! Compassion!	Les Liaisons Dangereuses
Fences	Deathtrap
Crimes of the Heart	A Beautiful Mind
Six Degrees of Separation	Terms of Endearment
Travesties	True West

19. **What would your title be if it identified the kind of story you are writing?** This title steps back from the story and identifies its genre, for example:

Pulp Fiction	Torch Song Trilogy
A Midsummer Night's Dream	Manhattan Murder Mystery
Love Story	A Soldier's Play
The Comedy of Errors	The Ghost Story
Rocky Horror Picture Show	The Play about the Baby
Bedroom Farce	Love Letters

20. **What would your title be if it made a literary allusion?** This title alludes to a famous saying, proverb, biblical passage, quotation, or literary source which reflects the plot or theme of the story, for example:

Of Mice and Men alludes to the saying "The best laid plans of mice and men oft go astray."

A Raisin in the Sun draws its title from a Langston Hughes poem which asks about a dream deferred: "Does it dry up like a raisin in the sun?"

Little Foxes echoes the biblical Song of Solomon when it describes "the little foxes that spoil the vines."

Shadow of a Doubt refers to the legal imperative to a jury to be certain beyond a shadow of a doubt when returning a guilty verdict.

You Can't Take It with You doesn't refer to an old adage. It is one.

You may need to do some research to complete this final round. Think about what matters most in your story and draw from another source to find a literary title.

WRAP-UP

Once you have a title, it may influence your story decisions, because, as you write or revise, it will always be somewhere in your mind as a guide. Later on, it will be a guide for the audience as well, because it will, by nature, signal what matters most during the story. Be sure you have the right guide in place. Here are a few questions to help evaluate any title you may be considering now:

- How well does the title fit the story? Does it stress the right stuff?
- Is the title unique?
- How well does the title match the mood and style of the story? If it's a comedy, for example, does it sound like one?
- Is it a memorable title that will stir up interest in your work? Remember that the title will be the first impression you make on an audience.
- How does the title look in print and how does it sound when you say it aloud? These elements can have a subliminal impact on its appeal.

> **Related tools in** *Character, Scene, and Story*. To continue fleshing out the big picture of your story, go to the "Building Your Story" section and try any stage 3 exercise, particularly "Different Sides of the Story" or "Coming Soon to a Theater near You!"

THE FOREST OF YOUR STORY

THE QUICK VERSION
Sum up what you know about the big picture of your story

BEST TIME FOR THIS
When you have a completed draft or are well into the story

SOMEWHERE THROUGH THESE TREES LIES A FOREST
When you're on the fourth page of the third scene of act 2 and you're try-ing to figure out what this particular character will do next or say next with that particular character at this particular time and place in the story, chances are you're not thinking thematically or pondering what this whole thing was supposed to be about in the first place. You may not be able to see the forest for the trees.

In the end, however, it's not about the details of the story so much as how they add up. As with any art, the whole is greater than the sum of the parts. By keeping the forest of the story in mind, you can keep the dra-matic journey on track as you maneuver the countless details that demand your attention. The term "forest of the story" here includes three basic ele-ments—plot, subject, and theme—wrapped together in one vision. What is the forest of your story?

ABOUT THE EXERCISE
This exercise offers questions to help you clarify how your story's plot, sub-ject, and theme interconnect. You can use the exercise either as a summary tool to reflect what you have learned from other big-picture exercises, or as an introductory tool to establish a broad context for other big-picture exer-cises that you may try later. Either way, you will be exploring your story in global terms.

As you address the exercise questions, keep in mind that there are no wrong answers. You can interpret and respond to each question any way you wish. You may learn the most from the questions that pose the most difficulty. Exercise examples are from the play *Doubt* by John Patrick Shanley.

■ **SUMMING UP YOUR PLOT**
1. A story is what happens among certain individuals in a specific time and place. In *Doubt*, Sister Aloysius, the principal of a Catholic elementary

school, becomes so obsessed with driving away a suspected child predator that she ends up shattering her own belief system. Briefly sum up the plot of your story.

2. Most stories raise a big plot question near the beginning. This question then remains unanswered through most of the story so that we must follow the entire dramatic journey in order to get the answer or to discover that there is no clear answer. The early scenes of *Doubt* stir up the questions "Is Father Flynn really guilty of child abuse? And, if so, how will Sister Aloysius prove it?" Think about what happens in the world of your characters. What big question is raised early on, but left unanswered through most of the story?

3. The big plot question is usually answered by the final outcome of the dramatic journey. In most cases, we had a sense of what this answer would be—we have been gradually prepared to believe it—yet it is not quite what we expected. In *Doubt,* we follow much of the story wondering whether or not Aloysius will be able to prove that Father Flynn is guilty. By the time we reach the end of the story, however, we realize that this quest has been more about her blind certainty than his guilt or innocence, so the big plot question is left unanswered. We are left with doubt. Think about the big plot question that spans the events of your story. What is the final answer? If there is no clear final answer, why is that?

4. Other exercises in this guide explore the idea that all human emotions can be boiled down to three basic feelings—fear, anger, and love. For example, anxiety, alarm, and grief are forms of fear. Irritation, hate, and rage are forms of anger. Joy, tenderness, and sympathy are forms of love. When all is said and done, *Doubt* might be seen primarily as a story of fear. Think about your story. Which primal feeling—fear, love, or anger—best describes its emotional landscape?

5. In *Doubt*, Aloysius's fear is what drives her to launch a crusade against the priest she suspects of wrongdoing, even though she has no real evidence to support her accusation. This fear might reflect worry about the well-being of the children of St. Nicholas School as well as concern about failing to live up to the duties of a principal. On a larger scale, Aloysius also may be demonstrating a profound fear of uncertainty and of the chaos that can result from operating outside a prescribed system of rules. Think again about the emotional landscape of your story. Briefly describe any connection you see between its primary emotion and its sequence of events.

■ **EXPLORING YOUR SUBJECT**

1. Though Shanley's play centers on the brewing scandal of a priest suspected of child abuse, the subject of the play is neither corruption in the Catholic church nor pedophilia. The subject is doubt. This is why the play ends not with the guilt or innocence of the priest, but with Sister Aloysius

experiencing for the first time the pangs of doubt. Think about your story at the highest level and in relationship to your plot. In one or two words, what is the real subject of your story?

2. Shanley's play explores doubt as a hallmark of wisdom and an opportunity for growth. Think again about your subject. In a little more detail, what is your story about? Expand your description of the subject by qualifying its meaning and making it more specific.

3. In Shanley's view, doubt in modern life has become something to be avoided rather than embraced. Expressing doubt is perceived too often as a sign of weakness and not as a sign of strength, especially in the world of politics and power. In media interviews, he has said that the play was inspired by—and in some ways serves as an allegory for—the U.S. invasion of Iraq in 2003. Why is the subject of your story important?

■ UNDERSTANDING YOUR THEME

1. A thematic statement reflects an important idea about the subject that the author believes and is trying to show as true. For example, the theme of *Doubt* is "Doubt leads to wisdom and growth." Think about your subject in relationship to your plot. What theme does this combination suggest?

2. The main character of the story typically embodies the theme. For example, the main character of *Doubt* is Sister Aloysius, one whose dramatic journey moves her from unwavering certainty to transformational doubt. Who in your story embodies your theme, and how?

3. While the main character's quest is meant to demonstrate the truth of the theme, certain forces oppose this truth. These include all of the obstacles standing in the character's path—from personal traits and conditions that weaken the character, to other characters or groups with opposing needs. These forces of antagonism embody a countertheme also at work in the story. If the theme is "Doubt leads to wisdom and growth," for example, the countertheme might be "Unwavering certainty gets the job done." The story then becomes a struggle between these opposing ideas. What is the countertheme at work in your story?

4. In many cases, the countertheme is embodied by the story's main antagonist. In *Doubt*, it is the protagonist Sister Aloysius who embodies the countertheme as well as the theme. At the beginning of the dramatic journey, she sees doubt as a sign of weakness and operates from a position of absolute certainty. By the end of the dramatic journey, she has begun to question her entire belief system. Who in your story embodies the countertheme, and how?

5. Think some more about your theme. Ideally, it raises a big universal question which is above and beyond the specifics of your story. Rather, it is a question about us in the audience: an inquiry into the human condition. While the plot raises its big question early on—this is what hooks us in and engages us emotionally—the theme may operate more slowly. In

some cases, it may raise its big question gradually over the course of the story. *Doubt* poses its big thematic question in the opening line when Father Flynn in a Sunday sermon asks his congregation, "What do you do when you're not sure?" Think about your theme. What big question does it raise on a universal level?

6. Because the big thematic question operates in the realm of higher truths and beliefs, the answer may be complex and have many different shades and dimensions. *Doubt* shows us that, when we are not sure of what to do, we can either cling to rules that protect us from the discomfort of uncertainty or use the power of doubt to explore new possibilities and gain new wisdom. At the end of the story, when Aloysius is finally able to experience and express doubt, she is in anguish yet also on the verge of becoming a new person. She has undone the certainties that until now have been blocking her growth. What is the answer to your big thematic question? Try to state the answer as simply yet truthfully as possible.

WRAP-UP

One of the most common dramaturgical problems is a weak throughline: a series of often good scenes that don't add up to enough when put together in sequence. By keeping the forest of the story in mind, you can make smarter decisions at the scenic level when you are focused on smaller story elements, such as what a character knows or doesn't know at this point in the dramatic journey, or what a character wants now or does next.

> **Related tools in *Character, Scene, and Story*.** To explore the big picture of your story from different angles, go to the "Building Your Story" section and try any stage 3 exercise, particularly "Different Sides of the Story" or "Coming Soon to a Theater near You!"

READY, AIM, FOCUS

THE QUICK VERSION
Clarify the big picture of the story by simplifying and prioritizing your story ideas

BEST TIME FOR THIS
When you feel ready to revise a completed draft

MANAGING THE ELEMENTS OF A DRAMATIC JOURNEY
We encounter many different elements in a dramatic story: a cast of characters who all have distinct needs and values, experience different emotions, and exhibit a gamut of behaviors as they tackle the problems and obstacles in their way. Meanwhile many different images come and go, and many different topics are debated from different points of view and for different purposes. Ideally, the combination of these elements creates a series of events that move us from the beginning of the dramatic journey to the end. All of these various elements are important, but in the end they are not all equally important. Some matter more than others. How well can you tell the difference?

ABOUT THE EXERCISE
The goal of this focusing exercise is to prepare you for the revision process by boiling your story down to a series of simple terms. Try to address each exercise topic with only one word or, if necessary, two words. Do not repeat a word that you have already given. These restrictions can be challenging but also enlightening. Consider doing this exercise more than once during revisions to see how your responses change or don't change.

■ IN A WORD (OR TWO) . . .
1. Sum up what your story is about.
2. Describe your main character.
3. Identify the most significant setting in your story. Use a noun.
4. Describe this setting. Use an adjective for the noun you just wrote.
5. Identify the most important time—when—story action takes place.
6. Describe your main character at the start of the dramatic journey.
7. Describe your main character at the end of the dramatic journey.
8. Describe the most important part of the transition: how your character moves from the beginning to the end of the dramatic journey.

9. Define your main character's goal in the story: what he or she wants overall.
10. Define the most difficult problem that your character must overcome in order to achieve the story goal.
11. Identify an important strategy that the main character tries—successfully or not—at any time in the story in order to achieve the goal. Use a verb.
12. Identify a second important strategy of the main character at any time during the quest. Use a second verb.
13. Identify a third important strategy of the main character at any time during the quest. Use a third verb.
14. Name something that tends to be highly valued in the world of your story.
15. Name something that is often very important in other places, but not so in the world of your story—for example, money might be very important in the business world but of little value in a religious commune.
16. Identify an important discovery that your character makes at any time during the story.
17. Identify something important that your character gains during the story.
18. Identify something important that your character loses during the story.
19. Rethink your answer to the second question and sum up who your main character is. Remember not to repeat what you wrote before.
20. Rethink your answer to the first question and sum up what your story is about.

■ IN A SENTENCE . . .
Sum up the main event of your story—what happens overall—in one sentence. Use any of the words you found in the first part of the exercise.

WRAP-UP
Before you begin to revise a completed draft, take the time to identify the most important elements that have emerged from your character and story choices. Even the most complex material can be boiled down to simple terms that can help guide you through the rest of the script development process.

> Related tools in *Character, Scene, and Story.* For another approach to identifying the key elements of your story, go to the "Building Your Story" section and try "List It."

SIX STEPS OF REVISION

THE QUICK VERSION
Revise the current draft of your script

BEST TIME FOR THIS
When you feel ready to revise a completed draft

WRITING IS REWRITING
Just as there is no one way to write a script, there is no one way to revise one. However, most dramatic writers would probably agree that, regardless of how and when it occurs, revision is one of the most important parts of script development. Once you have put your ideas down on paper and completed a draft, you can begin to look at your material with different eyes, evaluate what you see from this new perspective, and begin to refine the meaning and shape of what you have created.

In most cases, revision focuses first on how well the whole story works, how fully the characters have been developed, and how effectively the sequence of events has been composed. Once major character and story issues have been addressed, revisions can turn to smaller, though still important matters, such as cleaning up remaining issues at the scene and beat levels, and refining the dialogue.

It is not unusual for a dramatic script to undergo several rounds of revision. Some of this rewriting may occur before anyone else sees the script. Other revisions may take place after the script has been reviewed by others through dramatic writing workshops, development conferences, private readings, private or public staged readings, and—if the script makes it into production—the rehearsal process.

Dramatic scripts are meant to be seen and heard, so getting your characters off the page is vital to the revision process. If you have access to actors, you can set up a formal or informal reading of your work once you feel that you have a draft ready for this level of attention. In the early stages of revision, if the actors are good, such readings can work just as well in a living room as they do in a theater, and a small audience can sometimes be as useful as a large one in assessing a script's strengths and weaknesses. Aside from any comments that other listeners might share, you will learn a lot just by seeing what happens when the actors bring your characters to life in front of others.

If you do not have access to actors, you can trigger some of this discovery on your own by reading the script aloud and literally hearing your words. Some writers prefer to read the script aloud even if they have actors available to read it for them later.

ABOUT THE EXERCISE

This exercise offers practical guidelines for revising your script in steps, starting with a broad look at what you have so far, gradually narrowing your vision of the script down to its details, and then returning to the broader view. These guidelines are designed for a full-length script which centers on the dramatic journey of one main character. As with any exercise in this guide, however, these can be adapted to any story structure and writing process.

How you adapt the exercise will depend not only on the size and form of your script, but also the number of drafts you have completed so far. If this is your first draft, consider doing all six steps in the order given so that you can get a thorough review of your work. If this is a later draft, you may wish to abbreviate or skip some of these steps, depending on what your script still needs.

During the revision process, you can use almost any character, scene, or story exercise in this guide for additional support. In "Causing a Scene," the exercises most directly applicable to revisions include "Thinking in Beats" and any of the stage 3 dialogue exercises. In "Building Your Story," try "The Art of Grabbing," "Step by Step," or any stage 3 big-picture exercise during revisions. Be sure to review the troubleshooter at the end of the guide as well for further suggestions of exercises to consider when addressing common script problems.

■ STEP 1: DO A GLOBAL REVIEW OF THE SCRIPT

Is the story clear, complete, and interesting? Begin the revision process by reading your script from beginning to end as quickly as possible and preferably in one sitting. Jot down any ideas or questions that arise, and flag specific areas of the script that need more attention. As you do this, try to keep your focus on big issues and avoid getting bogged down in details. The goal of this global review is to move through the script with as little interruption as possible so that you can get a clear first impression of how the whole thing works so far. This impression is critical because it will provide a working context for all of the revisions to follow.

When making script changes after a global review, be sure of the following:
- The story adds up clearly to one main event.
- The subject and theme are clearly demonstrated by what happens in the story.
- What happens is always believable within the world of this story.
- The story prepares us intellectually and emotionally to understand why the crisis is a true crisis for this main character and not just a difficult situation.

- The beginning of the story raises a big question that doesn't get answered until the end.
- The conclusion is the result of everything that has happened and not a product of external forces, such as chance, accident, or any other last-minute plot surprise.

■ STEP 2: FOCUS ON ONE CHARACTER AT A TIME

Is each character necessary, distinct, and appropriately developed? A thorough character review requires a number of rereadings of the script so that you can see the story from each character's unique perspective. The goal of this review is to track the character's needs, feelings, and actions through the story as well as the larger transition that the character is undergoing. For best results, do each reading in one sitting so that you can clearly follow the character's overall arc of action and determine how well the character holds up as a distinct individual with a consistent core identity and a unique set of values and beliefs.

Start with the main character and review the script with only this character in mind. Reread only the scenes in which this character appears and, within these scenes, focus primarily on the stage directions and dialogue that apply to this character. As you note your observations and questions, try to stay focused on the larger issues of who this character is, how this character is causing the dramatic journey, and how this character is being affected by what happens. Be sure that the main character

- is someone whom we can care about and want to focus on;
- has an important goal that is clearly stated or implied;
- actively pursues this goal through ever-changing strategies;
- faces increasingly difficult challenges as the story evolves;
- has enough at stake to keep trying harder in spite of obstacles;
- is revealed and affected by what happens in the story.

Once you have analyzed the main character and identified issues to address, continue the character review by focusing in a similar way on each of the remaining characters in order of importance, with a focus on how each of these other characters is unique, why each is essential, and how each is changed or not changed by story events.

■ STEP 3: REVIEW STORY STRUCTURE

Does the story make sense intellectually and emotionally? Focus next on the chain of events that comprise the story. The goal this time is to see how the dramatic action flows, and whether or not the end of the story differs from the beginning of the story because of what happens in the middle.

Instead of approaching this chain of events in detail, look first at the most important events in the sequence: the inciting event that triggers the main character's dramatic journey, the turning point that ends each act and shifts the journey into a new direction, and the crisis and climax where the main character is most tested and revealed. These key events are the bold strokes of the story and can be important measures of the fundamental strength of the story structure.

Once you have analyzed the key events, you can review the throughline that connects these events scene by scene, act by act, from beginning to end. If you have not already created a step outline, this might be a good time to do one so that you can get an at-a-glance view of the story structure (see "Step by Step" earlier in this guide).

When reviewing story events, focus on them in relationship to one another: how they connect or don't connect, and why each is an important part of the whole chain. Check that no event simply repeats what has gone before, has no consequences later, or is an unnecessary detour from the throughline. As you do this, make sure that:

- The inciting event occurs during the story—not before it—and directly affects the main character.
- Each act ends with a turning point that is dramatically strong enough and different enough to draw us into the next act with a compelling new question.
- The dramatic action slowly rises to a crisis that forces the main character to make the most difficult decision in the story.
- Each dramatic event in the story is both unique and essential: without this event, the story would not make sense.
- Each dramatic event in the story is connected through cause and effect to at least one other dramatic event in the story.
- The sequence of events grows out of a changing emotional landscape that explains why and when things happen as they do.

■ STEP 4: FOCUS ON ONE SCENE AT A TIME

How well does each scene work dramatically on its own? With a strong throughline in place, you can begin to "think smaller" and analyze the details of each scene. Ideally each is a turning-point experience that changes the world of the story in either a good or bad way, and moves the dramatic journey closer to its ultimate success or failure. The goal of the scene-by-scene review is to ensure the dramatic integrity of each of these units. When making script changes during a scene review, be sure that:

- The characters each want something important and have an irresistible reason for wanting it here and now.
- Conflict is always present in some form throughout the scene.
- The scene is mostly about what's happening now and not about what happened in the past or somewhere else.
- Unless it is short, the scene unfolds in different beats of action that reflect a variety of character topics, strategies, and emotions.

- The beat changes are clean and make sense at a gut level.
- The main event of the scene is clear.

■ STEP 5: REVIEW THE SCRIPT TECHNICALLY

Is the dialogue effective and boiled down to its essence? Once the larger pieces of the story are in place, you can begin to approach the script technically and edit the remaining wordage of each scene for impact, density, and length. The goal of this refinement process is to heighten the language of the script and to eliminate any speeches, lines, or words that do not fit or are not really necessary. This is often when "darlings" die, scenes shrink, and stories tighten.

Just as much of writing is rewriting, much of rewriting is cutting. During this stage of revision, cut the story as much as you can without damaging the voice of any character, the main event of any scene, or the central throughline of the story. You may need to read through the script a number of times to accomplish this important task, cutting sometimes only a few words at a time, or a line here and a beat there. It can all add up to a major cut of several pages in the end. During this technical review, be sure that:
- The voice of each character remains distinct and true.
- Any unnecessary exposition has been eliminated.
- The dialogue leaves room for subtext that is knowable and adds another level of meaning to the scene.
- Unnecessary beats in each scene have been cut.
- Unnecessary speeches in each beat have been cut.
- Unnecessary words in each speech have been cut.

■ STEP 6: DO ANOTHER GLOBAL REVIEW

Is the story clear, complete, and interesting—or does it still need more work? Read your script again as quickly as possible. As with the first global review, the goal is to get a broad impression of how the whole script works. Jot down any questions that you still need to address and any tasks that you still need to complete. By this time in the revision process, these issues are likely to be small, though a larger new question or task can sometimes emerge when you return to the big picture of the story. Your findings will determine where you go from here.

WRAP-UP

The revision process is when many scripts really get written. As with any of the writing arts, however, your script will probably never be "finished": there will always be something more that could be done to make it just a little bit better. Hopefully, at some point, however, you will feel satisfied enough with your work to abandon the revision process, send your script out into the world, and leap into the refreshing process of starting something new.

Related tools in *Character, Scene, and Story.* For help with editing dialogue from a technical perspective, go to the "Causing a Scene" section and try "Anatomy of Speech."

Fixing Common Script Problems

Here in random order are twenty dramaturgical problems that often arise during new script development. Each description highlights the nature of the problem, briefly suggests how to approach it, and gives examples of specific guide exercises that can help you find a solution.

FALSE CHARACTER

Problem. The writer has not spent enough time getting to know the characters and has imposed artificial choices and actions on them to fit the prescribed structure of the story. These choices may look good at the moment but, in the big picture, the characters don't ring true. In addition to such characters imprisoned by plot, false characters include the stock character, such as the prostitute with a heart of gold, the two-dimensional villain who is nothing but evil, the author's mouthpiece who stops the show to deliver thematic messages, and the foil who exists in a scene only to ask the right questions so that another character can ramble on.

Solution. Double the time you spend fleshing out your principal characters. Know what traits, knowledge, and experiences make each one unique, and let the characters—not the plot—lead you to what happens next. To learn more about your characters, try any tool in "Developing Your Character," from "Basic Character Builder" to "In So Many Words." For difficult characters, be sure to try exercises that can lead to surprising discoveries, such as "Where the Character Lives," "Where the Character Works," "Into the Past," "The Secret Lives of Characters," or "The Dramatic Triangle." For a two-dimensional bad guy, try "The Noble Character" or "The Character You Like Least," or go to "Causing a Scene" and try "Good Intentions."

UNNECESSARY CHARACTER

Problem. Some characters are too much alike. They duplicate each other's functions in the story and sometimes even sound so much alike that their lines of dialogue are easily interchangeable. Other characters play such incidental roles that their presence barely matters—for example, the waiter whose only function is to serve cocktails in a scene that could have begun with the cocktails already on the table. In the end, the overall chain of events in the story would not be significantly affected if any of these redundant or utilitarian characters were removed.

Solution. Challenge the necessity for each character by imagining how the story would unfold without him or her. Know why each character is essential, how each differs from the rest, and what each contributes to the story. Get rid of characters who don't really matter, and make sure that each remaining character is distinct. To find greater contrasts among your characters, go to the section "Developing Your Character" and try such exercises as "Defining Trait," "Characters in Contrast," "Finding the Character's Voice," "Three Characters in One," and "In So Many Words." To analyze the importance of character relationships, try "Allies: Then and Now," "Adversaries: Then and Now," and "The Dramatic Triangle."

NO ONE TO CARE ABOUT

Problem. The principal characters fail to engage us because they are neither likeable nor empathetic, or because their needs and problems seem trivial, or because they are simply not very interesting. As a result, it's hard to care about what happens to them in the story.

Solution. Review the character's universal traits. Have you presented someone with whom we can empathize? Then look at what makes him or her unique. Is the character unusual enough to command attention? You may need to shift the balance between the ordinary and extraordinary so that a strange character becomes more familiar, or an everyday character becomes more unusual. You also may need to heighten the emotional impact of the character's dramatic journey. To make a character more engaging, go to the section "Developing Your Character" and try such exercises as "Getting Emotional," "The Noble Character," "Character as Paradox," and "Seven Deadly Sins." To increase a character's universality, go to the section "Causing a Scene" and try "Universal Truths and Lies." To heighten a character's dramatic impact, try "Good Intentions" and "The Emotional Storyboard."

NOT CLEAR WHAT THE CHARACTER WANTS

Problem. The character is saying and doing things in a scene, but seems to have little or no objective. As a result, the scene wanders in and out of various topics, but ends up going nowhere.

Solution. Make sure you know what the character wants in each scene and use that desire to drive the dramatic action. Even if the character is secretly up to something else, we need to sense that someone is trying to accomplish something important. In some cases, you can strengthen or clarify a character's objective by heightening the problem. To explore character needs, go to the section "Causing a Scene" and try "What Does the Character Want?"

NOT ENOUGH CONFLICT

Problem. The conflict in a scene has either dropped out or weakened to such a low level that the scenic event occurs too easily. As a result, the importance of the event feels diminished and the character's commitment to his or her objective has not really been tested. What's more, we have lost the opportunity to discover something new about the character's true nature by observing him or her under stress. One of the first signs of weak conflict is a scene that feels flat, talky, or expositional.

Solution. Know what the character wants and create obstacles that will make the objective more difficult to achieve. To explore character conflict, go to the section "Causing a Scene" and try "What's the Problem?" and "Heating Things Up."

NOT ENOUGH AT STAKE

Problem. The character doesn't have a strong enough reason to attempt a difficult or troublesome task. Either too little is at stake or nothing is at stake. As a result, it doesn't make sense for the character to tackle problems, take risks, or use up important resources in order to get something done.

Solution. Motivate your characters appropriately for the tasks they face: the greater the challenge, the stronger the motivation needs to be. At the scenic level, the stakes need to be high enough to make the scene happen. At the story level, the stakes need to be even higher: critical enough to push the main character to the end of the line and make compromise or surrender seem unthinkable. To explore character motivation, go to the section "Causing a Scene" and try "Good Intentions."

FALSE STARTS AND STOPS

Problem. It takes too long to get to the meat of the scene. There is too much setup and unnecessary delay before the core action begins. In some cases, the scene goes on and the characters keep interacting even though the core action has ended.

Solution. Know what the scene is really about. Then enter it as late as possible and get out as soon as possible. To explore a scenic event, go to the section "Causing a Scene" and try such exercises as "Basic Scene Starter" and "Scene in a Sentence."

STRATEGY GONE STALE

Problem. The conflict in a scene has grown static because the character has been trying the same unsuccessful strategy for much too long.

Solution. Use what you know about your unique character to find different ways to tackle a scenic objective. Some of these strategies may reflect a step-by-step action plan. Others may be spontaneous changes of behavior due to unexpected conflicts. Whether these strategies succeed or fail, they reveal different sides of the character, create the different beats of the scene, and bring variety to the dramatic action. To explore character strategy, go to the section "Causing a Scene" and try "How It Happens," "Character Adjustments," "The *Aha!*s of the Story," and "Thinking in Beats."

RETROSPECTIVE ELUCIDATION

Problem. The dramatic action comes to a halt so that characters can explain their past lives or share brilliant analyses of themselves and each other. This "all talk, no action" scenario tends to be launched in the absence of conflict and often with the help of a foil who prompts the explainer to keep telling more. When the term "exposition" is used negatively, it is usually to describe explanations like these.

Solution. Bring us into a scene only if something dramatic is about to happen, and keep the focus on the here and now. Use exposition sparingly—administer it in small doses—and don't reveal the past until you have created a question in the present that makes us want to know what happened before. To manage the challenge of exposition, go to the section "Causing a Scene" and try "There and Then," "Seeing the Scene," and "Talking and Listening." To keep the action more rooted in the present, try physical life exercises such as "Where in the World Are We?," "In the Realm of the Senses," and "The Voice of the Setting."

PUNCHES THAT DON'T LAND

Problem. The characters in a scene have clear objectives, problems, and motivations, but the conflict between them grows stale because neither character seems capable of affecting the other in a meaningful way. No one is vulnerable.

Solution. In drama, even the strongest characters have certain vulnerabilities that can expose them to unwanted physical, psychological, social, economic, or political effects. These vulnerabilities are often what fascinate us most about the characters we meet. Make sure that you understand the weaknesses of your characters as well as their strengths. Use this knowledge to disarm them in ways that reveal important truths about who they are, and turn the story in unexpected directions. To explore character vulnerabilities, go to the section "Developing Your Character" and try such exercises as "The Secret Lives of Characters" and "Seven Deadly Sins." To explore these vulnerabilities from an emotional angle, try "Getting Emotional" in the same section and "The Emotional Storyboard" in the "Causing a Scene" section.

NOTHING HAPPENING

Problem. The characters in a scene discuss various topics and engage in various behaviors, but it's not clear what matters most. Their interactions all seem equally important or equally unimportant. As a result, the dramatic elements cancel each other out and do not add up clearly to an important new story event.

Solution. Know the main event of each scene and be able to express it simply. To explore what matters most in a scene, go to the section "Causing a Scene" and try "Basic Scene Starter" and "Scene in a Sentence." To analyze the scene from a beat perspective, try "Thinking in Beats."

SOMETHING HAPPENING, BUT IT DOESN'T MATTER

Problem. A dramatic event occurs, but seems to have little or no impact on anyone in the story. Like a false dilemma, it comes and goes without consequence. Such events are often "darlings" that exist only for their own sake.

Solution. Identify the key events in the throughline of the story. Get rid of any that are not truly essential, and combine any that seem redundant. Know how each key event has changed the world of the story and show this impact in the dramatic action that ensues. To explore scenic events and how they connect or don't connect, try "The Roots of Action" from the "Causing a Scene" section, and "Step by Step," "Picturing the Arc of Action," and "Six Steps of Revision" from the "Building Your Story" section.

LACK OF FOCUS EARLY ON

Problem. We've been watching a dramatic story unfold, but we're not sure whose story it is, what type of dramatic journey we have begun, or what "rules of the game" apply or don't apply. We're more confused than intrigued by what's happening.

Solution. While there is no magic formula for dramatic storytelling, ten minutes is often a milestone in audience participation. By that time, we will probably have decided whether or not to go along for the ride. If you have given us a clear dramatic focus, we will be more likely to break through the intellectual challenge of trying to figure out who's who and what's what in the story, and ease into the more emotional process of becoming part of story events. To explore dramatic focus, go to the section "Building Your Story" and try such exercises as "Whose Story Is It?," "How Will the Tale Be Told?," "As the World Turns," and The Art of Grabbing."

MAIN CHARACTER TOO PASSIVE OR MISSING IN ACTION

Problem. The story was centered on one main character, but he or she has now stopped driving the action and has become a passive participant who only reacts to others and external events. This passivity occurs most often in the latter half of the script, where character initiative matters most. In some cases, the main character drops out of sight for long stretches of time while minor characters hijack the story. As a result, the main character becomes the story's least interesting member.

Solution. Know what the character wants—overall in the story and overall in each scene. Then make sure that the character always has a good reason to be working toward at least one of these objectives. To explore sources of character action, go to the section "Developing Your Character" and try "What the Character Believes," "Getting Emotional," and "Spinal Tap." To explore character needs at the scenic level, go to the section "Causing a Scene" and try "The Roots of Action," "What Does the Character Want?," and "Good Intentions." To explore character needs at the story level, go to the section "Building Your Story" and try "Inciting Event."

OFFSTAGE MORE INTERESTING THAN ONSTAGE

Problem. A critical turning point occurs offstage—either before the story, between scenes, or elsewhere during a scene—so that it must be reported to us by one of the characters. We are told, for example, that a new love relationship has begun or that an old one has ended. As a result, we follow the story intellectually rather than emotionally. One of the turning points often missing from a dramatic story is the inciting event: it happened in the backstory rather than in the here and now.

Solution. Remember that we want to be there for the best parts of your story. Make sure that all of the key turning points happen where we can experience them along with the characters. Put the inciting event onstage by starting the story either before this event occurs or while it is taking place. Then let the resulting twists and turns of the dramatic journey take place in front of us. If you are writing a play and can't physically put a big event onstage—such as a forest fire—make the onstage impact of the event more interesting than the event itself. To explore dramatic turning points and where they come from, go to the section "Building Your Story" and try "As the World Turns," "Inciting Event," "Turning Points," and "Crisis Decision."

WEAK THROUGHLINE

Problem. The story's arc of action is unclear, or difficult to follow, or just doesn't exist. We are told that things are different now, but we haven't experienced the change for ourselves. We see only the results and not the process. In some cases, important steps in the chain of events are missing. In other cases, there are steps that break away from the chain and lead nowhere. Sometimes we spend too long on one step of the story while the conflict grows stale. Other times we leap to a new step so abruptly that we don't know how we got there. Sudden surprises can be powerful storytelling tools, but too many leaps or illogical jumps can leave us watching the action from afar.

Solution. Look at the dramatic journey of the main character as a big step-by-step transition, from a starting point—such as social isolation—to a final destination—such as social connection. Make sure that the right steps are in place for this big transition and that the character's journey is one which is gradually but constantly moving forward. To map out your throughline, go to the section "Building Your Story" and try "Step by Step." To strengthen the throughline, try any stage 2 exercise in the section "Building Your Story," particularly "What Happens Next?," "Pointing and Planting," "Before and After," and "Twelve-Word Solution." To get a clearer global view of the throughline, try "Ready, Aim, Focus."

A CRISIS THAT ISN'T

Problem. The crisis decision near the end of the story is, from the main character's perspective, too easy, or, from the audience's perspective, too predictable. In some cases, there is no crisis decision.

Solution. The crisis decision is the most difficult and significant decision of the story. To make the decision worthy of its name, force your main character to choose not between good and evil, but rather between the best of two goods that cannot coexist or the least of two evils. This choice will be both difficult and unpredictable if each option means that something important will be gained and something important will be lost. To explore your main character's choices at the peak of dramatic action, go to the section "Building Your Story" and try "Crisis Decision."

NOT CLEAR WHAT HAPPENED IN THE STORY

Problem. The story doesn't know what it wants to be about. Perhaps there are two big, equally important events competing with each other and canceling each other out. Or there is simply no main event to hold things together. The story lacks focus.

Solution. Regardless of its size, scope, and complexity, think of your story as one main event. Then let all of the dramatic elements—from the cast of characters to the sequence of scenes—work together to make this main event happen. If there are two important subjects to address, make one more important than the other. Or find a third subject that encompasses the two. Know what your story is about and stick to it. To clarify your story's main event, go to the section "Building Your Story" and try any of the stage 3 exercises, such as "Main Event," "Your Story as a Dog," "The Incredible Shrinking Story," "What's in a Name?," "The Forest of Your Story," and "Ready, Aim, Focus."

A THEME THAT ISN'T

Problem. Above and beyond the plot of the story, there is no theme, or controlling idea, that holds the dramatic experience together. Or the theme is so small or so subtle that it is undetectable. The story seems to "stop" rather than "end," and the stopping point feels arbitrary.

Solution. Somewhere between drafts, take the time to think outside the plot and clarify what your story is really about. As an exercise, identify the subject in one or two words. Then, in a single thematic statement, express your point of view about that subject. This statement represents a truth that will be demonstrated by the story but never explained during it. Your high-level decisions about subject and theme can provide important guidelines as you enter the revision process. To explore these high-level elements, go to the section "Building Your Story" and try "What's the Big Idea?" and "The Forest of Your Story."

WAY TOO MANY WORDS

Problem. The writer has forgotten the power of the emotional life that actors will later bring to the script, or overlooked opportunities to use dramatic action, subtext, visual imagery, and physical life to show, not tell, the story. As a result, the script is bogged down in words. It may have unnecessary scenes, too many beats of action within some scenes, too many lines of dialogue within some beats, unnecessary repetitions, unnecessary explanations, or speeches that belabor the point.

Solution. Less is more. When you're ready to edit a completed draft, challenge every scene, every beat, and every line. Focus on boiling down the words to what is absolutely essential, and be sure that a scene's length is justified by its content. For best results, do this cutting in stages rather than all at once. You can reduce a heap of wordage by reviewing the script in rounds and making precise cuts here and there each time. To rework dialogue, go to the section "Causing a Scene" and try "Talking and Listening," "Unspeakable Truths," and "The Bones of the Lines." To convert wordage into imagery and other physical life, try "Seeing the Scene," "Where in the World Are We?," "In the Realm of the Senses," and "The Voice of the Setting." To analyze wordage from a beat perspective, try "Thinking in Beats."

Related tools in *Character, Scene, and Story.* For extra help with a scene that is difficult to write or revise, try "Fixing That Problem Scene" at the end of the guide.

GLOSSARY

Following are definitions of key terms used in Will Dunne's books for dramatic writers. While you may already be familiar with many of these terms, they are included here because their definitions highlight many of the dramatic principles underlying guide exercises.

act. A major unit of dramatic action that is typically composed of scenes and ends with a significant change, or reversal, in the dramatic journey. Most full-length plays today are structured in two acts; most full-length screenplays are structured in three acts.

adjustment. The attitude or emotion that a character manifests at any given time. The adjustment may be true (this is how the character really feels) or affected (this is how the character wishes to appear). At the scenic level, adjustments often change from beat to beat as characters make discoveries that shift them closer to, or further from, their scenic objective.

afterstory. Anything that will happen in the world of the characters after the story ends. Knowing this future can deepen the writer's understanding of what needs to occur or be revealed during the dramatic journey.

antagonist. One who opposes a main character's efforts to pursue a goal.

arc of action. The behavioral and emotional transition of a character during a specific period of time. A character typically has an arc within each scene as well as an arc that spans the course of the whole story.

backstory. Anything that happened among the characters in the past and will somehow influence them in the present. In the first scene, the backstory includes any relevant event that occurred before the story begins; in later scenes, the backstory expands to include whatever has previously occurred onstage or offstage.

beat. 1. The smallest unit of dramatic action. A scene is made up of beats; each centers on one topic, one behavior, or one emotion. Beats bring variety to the dramatic action of a scene and determine its structure and rhythm. 2. A pause in dialogue for dramatic effect. *This guide uses only definition* 1.

beat action *or* **objective.** The character need that drives one beat of a scene. Beat actions often are strategies or tactics that a character tries in order to achieve a scenic objective.

beat change. A shift in the dramatic action caused by a change of topic, behavior, or emotion, or by the entrance or exit of an important character.

behavioral objective. A character's need to get a certain response from another character. Operating at the beat, scene, and story levels, behavioral objectives boil down to four basic categories: to make another character feel good, to make another character feel bad, to find out something important, or to convince another character of something important.

character. A metaphor for a human being composed of a unique mix of physical, psychological, and social traits that are revealed and changed through dramatic action. This guide builds on the principle that character is the root of scene and story: it is usually character, not plot, that drives a dramatic journey.

Character 1. The main character of a scene: the one who drives most of the dramatic action and causes the scene to happen. Different characters may play this role from scene to scene. Character 1 is also often, but not always, the main character of the story.

Character 2. The second most important character in a scene. Different characters may play this role from scene to scene.

climax. The peak of action within a beat, scene, or story. At the beat level, the climax is usually a single line of dialogue or physical action; at the scene level, the climax may include one or more beats of action; at the story level, the climax may include one or more scenes.

conflict. Anything that makes a character objective difficult to achieve. Such obstacles may arise from the character's inner world, from other characters with incompatible needs, or from the current situation in the world of the story. The term *conflict* is often equated incorrectly with *argument*; however, argument is only one form of conflict. Also referred to as *obstacle* or *problem*.

crisis decision. The most difficult decision in the story. Traditionally, the crisis decision is made by the main character, reflects a choice between incompatible goods or the lesser of two evils, and triggers the story's climax and resolution.

deus ex machina. A solution to a problem which arises from coincidence or other external forces rather than from the character actions and story events that led up to it. The term refers to a device in ancient Greek theater where gods would arrive conveniently in chariots at the end of a play to solve everyone's problems.

dialogue. The words that characters speak as they talk and listen to each other in order to satisfy needs, address problems, or express ideas and emotions. In realism, dialogue has the feel of everyday conversation but is actually a heightened version of it. In nonrealism, dialogue may be stylized. Either way, the usual function of dialogue is to reveal character and advance the story.

dramatic action. Character interaction or other activity shaped and driven at its most fundamental level by three elements: objective, obstacle, and motivation.

dramatic journey. The main character's pursuit of an important but difficult goal and the effects of this pursuit on the character and the world of the story. Also known as the *quest*.

emotional life. The feelings of the character at any given time. Emotional life is both a cause and effect of dramatic action, and often minimizes the need for dialogue.

event. An important happening, positive or negative, in the world of the story—for example, something is achieved or not achieved, discovered or not discovered. Dramatic events often center on a beginning, end, or change of some kind.

exposition. Explanation or description of that which cannot be observed here and now, such as past or offstage events in the world of the story, or the inner life of a character. Though often viewed as negative, exposition can be a vital and powerful part of dramatic storytelling when used judiciously to expose specific character traits, ideas, and facts.

feather duster. An expositional scene in which characters explain things to each other, often at length, only for the sake of the audience. The term refers to old-fashioned dramas that would begin with servants dusting the room and gossiping about their employers so that the author could set up the story.

foil. A character who exists in a scene only to ask just the right questions and lend an eager ear so that another character can ramble on about all of the things that the author wants him or her to say for the sake of the audience.

foreshadowing. Preparation for a future story revelation or development. In the case of a "plant," this preparation may be transparent so that its real purpose is not known until later. In the case of a "pointer," this preparation calls attention to itself in order to generate anticipation of what might happen later.

fourth wall. The imaginary wall that separates the audience from the events on stage or on screen. In some cases, such as stories that feature a narrator, characters "break the fourth wall" to address the audience directly.

French scene. A unit of action demarcated by the entrance or exit of a principal character. Each time a new configuration of characters occurs, a new French scene begins. Ideally something important happens in each French scene.

genre. A category or type of dramatic story characterized by a certain style, form, or subject matter. Through the ages, a variety of genres and subgenres have evolved as blends or subsets of the two basic theatrical genres: comedy and tragedy.

given circumstances. The current situation in the world of the story, including any fact, event, state, or condition that will affect how a scene begins or unfolds. Each scene occurs within a unique set of given circumstances.

inciting event *or* **incident.** The phenomenon, large or small, positive or negative, that sets the dramatic journey into motion by upsetting the balance of the character's life and arousing the story goal or superobjective. The inciting event is often the first important event in the story.

interior dramatization. Imagery, sound, or dramatic action that suggests or depicts what is going on in a character's mind, such as a memory, idea, or perception.

interior monologue. Words spoken by a character that can be heard by the audience but no one in the story. Interior monologues typically reflect what a character is thinking and feeling. Also known as *soliloquy*.

measure of success. A specific statement, action, event, or other outcome that would indicate that a character's objective has been achieved.

melodrama. A story dictated more by plot demands than by character motivations so that exaggerated conflicts and emotions can be presented to the audience for "dramatic effect."

monologue. A long speech in which a character speaks to the self, or to someone else who is present or not present, or to the world at large.

motivation. Why a character says or does something. Motivation is a basic element of dramatic action and reflects something at stake for the character.

nonrealism. A storytelling style that creates an artificial reality. It may feature unusual or otherworldly situations, intellectual themes, stylized speech, archetypal characters, and imaginative devices such as exaggeration, distortion, fragmentation, repetition, symbolism, or direct address to the audience.

objective. What a character wants. A basic element of dramatic action, an objective may be behavioral or physical and, depending on its size and importance, may drive a beat (*beat action*), scene (*scenic objective*), or whole story (*story goal*).

obstacle. Anything that makes a character's objective difficult to achieve. Obstacle is a basic element of dramatic action. Also referred to as *conflict* or *problem*.

physical life. The specific setting for a scene as well as the objects in it and the physical elements that compose it.

physical objective. The desire or need to complete a physical task.

pivotal object. A thing that has special positive or negative meaning for the characters and significantly affects their interaction in a scene. The pivotal object often embodies what the character most values or fears here and now.

plant. A speech, action, image, or object that will make a future story development understandable and credible to the audience by discreetly paving the way for it. Ideally, a plant's true purpose is not known until its payoff occurs later on.

pointer. A speech, action, image, or object that paves the way for a future story development by overtly suggesting that it might happen. Unlike a plant, a pointer draws attention to itself in order to make the audience anticipate an outcome.

point of attack. The precise moment when a story or scene begins.

point of view. The vantage point from which the story will be revealed to the audience. This vantage point may be unlimited or limited.

protagonist. A classical term for the main character of a dramatic story. The role of protagonist may be played by more than one character.

quest. What the main character is after in the story. Also known as the *story goal* or *superobjective*.

realism. A storytelling style that creates the illusion of real life without acknowledging the audience. It typically features "slice of life" situations, emotional themes, everyday speech, and characters with whom we can empathize.

resolution. How things end up for the characters; the final outcome of the story. Also referred to as the *denouement*.

reversal. A turning-point experience, positive or negative, that sets the dramatic journey into a radically different, often opposite, direction. Each act of a dramatic story typically ends with a reversal.

rule of three. The storytelling principle that something which is said or done three times is funnier, more important, or more dramatic than something which is said or done any other number of times. This "rule" suggests that thrice provides the best emphasis for an important fact or action, since once is not enough to stress something, twice seems like a mistake, and four times feels repetitious.

scene. A unit of dramatic action that is driven by a character's need to accomplish something important and unfolds in one setting in real time. Most scenes add up to one main event that changes the world of the story in a good or a bad way.

scenic objective. The character need that drives most of a scene. Once aroused, either prior to the scene or during it, the scenic objective does not change until it is achieved or reaches a point of failure.

sense memory. A technique in which actors relive a past experience emotionally by recalling a physical detail from it. Writers can adapt this technique to explore their characters at a visceral level.

speech. What a character says at one time. A speech may be as short as one word or as long as several pages, depending on the complexity and importance of the content. Also referred to as a *line*.

spine of the character. The root action from which all of the character's other actions flow.

step outline. A writing or revision tool that gives the writer an at-a-glance view of the story structure by listing the key events in the order in which they happen.

story. The series of events that occurs when a character pursues an important goal that is difficult to achieve.

story goal. The character desire or need that is aroused by the inciting event, drives most of the story, and does not reach its conclusion—whether successful or unsuccessful—until the story ends. Also known as the *quest* or *superobjective*.

story structure. The selection and sequence of events used to depict a story. Classically referred to as *plot*.

strategy. How a character attempts to achieve an objective. Different strategies create the different beats of a scene. Also known as *tactics*.

style. The manner in which characters and story events are depicted. The style of a dramatic work may be realistic or nonrealistic.

subtext. Character thoughts and feelings that influence character behavior but are not stated in the dialogue. Subtext is that which remains "between the lines."

superobjective. See *story goal*.

suspense. A state in which the audience is in two places at the same time: the present (what is happening here and now in the story) and the future (what might happen later in the story as a result of what is happening now).

theme. A universal idea that the writer believes to be true and attempts to demonstrate through the characters and story. The theme is usually not stated in the dialogue but is often reflected most clearly in the crisis, climax, and resolution of the story. Also known as *controlling idea* or *premise*.

throughline. The spine of the story: the key events and how they connect so that the dramatic journey maintains a forward movement from beginning to end and enables a transition to occur.

turning point. A dramatic event, large or small, positive or negative, that creates an observable change in the world of the story. A major turning point is sometimes referred to as a *reversal*.

voice. How a character expresses thoughts and feelings through language. This voice is a core component of character identity and speech.

ACKNOWLEDGMENTS

Thank you to the dramatic writers with whom I have worked individually and in groups over the past twenty-eight years and from whom I have learned so much. This guide would not exist without them. Thank you as well to the dramatic writers whose plays and screenplays are cited in this guide. Their work is an ongoing source of insight and inspiration as I develop exercises for the writers in my workshops. Thank you also to my own teachers and mentors, particularly: Lloyd Richards, Jean Shelton, Wendell Phillips, Stella Adler, Corinne Jacker, and Robert McKee.

Looking back to the early days of this guide, I wish to thank those who each in their own way helped put it on a path to publication, particularly: Susan M. Bielstein, Kim Pence, Alan Johnson, Christopher Rhodes, Joan Vanderbeck, Marion Bundy, Ruth Kirschner, Ralda Lee, Nion McEvoy, and Jay Schaefer.

Most importantly, I thank the University of Chicago Press and the staff with whom I have worked on this project: my editor Paul Schellinger, who championed this guide, and my copy editor Carol Fisher Saller, who helped refine it. I also give special thanks to the theater experts who through the Press were generous enough to review my proposal and manuscript and offer invaluable suggestions and support: Arthur R. Borreca and Dennis J. Reardon.

Chicago Guides
to *Writing*, Editing,
and Publishing